MACHIAVELLI IN AMERICA

MACHIAVELLI IN AMERICA

THOMAS BLOCK

Algora Publishing
New York

Library of Congress Cataloging-in-Publication Data —

Block, Thomas.
Machiavelli in America / Thomas Block.
    pages cm
Includes bibliographical references and index.
    ISBN 978-1-62894-067-1 (hard cover: alk. paper) — ISBN 978-1-62894-066-4 (soft
cover: alk. paper) — ISBN 978-1-62894-068-8 (ebook) 1. Machiavelli, Niccolr, 1469-1527—
Influence. 2. United States—Politics and government—Philosophy. 3. Political culture—
United States. I. Title.
    JC143.M4B575 2014
    320.973—dc23
                    2013049444

Printed in the United States

For my wife, Debbie,
who believes that change can come
from within the political system.

TABLE OF CONTENTS

Introduction

Many people are familiar with the controversial thinking of the 16th-century Florentine political philosopher Niccolò Machiavelli (d. 1527). His influence has been so widespread that the word "Machiavellian" has been incorporated into our language as a pejorative, equated with "cunning, duplicity and bad faith."[2]

What might be less well known is Machiavelli's influence on the contemporary American political panorama. The long-dead Florentine thinker's ideas still inspire political actors. More importantly, in 21st-century America, following his counsel leads to electoral victory. The more "Machiavellian" the American politician, the more likely they are to win.

Machiavelli in America examines this disturbing dynamic. First looking at Machiavelli and his ideas, the study then examines the specific way in which his guidance influences political society today. At the end of the book, I offer one activist response — a method for those of us who believe that "Machiavellian" and "American politics" shouldn't be synonymous may fight back. *Machiavelli in America* proposes one specific strategy for combatting the pernicious energy that too-often defines American politics.

Le Plus Ça Change

> Whoever considers present and ancient things easily knows that in all cities and in all peoples there are the same desires and the same humors, and there always have been. So it is an easy thing for whoever examines past things diligently to foresee future things in every republic.[3]

Since Niccolò Machiavelli's era, the world and its inhabitants have undergone major changes in technology, organizations of countries, social consciousness and interaction, energy use, transportation and variations in other aspects of human society.

Oftentimes, these transformations have been presented as "progress." Empires have risen, to be replaced by better, more humane ones. Religions have spawned other, more refined holy paths. The number of poor in the world has been eased, while violence appears to be abating as we ascend into the 21st century.[4] Yet through it all, human nature — that which lies at the heart of all of these innovations — remains constant. The driving force behind all human history remains as invariable as atoms.

Machiavelli assured that there was no greater place to search for clues to how things will be in the present and future than the past. The constancy of the human character assured that whether history was being written by the Athenians and Melians (415 B.C.E.), Guelphs and Ghibellines (12th and 13th century Italy), or Democrats and Republicans (21st century), the dynamic behind the political and social machinations remained the same. The same human nature defined the conflict in each situation.

This invariable characteristic of humankind inspired the Florentine philosopher to develop one of the most enduring political treatises in human history, *The Prince*. Persistent because its distasteful analysis of human social and political life appeared, and still appears, to be correct. That is to say, the Machiavellian prescriptions described for attaining and retaining power *work*.

For Machiavelli selfishness defined the primary motivation for all human activity. A narcissistic desire lay at the heart of the human temperament, pitting individuals against each other with the sole desire to advance their own personal interests. Society simply provided the framework within which each person might master those around him or her.

As Machiavelli scholar Harvey Mansfield (William R. Kenan Jr. Professor of Government at Harvard University) noted:

> For Machiavelli, there is just one beginning — necessity. Every human institution begins without an inheritance from God or nature . . . We begin bare, unprotected, insecure and justly fearful.[5]

Machiavelli, being a man of letters, added nuance to the animal bases of his political philosophy. He discussed the social motivators of fear and propaganda, the fraud of religion and language, as well as the importance of sometimes applying outright violence. However, the foundation of his political ideology remained straightforward: *everyone* in a society acts primarily for personal gain. And for a politician to succeed in mastering this world, he had to either manipulate or frighten people into believing that their interests allied with his own.

THE IMMUTABILITY OF HUMAN NATURE AND TODAY'S AMERICA

Machiavelli assured that any statesman wishing to master the unruly mob of society had to do so with the understanding that human traits are eternal. Far from ruling in the hopes that things might get better, political leaders must implement all programs with the appreciation that humans are often mean, small and selfish. As Machiavelli noted:

> Whosoever desires to found a state and give it laws must start with assuming that all men are bad and ever ready to display their vicious nature, whenever they may find occasion for it.[6]

It was this claim of humanity's unchanging "vicious nature" that inspired me to write this book. Are we really this bad, I asked myself? Is human political interaction defined more by Josef Stalin (d. 1953; Russian dictator from 1941-1953) or Benito Mussolini (d. 1945; one of the key figures in the creation of fascism) than Gandhi or Martin Luther King Jr.? And even when a Gandhi does gain an occasional political victory, he does so by living sexless and eating nuts for most of his life, before being gunned down in cold blood. Hardly the model that most of us want to follow in remaking the world.

Even more provocative, however, was my growing awareness that Machiavelli's ideas are central to the American political process. The far-off Florentine is perhaps the single most important political advisor in the United States *today!* This fact will be explored in detail below.

Until we look in the mirror of American politics and see Machiavelli's smug visage staring back at us, we won't be able to move beyond the selfish, narrow and destructive cycle that we in this country — and around the world — find ourselves. Choosing between bad and worse for virtually all political leaders will not, in the end, help us find our way to a better world.

In this inquiry, I examine the Florentine's ideas, and then explore how they reverberate in American society. Prescient or simply lucky, Niccolò Machiavelli foretold the American political dynamic. Many of us in the voting public may not be aware, but Machiavelli and his writings were important not only at the seminal point in American history — its founding — but continue to be so today.

As Renaissance scholar Paul Grendler noted:

> After World War II, [Machiavelli] came into his own as an advisor to American policymakers. Today, Machiavelli's influence on political policy may be greater than at any time since he served the Florentine government. Machiavelli has become American.[7]

If human nature is, as Machiavelli assures, mean, small and selfish. And the Florentine's worldview permeates American political life, then what hope can there be? The United States is currently the richest and most powerful nation in the world, equivalent to Rome of the Ancient World or the Papacy of the Renaissance. While some of us might hope that it would use its vast power for the common good, the Machiavellian reality is that instead it often uses it to satiate base animal desires through political, economic and military domination.

Machiavelli's American program works beautifully for successful power management.

It doesn't always make the planet a better place to live.

MACHIAVELLI: BECAUSE IT WORKS

Machiavelli's program concentrated on subjugation and mastery. He did not concern himself with the common good, democracy or human rights. "I have thought it proper," he wrote, "to represent things as they are in a real truth, rather than as they are imagined."[8]

And the way things *are* in truth has little to do with utopias or universal justice.

Yet a question lingers: *why* do Machiavelli's ideas work? Why do Gandhi's theories, or those of Thomas Merton (d. 1968), Simone Weil (d. 1943), the Sufi saint Jallaludin Rumi (d. 1273) and even Jesus Christ simply provide a backdrop against which the truth of Machiavellian ideals are thrown into relief?

For Machiavelli, the concepts of moral philosophers and actors from Socrates to the Sufis and the religions within which they operated were certainly important. But only because they provided a fraudulent tool for the relentless, morally unhinged pursuit of power. In terms of their direct relation to political reality, however, he considered them as meaningless as music. Machiavelli never once mentioned in his writings the concept of the "common good," or even human conscience.[9]

Machiavelli's ideas continue to fascinate and function for precisely this reason: they deal with the world as it is. His leadership model has not only inspired many of America's most successful politicians. They have also instigated shelves full of recent books, bearing titles such as *The New Machiavelli: the Art of Politics in Business; A Guide to the Corporate Machiavelli; Machiavelli on Modern Leadership; The Modern Machiavelli; What Would Machiavelli Do*[10] and a host of other treatises, most of which inform today's leaders how to apply Machiavellian ideas to the worlds of politics and business.

Renaissance scholar Paul Grendler made note of specific contemporary American political officials and advisors who look to Machiavelli's books for political counsel. He assured that admirers of the Florentine's thought attained key positions in the administrations of Ronald Reagan, George H. W. Bush and George W. Bush, spanning the last two decades of Republican presidential administrations. He specifically named former U.S. Deputy Secretary of Defense Paul Wolfowitz; former conservative presidential candidate Alan Keyes; Supreme Court nominee Robert Bork; former Secretary of Education Robert Bennett; Supreme Court Justice Clarence Thomas and conservative columnist and pundit William Kristol, among others.[11]

Human Constancy: The Amygdala

> There is no need of gods or conspiracies to make men rush headlong into the most absurd, self-inflicted disasters. Human nature suffices.[12]

Richard Gregg (d. 1974; a social philosopher said to be the first American to develop a substantial theory of nonviolent resistance) said: "Governments are the institutionalized forms of our habitual inner attitudes. Each one of us is partly responsible."[13] But what are these "habitual inner attitudes" which have led Machiavelli to be a more relevant contemporary political advisor than Mahatma Gandhi?

Human experience is situated in the brain. Like the computer, the brain was not created of a piece, regardless of what fanatical religious believers might propose. It emerged through an evolutionary process, with new cortical structures being built on top of old.

We share much with earlier forms of life, from fish to rats. Later neural additions — those that separate us from the more primitive animal species — were simply added on top of the earlier structure. The human animal is still beholden to the primal aspects of our brain stem. These prehistoric drivers control necessary facets of life, from breathing to eating to modulating emotional responses.

It is vital to grasp this Erector Set™ quality of the mind. Machiavelli's political philosophy does not emerge from an appreciation of the most recent (evolutionary) features of the human brain structure, those contained in the neo-cortex. These latest facets of the neural architecture define what makes us most "human." Here resides the brain structure supporting consciousness: introspection, advanced learning and moral thought.

Machiavelli's system bypasses this center of academic learning and spiritual understanding to access a far more powerful and primitive aspect of the human character, the subcortical amygdala. In this ancient neural bundle sub- and pre-conscious decisions are made that propel the vast majority of individuals in their actions.

The amygdala, a small, nut-sized structure situated at the base of the human brain stem, stands at the center of the human condition. In humans and other animals, this brain structure is linked to both fear responses and pleasure. Its size has been shown to positively correlate with aggressive behavior across species. The larger the amygdala, the more aggressive the individual.

It is also linked to the neuroses that sometimes define humanity's interaction with the world around it. Conditions such as anxiety, autism, depression, post-traumatic stress disorder and phobias are suspected of being linked to abnormal functioning of the amygdala.[14]

It is here, deep in the recesses of the human brain, that Machiavelli's ideas take root. Pre-conscious motivations around which our thoughts and beliefs form often stem from primal survival impulses originating in the amygdala. These are then re-interpreted by the consciousness and shaped into thoughts and beliefs.

It Is Better to Be Feared than Loved

> Since men love at their own pleasure and fear at the prince's pleasure, a wise prince must base himself upon that which is his, not upon that which is other men's.[15]

Machiavelli posited that a prince's surest method of controlling people was by inspiring fear. By frightening them into following the leader. Love, respect and bribes might sometimes be efficacious in inspiring a population, but only heartfelt terror would always work.

The amygdala helps control fear responses. Machiavelli's contention that it is better to be feared than loved has its basis in the human brain stem. When people cause others to feel fear, they have accessed a primitive aspect of humanity, one existing beyond rationalizing or conscious thought. We feel the fear first. Then we interpret it with our higher brain functions.

Fear stands at the heart of civilization. It is more important to human society than love, compassion or the search for a common good. Fear drives us to action in ways that the other, higher aspects of our character are unable to do. As Machiavelli assured, and I will concur throughout this study, fear has been at the center of political experience through all times, including today in the United States.

The power of this insistent, unconscious emotion is a leftover from a time when survival depended on it. To be afraid of what lurked in the dark was necessary to early humanity. It remains so for every animal from starfish to wildebeest. Death comes in a split second when awareness is at a lull. Fear keeps the senses tingling and the ability to avoid danger at a maximum.

Long before Machiavelli distilled this ancient dynamic into his brutal political program, some of humanity's greatest thinkers acknowledged this pre-human facet lying at the center of human experience. The Greek philosopher Aristotle (d. 322 B.C.E.) maintained:

> Man, when perfected, is the best of animals, but if he is isolated from law and justice, is the worst of all . . . That is why, if he is without virtue, he is a most savage being, and worse than all others in the indulgence of [his] lust and gluttony.[16]

And the Islamic mystic Jallaludin Rumi said:

> Man is a mixture of animality and rationality, and his animality is as inseparable a part of him as his rationality. He is like a torrent in which mud is mixed. The clear water is his rational speech, and the mud his animality.[17]

Machiavelli noted and then explained how leaders might exploit this innate aspect of humankind:

> It is necessary for the prince to know how to use both the beast and the man. This part was taught to princes covertly by the ancient writers, who write that Achilles, and many other ancient princes, were given to Chiron, the centaur, to be nourished that he might raise them under his discipline . . . a prince is constrained by necessity to know well how to use the beast.[18]

The most certain way to "use the beast" was, according to the Florentine political thinker, to inspire fear in people.

MACHIAVELLI ON THE BRAIN

> That whereby man differs from the lower animals is but small. The mass of people cast it away, while the superior men preserve it.[19]

The bases for Aristotle's "animal nature," Rumi's "mud" or Machiavelli's "Chiron" are localized in humanity's hard wiring. What's more, it has been scientifically proven that the animal in humanity is more powerful than the rational, as Machiavelli contended. Human beings are captives to the primal neural aspects of their carnal selves, rather than master of them.

Even more disturbing, it has been shown that Machiavellian techniques of relating to others are innate to animals, and therefore to man.

> A group of comparative primatologists studying the evolution of intelligence in primates (apes, baboons, chimpanzees, monkeys and man) coined the term "Machiavellian intelligence" to explain certain kinds of behavior. They discovered that baboons and monkeys purposefully deceived and manipulated others in order to obtain desired personal ends . . . They see it as an essential part of intelligence in primates, including man . . . It might be called social problem solving unchecked by morality.[20]

The author of this passage continued on to note that "Machiavellian intelligence postulates that intelligence begins in cunning, deceit and manipulation."[21]

Animals have no, or very little, morality. Humans, at their best, can and do behave in a moral way. However, our species is still molded by an animal past where morality plays little role, leaving society too often with "social problem solving unchecked by morality." Oftentimes in communal and political situations, the higher aspects of the human being melt away, and "Machiavellian intelligence" rules.

Joshua Greene (a researcher at Harvard University and leader in the field of moral psychology) has explored this dynamic in detail. He noted: "Most of the time when we are deciding the right thing to do, what's happening in the brain is an emotional response, not a reasoned one."[22]

Decisions on right and wrong, morality and religion and a host of other fundamental aspects of an individual's belief system are made in areas of the brain far more primitive than the higher functioning neo-cortex. The rational self then *interprets* these pre-conscious messages. The logical and moral are held hostage to the more primal, emotional aspects of the character, exactly as Machiavelli proposed. Only in the greatest humans — Gandhi or Jesus or Rabbi Abraham Joshua Heschel (d. 1972) or Rumi (or perhaps yourself) — does the neo-cortex wrest control of the thought and action, to make an individual both moral and truly conscious.

This human nature explains the difference between what many people say and study in religious institutions over the weekend and the way they spend the rest of their week. Their actions are often driven by the Machiavellian desire to succeed in life at any cost, not the soothing messages of their spiritual formation.

This dynamic can be clearly seen in political and social decisions. It has led American society in recent times to take from the poor to give to the rich, start war after war of choice over the past 50 years and chew the marrow out of the bones of poor Mother Earth herself. Although this last one — as evidenced by the fouling of our earth and depletion of vital resources — might lead to the downfall of civilization itself, our species is so driven by primal needs that we cannot stop ourselves. Like a dying addict, unable to give up smoking or heroin or alcohol.

A Fundamental Problem

> Five or six times a day man experiences involuntary disappointment and pain. Absolutely these things do not come from him; therefore, they must come from other than him, and so he is subject to that other.[23]

The first step on the road to recovery is acknowledging the illness. As long as we (as a society and species) reward Machiavellian intelligence with social success and electoral victory, we are sick. The Chinese philosopher Lao Tzu (c. 6th century B.C.E.) said: "first realize that you are sick; then you can move toward health."[24] Once we admit our challenge, however, an even more difficult task is to develop a *response* to Machiavellian intelligence. One that operates in the world of emotion and the subconscious, and masters them for the common good.

This book is one attempt to acknowledge our shared illness as well as to propose a solution. If we continue to be driven by primal urges and fears, we will soon find ourselves headed off a cliff caused by warfare, gluttonous use of resources, ethnic hatreds and other behaviors in which messages from the amygdala metastasize in human experience.

Machiavellian Politics

> In the footsteps of Machiavelli many American politicians seek to gain the support of the electorate by any conceivable method. They chatter, coax, and cajole, and if this is ineffective, they pretend, deceive, and promise the world. Since people are taken in by appearance, politicians appear devout and loyal; yet, in political theory, it is better to be a clever winner than to be a devout loser. Indeed, many American politicians are instinctively Ma-

chiavellian, denying the relevance of morality in political affairs and holding that craft and deceit are justified in pursuing and maintaining political power.[25]

Contemporary scientists have explored how brain chemistry affects politics. According to a 2011 study, people with different political views have different brain makeups.[26] It was demonstrated that people with conservative views[27] have a larger amygdala than those with more progressive stances.

Additionally, as was noted, the size of the amygdala correlates positively with aggression, leading more conservative members of society to be more violent in considering political options. Not to say that conservatives would stab someone in the grocery line. But they are more likely to support aggressive political responses to social and geopolitical issues. Science writer Joanna Schaffhausen noted in *The Biological Basis of Aggression*:

> A large body of research implicates the amygdala as a key brain structure for mediating violence. In animals, electrical stimulation of the amygdala augments all types of aggressive behavior, and there is evidence for a similar reaction in humans. It is also possible to increase aggression through modulation of the amygdala.[28]

Researchers have recently begun to examine the amygdala and how it affects political decisions.

> The difference in brain structure could explain some of the traits that distinguish conservatives and liberals, researchers said. People with larger amygdalae tend to respond with more aggression in situations where they feel threatened and are more sensitive to fear and disgust.[29]

It's easy to see how accessing this aspect of political supporters would be advantageous. The amygdala shoots primal, emotional stimuli into the neocortex, where these motivators are then interpreted within the conscious structure of a personality. By attaching this fear and disgust to a political adversary, one can gain advantage. Machiavelli understood this, as do most successful politicians and leaders.

Even individuals who might not have overlarge amygdalae are susceptible to suggestion by those with high "Machiavellian intelligence."

> Research has found that political orientation is influenced by short-term events related to fear and disgust. Thus, simply asking persons to wash their hands caused their views to become more conservative. Reminding persons of the existence of threats such as terrorism caused political views to become more conservative.[30]

This dynamic was explicitly examined in an article in the *Washington Post* entitled "The World is Safer, but No One Will Say So," on the eve of the 2012 presidential election:

> There's one foreign policy fact that President Obama and Mitt Romney dare not mention this election season. No American general will speak of it. Nor will it displace the usual hot topics at Washington's myriad foreign

policy think tanks. Measured by most relevant statistics, the United States — and the world — have never been safer . . . The candidates' rhetoric, however, suggests that the globe is ablaze.[31]

The reason is clear: fear works. Even if these politicians were dealing with a more thoughtful electorate, one with smaller amygdalae, the citizens could still be bent to the leader's will through aggressive language and fear mongering. Members of the public may be viewed as a *tabula rasa*, to have fear and aggression smeared over them. This turns them into partisans for the very leader who is frightening them.

Politicians, or Machiavelli's "princes," understand how to stimulate fear to manipulate their audiences and thereby achieve the goal of leadership. The political goal is to forge an "us" against a "them" by situating the fear response in someone or something outside of the chosen group (be it homosexuals, Democrats, Arabs, immigrants or other). Then the motivator (politician) of the primal fear stimulus offers him or herself as the palliative, capable of stemming the sense of dread emitted from deep within the individual's psyche and focused on the outside stimulus.

As the 2012 election cycle drew to a close, Republican vice presidential candidate Paul Ryan (R-WI) utilized exactly this motivation in describing the terrifying result of his opponent's victory:

> Representative Paul D. Ryan accused President Obama on Sunday of taking the country down a path that compromised Judeo-Christian values and the traditions of Western civilization . . . "It's a dangerous path," Mr. Ryan said, describing Mr. Obama's policies. "It's a path that grows government, restricts freedom and liberty and compromises those values, those Judeo-Christian, Western civilization values that made us such a great and exceptional nation in the first place."[32]

This is Machiavellian intelligence. And it still reigns supreme in the worlds of politics and business. The linkage between the amygdala and politics makes explicit the neurobiological bases to Machiavellian theory.

Chaos and Control

> Without "ordered government," human beings exist in a condition of "ambitious license," where "everything is full of confusion and disorder." To escape this natural condition, they need to be constrained by a "new prince" who comes to power by the ruthless use of force.[33]

Chaos represents the birthplace of fear. Fear of an ungovernable power which lies within us, of a pathological anarchy which might be unleashed if we do not somehow control ourselves through social boundaries and civilizing conventions. Security for individuals and societies is the antidote to the terror of a violent anarchy lurking within the human soul. Political culture represents one method of controlling these aggressive urges.

Fear — the manipulating impetus utilized by those with high "Machiavellian intelligence" — pairs naturally with this threat of internal chaos. Politicians, however, must remove the chaos from the internal experience of his or her constituents, situating it in an enemy. In this way, a politician may bring citizens together around his or her leadership, promising to annihilate the chaos out there, safeguarding the followers.

George W. Bush once said (February 2008), as he was attempting to gain support for a piece of security legislation: "At this moment, somewhere in the world, terrorists are planning new attacks on our country."[34] The hypothetical terrorist attacks represented the potential chaos. Those who stood between President Bush and his legislative goal were portrayed as being on the side of chaos.

Richard Gregg noted that governments represent the institutionalization of this interior dread of chaos. They are manifestations of our terror, not ameliorations of it. Each individual leader is sometimes little more than a mirror of humanity's primal fear.

Or as the Muslim mystic Jallaludin Rumi asserted:

> When I see distinctly that a hundred thousand forms without bound and hosts without end, multitude upon multitude, are held captive by a person who is held captive in turn by a miserable thought, then all these are prisoners of that one thought.[35]

It is that single thought that expresses something deep within the soul of each of us.

Chaos and Control II

> Necessity is always one's own necessity, that is why necessity overpowers any human capacity of detachment.[36]

"Detachment" is the first step toward intellectual understanding, where the neo-cortex can play a governing role over thoughts and emotions. The place where "necessity overpowers detachment" represents the nexus of Machiavellian theory and human biology.

However, each of us enjoys the belief that we are master of our own thoughts and feelings. It is in this disconnect that a whole range of beliefs — some even completely independent of reality — take hold in society. Examples of this type of (incorrect) belief are that the Earth was flat (we got over this one); that humans play no role in global climate change (in 2010, half of all Americans believed that[37]); that President Obama is a Muslim (17% in 2012[38]); that Iraq had weapons of mass destruction prior to the 2003 war (63% of Republicans in 2012[39]). These and a host of other completely false beliefs are held tight due, ultimately, to a fear of chaos buried deep in our brains.

The views are born of fear and then are held tightly regardless of what the facts of the matter might be.

Faith in the autonomy of the individual self, in one's own ideas and thoughts and beliefs, is a means to fend off chaos while at the same time creating it. It represents a stylized image of the self and the world. One that helps twist nuance and muddy reality into a hardened, though often false, vision of the universe and our place within it.

What's more, individuals become attached to their versions of reality, false though they may be, as these chimerical images become enmeshed with their own existential sense. The great Muslim spiritual thinker Abu Hamid al-Ghazali (d. 1111) noted: "You only truly possess that which cannot be lost in a shipwreck."[40] For the vast majority of humans, however, their beliefs and thoughts define them. These must be held onto or the sense of self unravels. And then the chaos lurking just below human consciousness explodes into the human psyche.

Ronald Lindsay, president of the *Committee of Skeptical Inquiry*, was quoted in the *Washington Post* addressing the underlying motivation for people choosing their inklings over truth. He was discussing a question in American politics which may have been forgotten by the time you read this: whether or not President Barack Obama was actually born in the United States, otherwise known as the "birther" controversy. But the dynamic he explored holds true for any set of deeply held beliefs:

> If you have a pre-commitment to your view, and that point of view is important for your identity — if you are emotionally attached to it — your emotion is going to shape your reasoning process. You'll be presented with facts, but you'll find some way to minimize the significance of those facts.[41]

This construction — holding onto unfounded beliefs and having them color one's view of the world — represents the beginning of chaos, as it demarcates the first step away from truth. And it is here that Machiavellian political tactics make their inroads and allow a political theory based on fraud and raw power to continue to hold sway in our world.

EMOTIONAL MATURITY: ELUSIVE AND RARE

We live in a world of unreality and dream. To give up our imaginary position at the center . . . means to awaken to what is real and eternal, to see the true light and hear the true silence.[42]

Machiavelli's influence on modern and contemporary politics is undeniable. It's as if he brought out of the shadows some widely held secret — something that all political leaders prior to his time had thought but dared not utter. The resiliency of his ideas is astounding, and it only seems to grow with time. As was earlier noted, "Machiavelli's influence on political policy may be greater than at any time since he served the Florentine government."[43]

Niccolò Machiavelli did not concern himself with what might or should be, but with what is. And, as Machiavelli assured and politicians have forever proven, it is the least emotionally mature among us who are driven the most powerfully to control the world by leading it. The least emotionally mature (that is to say, those "whose lust overcomes [their] intellect"[44]) externalize their primal emotional stirrings, centered in the amygdala. Machiavelli's prince is often one who "tends to be more rigid and closed-minded, less tolerant of ambiguity and less open to new experiences."[45]

The people who are driven most by their unconscious impulses, who most desperately need control, glory, power and wealth to have a sense of self-worth, are those who best master the Machiavellian game of worldly success. These leaders in business and politics are the ones I will be discussing throughout this study. They are the least spiritually healthy among us, yet the most temporally important. It is these men and woman who stand behind every war, every clear-cut forest, every oil spill, every homeless veteran moldering on the streets of countries around the world.

Spiritual realization represents the antithesis of the brain that "tends to be more rigid and closed-minded." Spirituality concerns a deep study of the self, an attempt to have the higher aspects of the brain structure (the neocortex) control the lower (amygdala). As Confucius advised: "Attack the evil that is within yourself, rather than attacking the evil that is in others."[46] And Shems-i Tabrizi (d. 1248), Rumi's teacher, said: "The measure of life that you do have should be spent in investigating your own state"[47] of mind.

Truly spiritual people yearn for self-awareness, not worldly success. These men and women eschew worldly gain and power. In fact, they view temporal success with great suspicion. As Rumi noted:

> Not all gallows are made of wood. Official positions, exalted rank and worldly success are also very high gallows. When God wishes to catch someone, He gives him a great position or a large kingdom in the world. All that is like a gallows on which God puts them so that all people may be aware.[48]

Ergo, it is those least qualified — those furthest from controlling the primal emotional drivers deep within the human brain — who climb onto Rumi's gallows and wrest control of the levers of society through their unrelenting application of Machiavellian tactics to the social and political worlds.

TRUTH

> Nature is synonymous with Truth. To lie deliberately is to blaspheme. And likewise to lie without realizing it. Because the involuntary liar disrupts the harmony of nature. Nature gave him the resources to distinguish between true and false. And he neglected them.[49]

Before descending into the social reality where Machiavellian rules are the order of the day, it is important to consider truth. It is a force often irrelevant and even oppositional to what is considered objective reality, yet it sits at the center of all political and social conversations. It is often ignored or even actively eschewed.

The conservative columnist Cal Thomas put forward an interesting proposal concerning the insertion of truth into politics:

> Before an election, have candidates take a lie detector test. Put it on TV and/or the Internet. A panel of reporters or other experts could ask the questions, just like they do in presidential debates. In fact, this could be a five-minute segment at the end of the debates. "And now, to the lie detectors..."[50]

Ha, ha, ha! Political participants on either side of the aisle would never accept common sense remedies such as this one. It would too easily and clearly unmask the whole pernicious system. Lie detector tests are for criminals, not for politicians, they would aver.

Within the social and political realms, we — as a culture and a species — rarely attempt to find the place of truth. We opt instead for a dubious objectivity that often represents little more than a midpoint between two opposing political or social opinions. This objective reality merely reflects popular attitudes, subject to polling data, gut reactions, propaganda, a narrow reading of history, the weight of tradition and a basket of other impressions. Truth is shunted into the shadows of social, cultural and political conversations.

The 20th-century prophet Thomas Merton addressed this disconnect between truth and the narrative of accepted reality:

> The process which Kierkegaard calls "leveling" is that by which the individual person loses himself in the vast emptiness of a public mind. Because he identifies this abstraction with objective reality, or simply with the "truth," he abdicates his own experience and intuition.[51]

While truth and objective reality are certainly different, it is beyond the scope of this work to provide a definitive philosophical definition of truth. As the *Stanford Encyclopedia of Philosophy* noted, "Truth is one of the central subjects in philosophy. It is also one of the largest. Truth has been a topic of discussion in its own right for thousands of years. Moreover, a huge variety of issues in philosophy relate to truth, either by relying on theses about truth, or implying theses about truth."[52]

In terms of this book, truth is not a philosophical issue. Within the political and social ambits, we can uncover an ideal of truth that has more than relative meaning. There are opinions, issues and concerns that are closer to actuality than others. However, these almost always become lost in the muddle of political speech, partisan warfare and the desires of the ruling or moneyed class in any society.

For instance, the national narrative in the United States includes the notion of "manifest destiny." In textbooks and the national chronicle, this is often represented as the country being the new Israel, a land of gentle, civilizing suasion, with Europeans aiding the primitive natives who inhabited the country before the coming of the Caucasian saviors. The truth, however, is far different, as the United States was forged from genocide of the Native Americans and then built on the backs of nearly 300 years of slave labor.

Further, specific truths exist in contemporary society — that human activity contributes to global warming, that the ubiquitous use of plastics is a cause of cancer and the United States is a nation of growing inequality. However, within the world of politics, these are treated as opinions. The media presents them alongside opposing points of view, complete with polling data and party affiliation. Truth in the political world is viewed with great suspicion. Telling the truth is frowned upon. As journalist Michael Kinsley (b. 1951) noted: "A gaffe is when a politician tells the truth — some obvious truth he isn't supposed to say."[53]

Within the world of Machiavellian intelligence, political speech becomes hostile to truth. As the 20th-century prophet Simone Weil (d. 1943) noted: "on inspection, almost all the words and phrases of our political vocabulary turn out to be hollow."[54] They are hollowed out so truth can be obscured, and a shared social reality — as proposed by the economic and political princes — can overwhelm it. It is those who master the realms of propaganda, social myth and public lying who become princes in our world, while the truth-tellers and self aware spend their time in quietude, barely affecting the public square.

This is the arena in which Machiavellian actors are at their strongest: overwhelming truth to shape reality. However, the objective reality they propose is, in many instances, so far from the truth as to have little relation to it. "Reality" describes the external world that we appear to live in, as defined by politicians, the media, popular culture, advertising and other means of presenting a narrative of a shared history, society or realm. Reality can be controlled through propaganda and the mass media. It takes on a life of its own.

> Agreement between several men brings with it a feeling of reality. Divergence, where this agreement is concerned, appears as sin. The state of conformity is an imitation of grace.[55]

The difficulty with inserting truth into the general human narrative has been well documented. The 18th-century Jewish spiritual leader Baal Shem Tov (d. 1760) stated: "What does it mean when people say that Truth goes all over the world? It means that Truth is driven out of one place after another, and must wander on and on."[56] Political reality, on the other hand, as proposed by a respected media organization such as CNN, can be viewed simultaneously in more than 200 countries around the world, giving it the veneer of truth that a lone voice can never create.

Machiavelli, ever aware of this fundamental human dynamic as well as methods to exploit it, noted:

> The vulgar are taken by what seems [to be] and by the outcome of the thing, and in the world there are only the vulgar; and the few don't stand a chance against them when the many have so many upon whom to lean.[57]

He also noted:

> The great majority of humans is satisfied with appearances, as though they were realities, and are often more influenced by the things that seem than by those that are.[58]

Of the many pithy statements that we can cull from Machiavelli's writings, this might be one of the most chilling. Because it is true: we have a world that often divorces social reality from truth. This leaves us, as Simone Weil bitterly noted, with a "present situation more or less resembling that of a party of absolutely ignorant travellers who find themselves in a motor-car launched at full speed and driverless across broken country."[59]

And far from attempting to ameliorate the situation, the vast majority of successful politicians simply exploit it, only deepening the crisis.

A Response to Machiavelli

> It has been a common view among political philosophers that there exists a special relationship between moral goodness and legitimate authority . . . Rulers were counseled that if they wanted to succeed, they must be sure to behave in accordance with conventional standards of ethical goodness. It was thought that rulers did well when they did good; they earned the right to be obeyed and respected inasmuch as they showed themselves to be virtuous and morally upright. It is precisely this moralistic view of authority that Machiavelli criticizes at length . . . For Machiavelli, there is no moral basis on which to judge the difference between legitimate and illegitimate uses of power.[60]

The ensuing voyage through Machiavellian politics can appear grim, especially as we explore how the Renaissance philosopher inspires politicians in our era. However, this exposition does not end in a hopeless jumble. The final chapter of the book proposes a response to Machiavelli. I outline a specific approach for how we might begin to turn our political system away from what is known as "realpolitik" (another name for Machiavellian realism) to the kind of morally centered social world envisioned by prophets from Marcus Aurelius (d. 180) to Thomas Merton and Simone Weil.

A "Moral Ombudsman" — a non-profit group developing a moral code for social and political interaction, using the thoughts of our greatest religious, spiritual and social thinkers over the past few thousand years — would examine our contemporary political milieu from a true moral center, that place that lies at the heart of all religions. Additionally, this activist think tank would use some Machiavellian means to influence the public discourse for the greater good.

A specific program for the Moral Ombudsman is addressed at the end of this study. It is vital to note at this juncture, however, that this proposition moves beyond the teachings of individual religions, which often divide people from each other, into the highest realm of the human spirit. It utilizes spiritual (not religious, per se) thinking to examine and influence human political interactions.

Within political life, religious institutions often appear to be little more than super energized partisan arms. However, spirituality represents the unifying force at the heart of all sacred paths. It centers on an individual's search for a direct relationship with the Divine, in whatever form he or she imagines It. A solitary and meditational path, it represents one in which the searcher concentrates far more on the quality of their own character than that of those around them.

In addition, spiritual adepts attempt to understand the world — the living beings, the ecosystem, the universe in general — as a seamless whole, united through sub-atomic physics as well as heart and soul. It is rare that a spiritually-centered person would attempt to achieve personal gain at the expense of another person or community.

Although religion in America has become politicized and is used, too often, as a Machiavellian tool (something that the Florentine philosopher heartily endorsed), this misuse of human spirituality cannot erase the fact that the moral and social coalesce at the heart of all religions. It is this energy that must be unearthed and brought to bear on the social and political worlds, to counteract the spiritually immature, Machiavellian aspects of our culture.

If we do not do this, our greedy, selfish and self-destructive primal nature is going to win — and all of us here on this earth are going to lose. As a recent cartoon in *The New Yorker* stated, showing one child sharing a story around a fire with a few other tattered kids: "Yes, the planet got destroyed. But for a beautiful moment in time we created a lot of value for our shareholders."[61]

This tipping point is coming soon. There is no time for delay. Those who want to work for the common good must work and work hard, if we are to survive with a semblance of the civilization that we have so painstakingly built here together.

One approach to this appears in the final chapter of this book.

CHAPTER ONE: NICCOLÒ MACHIAVELLI

> Today Machiavelli is variously said to be the teacher of modern
> nationalism and the modern concept of the state; the founder or an
> important precursor of modern social science understood as the
> realistic, empirical and value-neutral study of man and society; and
> — most recently and fashionably — a founder or important early
> representation of the tradition of modern civic republicanism.[62]

Machiavelli's shadow lurks behind many of today's theories in history,
science and politics. His far-off counsel continues to inspire not only politicians in the United States and around the globe but also social and natural
scientists.

Niccolò Machiavelli (1469-1527) was born in Florence, the third child
of attorney Bernardo di Niccolò Machiavelli. The scion of a long line of Florentine political actors, Machiavelli descended from a series of Marquesses
of Tuscany. In his lineage were thirteen *"Gonfalonieres* of Justice," or titular
heads of the Florentine City Council.

Well educated and erudite, Machiavelli was elected president of the second chancery (1498), after the expulsion of the Medici family from power
and restoration of the Florentine Republic. The Medici ruled in Florence
and Tuscany throughout most of the Renaissance (late 14th through 18th centuries), with the notable exceptions of 1494–1512 and 1527–1530, the first
period of which coincided with Machiavelli's life. The Florentine Republic
appointed him to a council responsible for negotiation and military affairs.
He spent more than a decade carrying out diplomatic missions to France,
Spain, Germany, the Papacy in Rome and the Italian states between 1499 and
1512. Between 1503 and 1506, Machiavelli was responsible for the Florentine
militia, including the City's defense.

In August 1512 the Medici defeated the Florentine Republic at Prato. The Florentine city-state and the Republic were dissolved. Machiavelli was deprived of office in 1512 by the Medici, and in 1513 was accused of conspiracy and was arrested and imprisoned. Despite undergoing torture (being hanged from his bound wrists, dislocating his shoulders), he denied involvement in any plot against the Medici and was released. Now a middle-aged man of 44, he retired to his estate and devoted his final fourteen years to writing the political treatises for which he is known.

As Max Lerner (d. 1992; Max Richter Professor of American Civilization, Brandeis University) told it:

> Finding himself after fourteen years deprived of his job, he felt shut in like a bird in an iron cage. More and more he retreated to his study and his mind. From them came *The Prince*, *The Art of War*, *The Discourses*, *The History of Florence*; various plays, poetry, stories, biographical sketches. The civil servant, the politician, the diplomat, the military organizer had become a man of letters.[63]

As a thinker Machiavelli belonged to a school of Florentine intellectuals concerned with an examination of political and historical problems. In his own lifetime, he achieved some fame as a historian and playwright, but with *The Prince* he hoped to regain political favor. In the end, however, it was *The Prince* that prevented him from leaving the soft prison of his intellectual pursuits and rejoining political Florence.

In 1527 the papal armies were defeated and Rome was sacked by the soldiers of Charles V, who was both the king of Spain (as Carlos I) and the Holy Roman Emperor. At this, the popular party in Florence overthrew the Medici and for a short time restored democratic government. Machiavelli hurried back to Florence, eager to regain his post as secretary. But he never stood a real chance. *The Prince*, circulated in manuscript, had made him enemies; the small dull men who dispensed office feared his brilliance and his wit. Mercifully Machiavelli fell sick and never learned that the final vote of the council was overwhelmingly against him.[64]

Throughout his time of enforced reflection and writing, Machiavelli despaired of the opportunity to remain directly involved in Florentine political matters. After a time he began to participate in intellectual groups in Florence and wrote several plays that were popular and widely known in his lifetime. Still, for him as for many disaffected citizens of all eras, politics remained a passion.

In a letter to Francesco Vettori (d. 1539; a diplomat, politician and writer who served both the Florentine Republic and Medici regime), Machiavelli described his time in exile from political life:

> When evening comes, I go back home, and go to my study. On the threshold, I take off my work clothes, covered in mud and filth, and I put on the clothes an ambassador would wear. Decently dressed, I enter the ancient

courts of rulers who have long since died. There, I am warmly welcomed, and I feed on the only food I find nourishing and was born to savor. I am not ashamed to talk to them and ask them to explain their actions and they, out of kindness, answer me. Four hours go by without my feeling any anxiety. I forget every worry. I am no longer afraid of poverty or frightened of death. I live entirely through them.[65]

Machiavelli died in 1527 at the age of 58. His most important work was not published until 1532.

THE WORKS

> May I venture a guess as to the reason why we still shudder slightly at Machiavelli's name? It is our recognition that the realities he described are realities; it is that men, whether it is in politics, or business, or private life do *not* act according to their professions of virtue; that leaders in every field seek power ruthlessly and hold onto it tenaciously; that the masses who are coerced in a dictatorship have to be wooed and duped in a democracy; that deceit and ruthlessness invariably crop up in every state.[66]

Machiavelli wrote prolifically. One of his most successful plays, the *Mandragola* (mandrake), offered an in-depth look into Machiavelli's world, a comic parallel to *The Prince*. Both are works of practicality and the pursuit of happiness at the expense of others. The play was both performed and printed within Machiavelli's lifetime.

Machiavelli's best-known works, however, were his political treatises: *The Prince* (first printed in 1532) and the lesser-known *Discourses on the First Ten Books of Titus Livius* (first printed in 1531). Both outlined his theories for ascending to and retaining political power. Machiavelli's ideas of statecraft may be succinctly embodied by this pithy maxim: the ends justify the means.

According to the Florentine philosopher, any methods, however distasteful or even illegal, may be applied to political pursuits so long as they are successful. Violence may be necessary for the effective transfer of power and introduction of new legal institutions. Force may be used to eliminate political rivals, to coerce resistant populations and to purge previous rulers who would inevitably attempt to regain their power. Machiavelli has become infamous for this political advice, and he is remembered in history most often as an adjective: "Machiavellian."

THE PRINCE

> Machiavelli and the founders of modern democracy believe that to rule is not essentially to follow the laws of nature and reason but rather to succeed in asserting one's will over others.[67]

Machiavelli wrote *The Prince* during 1513, a few months after his arrest, torture, and banishment by the incoming Medici regime. The accepted theory is that he penned the short treatise to ingratiate himself to Lorenzo di Piero de' Medici (d. 1519) in a failed attempt regain his position in the Florentine government.

The Prince rose almost immediately to social importance due to its impertinently honest look at the civil world. The political program that Machiavelli developed appeared to work quite well. Since its original distribution in manuscript form in 1513, it has become one of the most important handbooks of power ever written.

Perhaps for the first time in human history, Machiavelli presented a vision of social interaction completely devoid of moral and ethical constraints. As Angelo Codevilla (professor of international relations at Boston University, as well as translator of *The Prince*) noted: "Machiavelli's practical maxims freed us all from the myth that government is about the pursuit of goodness."[68]

The Prince has been identified as one of the first works of modern political philosophy in which effective truth is taken to be more important than an abstract ideal. As Machiavelli stated:

> Because how one ought to live is so far removed from how one lives that he who lets go of what is done for that which one ought to do sooner learns ruin than his own preservation: because a man who might want to make a show of goodness in all things necessarily comes to ruin among so many who are not good. Because of this it is necessary for a prince, wanting to maintain himself, to learn how to be able to be not good and to use this and not use it according to necessity.[69]

Machiavelli composed *The Prince* as a practical guide for ruling. It was not theoretical or abstract. It presented a menu of policies and actions to aid rulers, outlining the advantages and disadvantages that attend various routes to power; how to acquire and hold new states; how to deal with internal insurrection; how to make successful alliances; and the central importance of maintaining a strong military and undertaking wars.

In structure *The Prince* comes in four parts. Chapters 1 to 11 are a discussion of the types of states (principalities), classified by the manner in which they were created, organized and governed. Chapters 12 to 14 are a discussion of military affairs, in particular the militia. Chapters 15 through 19 are a catalog of the real virtues needed by a prince. These are the chapters that stand in such sharp contrast to the humanist literature, not to mention the medieval literature, which preceded Machiavelli. Chapters 20 to 25 are further comments on psychological factors . . . Machiavelli consciously sought to refute the humanists while copying their literary form.[70]

Broadly speaking, Machiavelli's discussion was guided by the underlying view that lofty ideals translated into bad government. This premise was especially true with respect to personal virtue. Certain virtues may be admired for their own sake, but for a prince to act in accordance with classical ideas of virtue was often detrimental to the state.

Machiavelli redefined the ideal of virtue from a personal quality of steadfastness and ethical behavior to an amoral individual force leading to victory.

As Carnes Lord (professor of military and naval strategy at the Naval War College) noted in "Machiavelli's Realism":

> Machiavelli develops a notion of *virtù* that is intended to supplant the traditional accounts of moral virtue or human excellence available in the classical as well as Christian traditions. Machiavelli's alternative account emphasizes the aspects of virtue that have to do with manliness, daring and courage. Thus he makes virtue appear not as the good order of the soul, as it is presented in traditional teachings, but rather as an instrument for acquiring and enjoying the "good things in life" in the vulgar sense of that term.
>
> The "virtuous" prince in the new and true sense of the word is one who recognizes the imperative of aggrandizement at the expense of others and does whatever is necessary to secure both himself and his country against foreign threats. Accordingly, he points to military force as the primary element of statecraft.[71]

In addition to the ideal of virtue being twisted and then exalted, Machiavelli's *Prince* developed a moral universe that was entirely relative. Certain vices may be frowned upon, but vicious actions were sometimes indispensable to the good of the state. So while fraud, murder and corruption should sometimes be avoided, in other instances they represented the precise course of action to be undertaken by a "virtuous" prince.

Machiavelli combined this idea of moral fluidity with another: the theme that obtaining the support of the populace was the best way to maintain power. However, this support was not maintained by upright behavior or inspiring love in the subjects. Machiavelli famously stated that it was "better to be feared than loved," as "men loved at their pleasure, but feared at that of the prince." Fear was the most effective technique of inspiring people to follow the prince.

Therefore, the appearance of virtue (in the classical sense) was more important than actually having it, which Machiavelli considered a liability. To *have* moral qualities meant that the prince would not be able to undertake the actions necessary to inspire fear in his subjects. However, it was necessary to *appear* to be moral, so that people would fear the prince not only on a personal level but also out of respect and, in the best of cases, awe, as the prince's actions would appear to be allied with the will of God.

Machiavelli stated:

> Morality interferes with efficiency, therefore it is absurd to concern oneself with moral questions that in any case are practically meaningless, since the vicissitudes of the power struggle may demand at any moment that they be thrown aside as useless baggage.[72]

This led to a political system based in subterfuge and violence. As Harvey Mansfield noted in *Machiavelli's Virtue*: "Machiavelli makes the politics of the new prince appear in the image of rape."[73]

The *Prince* is hardly a museum piece, consigned to history and studied only by academics. It might well be the most important living document of political philosophy, informing politicians today. Angelo Codevilla, translator of *The Prince*, noted:

> The *Prince* is not a handbook about wielding power in a bygone time. It is a key part of our civilization's debate about how human beings get along with one another. Its teachings are essential to understanding Machiavelli's time, our own, and all others, as well.[74]

As we will see in sections further along, *The Prince* and Machiavelli's ideas developed in *The Discourses on the First Ten Books of Titus Livius*, *The Art of War*, *The Florentine Histories* and other writings became embedded in 18th and 19th century political thought, and continue to be bedside reading for contemporary political actors.

THE PRINCE AND THE CHURCH

> Under Pope Paul VI, in 1557, [*The Prince*] was put on the Index [thereby banning it]. What is ironic about this is that the Church princes, like the secular princes, were among the principal followers of Machiavelli's precepts. As Lord Acton [d. 1902; an English historian], himself a Catholic, points out, the arguments used to excuse the massacres of the religious wars were often drawn from Machiavelli.[75]

The *Prince* was not immediately accepted by all quadrants of Florentine life. As was noted, even when it was circulating in manuscript form it so horrified some of Machiavelli's contemporaries that they scuttled his attempt to return to Florentine civic life in 1527.

Additionally, its precepts were in direct conflict with the dominant Catholic and scholastic doctrines. Church elders certainly applied Machiavellian ideas, sticking closely to their "do as we say and not as we do" ethic. Nonetheless, for appearance's sake they presented themselves as deeply offended by the Florentine philosopher's ideas. Within twenty-five years of its publication the Catholic Church banned the book, effectively expanding its readership into the European halls of power. By 1559, when there were approximately fifteen editions of *The Prince* in circulation, Pope Paul IV put it on the Index of Prohibited Books in the "banned absolutely" category (meaning that Catholics were forbidden to read it). It was only in 1966 that the Index was altered to allow Catholics to read previously banned books that had been published prior to 1600. Yet, as Jonathon Green, who wrote an encyclopedia of censorship, pointed out, these books "are to be considered as much condemned today as they ever were."[76]

DISCOURSES ON THE FIRST TEN BOOKS OF TITUS LIVIUS

Machiavelli's *Discourses on the First Ten Books of Titus Livius* expanded his exploration of the political system. *The Prince* dealt with the aspects of ruling for a unitary executive, one who must control not only the passions of the general population but also the nobility. The *Discourses* examined the structure and benefits of a republic, a form of government based on some level of popular consent and control. He examined democratic government with the familiar Machiavellian bent. Even in a democracy, the ends [still] justified the means. Provided the leader could get away with it, of course!

Alone in his study after a hard day working on his lands, Machiavelli peered back through history and saw other approaches to running a country than that of individual rule. In ancient Greece and Rome, as well as recent Florence, he saw governments that involved more input from the general population. Ancient Rome stood out for Machiavelli as the height of political achievement, due to its longevity and vast geography. He penned the *Discourses* to explore its manner of attaining and retaining power, in a government where the general population could not be completely subjugated as in a principality, but must be seduced, coerced and threatened into acquiescence.

Machiavelli wrote the *Discourses* in the form of a longer commentary than *The Prince*, using Roman historian Titus Livy's (d. 17) work *The History of Rome* as his literary template. Livy's work comprised a commentary on the history of Rome from its founding in 753 B.C.E. to 194 B.C.E.

> In the *Discourses*, Machiavelli offered analyses of the principles and institutions of successful and enduring republics, that is, states in which the people have a large or small participation in government. Above all, he discussed the political, religious and military institutions needed for a successful republic... The *Discourses* differs from *The Prince*, because it studies republics and goes far beyond advising a ruler. But the basic political principles are the same.[77]

The *Discourses* included both empirical observations from the surrounding political milieu in Italy, as well as historical generalizations from ancient Rome, Greece and other eras. As Machiavelli himself did not make a sharp distinction between the past and the present, believing that all ages were fundamentally similar and human nature constant, he interspersed historical and contemporary observations to build his argument. Machiavelli insisted that the laws in force in human affairs are as unchanging as those of the sun and the elements.

The text was composed of three books. In *Book I* Machiavelli focused on the internal structure of the republic. *Book II* concerned matters of warfare, which Machiavelli asserted time and again were the most important aspect of statecraft. A concept verified by the ensuing half millennia of history.

Book III was perhaps most similar to the teachings of *The Prince*, as it concerned individual leadership. Taken together, the three books provided guidance to those trying to establish or reform a republic. However, Machiavelli's advice also included a very long section on conspiracies, providing advice to people seeking to overthrow a republic as well as those trying to establish one.

Power was Machiavelli's currency. He was less concerned with who wielded it.

OTHER IMPORTANT WRITING

Machiavelli also penned other works that expanded his political vision. *The Art of War* dealt with Machiavelli's most important art of statecraft. As his protagonist, Lord Fabrizio Colonna (considered by some historians to be Machiavelli's *doppelganger*) stated at the outset, the book was written, among other things, "to honor and reward *virtù*." Of course, the *virtù* in question was not the historical, morally based version but Machiavelli's perversion of it, a stew of greed, force and courage. Machiavelli also asserted again that the military was of vital importance in striving for the public good. He noted in the preface that the military was like the roof of a *palazzo* protecting the contents.

Written between 1519 and 1520 and published the following year, it was Machiavelli's only nonfiction work to be printed during his lifetime. *The Art of War* echoed many themes, issues and proposals from his earlier, more widely read works, *The Prince* and *The Discourses*. His ideas concerning war were not created in a vacuum. Machiavelli had served for fourteen years as secretary to the Chancery of Florence and "personally observed and reported back to his government on the size, composition, weaponry, morale and logistical capabilities of the most effective militaries of his day."[78]

Although now considered a lesser work, *The Art of War* had resonance among Machiavelli's contemporaries. Some of the recommendations made in the book — those on training, discipline and classification, for instance — gained increasing practical importance in early modern Europe when armies came to be composed of professionals culled from different social strata. Due to the importance that Machiavelli placed on war, and his development of the idea of limited warfare as a political tool, he felt that this was his most important work.

Another book was his *History of Florence*. In 1520, Pope Leo X (himself a member of the Medici family) commissioned Machiavelli to write this history. In 1525, Machiavelli presented Pope Clement VII (yet another member of the Medici family) with eight books following the history of the city from its origin up to 1492. Machiavelli's *History of Florence* not only stands as a monumental literary work but also as a vehicle that led to Machiavelli's reinstatement into Florentine society. After he presented it to the Pope, Machiavelli received an appointment as a negotiator for the wool guild, as well as receiving work with the Franciscans and commissions for other writing projects for members of the Medici clan.

The composition of the work presented a problem, however, for the commission was not meant to give him the opportunity to eulogize republican Florence — of which Machiavelli had been the Secretary, but had taken place out of the ambit of Medici control. He was expected to pen a treatise that showed the present state of things (i.e., a Medici principality) as a natural political evolution from earlier Florentine history.

Books I, II, III, and IV narrated the city's history before the Medici ascension, while the last four chapters spoke of the fight for power that ended with the Medici lordship. The final book closed with the death of Lorenzo il Magnifico in 1492 and the end of the fragile peace occasioned by Lorenzo's politics of balance. What remained unexamined was the decline of the Medici (under Piero the Unfortunate, 1492–1494) and then the period of Girolamo Savonarola's rule (1494–1498) and the Florentine Republic (1498–1512).

Machiavelli used the opportunity of the Medici commission to situate his political theories within his country's own history. The major themes in *The History of Florence* were the necessity of basing strong government on the consent of the people, even if this consent had to be garnered using coercive or violent means. It also utilized Florence's history to point out the inevitable corruption of the state if it tolerated political factions. As a scholar Machiavelli relied heavily on the details related by earlier chroniclers, but he shaped and combined his material to make it fit with his worldview. As with all his works, he used history to provide lessons that he considered valid during all eras.

MACHIAVELLIAN THOUGHT

> All modern thinkers who have wanted to be free to think without regard to the constraints of natural and divine law are the fruits of the Machiavellian revolution.[79]

More than just a political theorist, Machiavelli is considered by many scholars to be the father of modern thought, offering a new approach for understanding the world that affected scientific, social and philosophical thinking. His "clear minded" and amoral presentation of political reality inspired the vision of thinkers in a variety of other fields. Professor Steven Forde noted in "Machiavelli's Liberal Republican Legacy":

> Bacon, Descartes and other knowing or unknowing disciples of Machiavelli applied the new understanding to the natural world and created a science devoted to controlling nature for the sake of easing man's estate. In the process, they furthered Machiavelli's wholesale assault on the older moral philosophy.[80]

Machiavelli's innovation was his faith in human reason as an instrument not only to analyze the world but also master it.

THE TUTOR OF PRINCES

According to Machiavelli, humanity's war with fortune affected all interactions. And mastering fortune often centered on controlling those around one. This was not an easy task, as Machiavelli held a dim view of human nature. "It is necessary to whoever disposes a republic and orders laws in it to presuppose that all men are bad."[81] As Paul Carrese (professor of political science at the United States Air Force Academy) noted: "Machiavelli replaces [Aristotelian ideas of] progression toward a set end with a chaotic natural world that permits only the fittest, most adaptable beings to survive."[82]

To this end, Machiavelli did not look to the same models that political leaders had been emulating up to that time (the lawgiving Moses; the gentle Jesus; the political ideals of Plato or Aristotle). Instead, he proposed Chiron, half man and half beast, as the tutor of princes.

> You therefore must know there are two kinds of fighting: the one with laws, the other with force. The first is proper to man, the second to beasts: but because many times the first does not suffice, it is expedient to recur to the second. Therefore, it is necessary for a prince to know well how to use the beast and the man.[83]

Machiavelli proposed a rule for political actions that horrified the moral senses but, if history is examined clearly, has proven to represent the truth. He noted: "When the act accuses, the result excuses."[84] Whatever actions undertaken to master *fortuna* (the word Machiavelli used to refer to fate) or attain political victory would be excused if the actor was successful. Machiavelli absolved triumphant leaders of all blame or responsibility for any act necessary to attain and retain power:

> A wise mind will never censure anyone for having employed any extraordinary means for the purpose of establishing a kingdom or constituting a republic . . . when the result is good, it will always absolve him from blame.[85]

MOSES: THE TUTOR OF PRINCES

The perfect historic prince for Machiavelli — the one who well understood that man was "part human and part beast," and to be ruled correctly must be mastered — was the Biblical Moses. Not because he was a lawgiver or peace loving leader, but because he appreciated how to use power to terrorize his own people to retain control over them.

In discussing Moses, Machiavelli approvingly noted that the Jewish king "killed numberless men" to force his laws upon Israel. While he wasn't proposing that the slaughter of his followers was good, he did contend that drastic times called for drastic measures. And Machiavelli considered no measure too drastic.

We read in Exodus 32:26-28 of Moses' subjugation of the restive Jewish population after he had returned from Mount Sinai with the Ten Commandments only to find the Jewish people worshipping a golden calf:

> Then Moses stood in the gate of the camp and said: "Whoso is on the Lord's side, let him come unto me." And all the sons of Levi gathered themselves together unto him. And he said unto them: "Thus saith the Lord, the God of Israel: put ye every man his sword upon his thigh, and go to and fro from gate to gate throughout the camp, and slay every man his brother, and every

man his companion, and every man his neighbor." And the sons of Levi did according to the word of Moses, and there fell of the people that day about three thousand men.[86]

Moses's willingness to slaughter his own people represented the height of Machiavellian *virtù*. As Harvey Mansfield noted in *Machiavelli's Virtue*, Moses's actions represented the Machiavellian dictum that it was occasionally necessary to enforce sensational and even unjust executions to master the population:

> Gratitude [in the prince's subjects] can be manufactured if a prince mixes some deliberate but unexpected actions of injustice with his justice . . . a few sensational, shocking executions, especially if they are "extraordinary" and hence of doubtful legality, or even blatant illegality, will cause his beneficiaries to keep their eye on him and come to his side when he needs their help, not merely when they want to give it.[87]

VIRTÙ

> One can either be an excellent ruler or a morally good man, but not both, for it is in the nature of politics that such goods as order and prosperity cannot be secured without unjustly injuring a great many individuals not only as a matter of exception but on a recurrent basis.[88]

Machiavelli's novel interpretation of *virtù* twisted a moral concept into one based in mastering fate and imposing individual will. Although the Merriam-Webster Dictionary defines virtue as, above all, a "conformity to a standard of right: morality" and "a particular moral excellence," Machiavelli reconfigured the idea. As Leo Strauss (d. 1973; professor of political science at the University of Chicago) remarked in *Thoughts on Machiavelli*:

> [The prince] certainly need not possess and exercise moral virtue proper . . . But he must possess that virtue which consists of "brain" or "greatness of mind," and manliness combined — the kind of virtue possessed by the criminals Agathocles and Severus. This is the most obvious message of *The Prince* as a whole. Whereas moral virtue and republican virtue are the affects of habituation and hence of society, this kind of [Machiavellian] virtue which we have now encountered is natural. Its ground is . . . the natural desire of each to acquire wealth and glory.[89]

This flew in the face of at least a millennium of moral and political thought. Going back to the Roman philosopher Boethius (d. 525), virtue had been defined as a quality by which men imposed moral form on *fortuna* (fortune or fate). It did not propose mastering fate like a bitch, as had the Florentine philosopher, but rather to gently impress goodness onto her through ethical thought and action. Civic humanism, in this historic construction, identified the good man with the social actor, the citizen, thereby politicizing virtue and rendering it interdependent with the virtue of others.[90] Virtue was a social grace infused with morality.

Machiavelli's *virtù*, however, was a solitary affair. It defined the way in which a single man acted not only on his subjects, but history itself. It was in this light that Machiavelli viewed Moses and his actions upon his return with the Ten Commandments, when he found his people worshipping the idol. The virtue Moses displayed was prototypically Machiavellian: he slaughtered 3000 individuals with the help of the Levites to regain control of his restive people.

This concept of *virtù* was not only central to the Florentine's ideas of power and leadership, it can also help the rest of us appreciate why the morally good do not rule in this world. In the world of spirituality and civic mindedness, a different idea of virtue reigns than that of Machiavelli. Scholar Harvey Mansfield addressed the divide between Boethius's idea of virtue and Machiavelli's:

> Humility is the modern virtue; it is the virtue of weakness, the virtue that makes a virtue of weakness. To Machiavelli, it is the outstanding example of the fraud he recommends . . . Machiavelli, with his hidden virtue, appropriates the Christian virtue that won the victory over ancient virtue, and uses it against the Christians, thus reversing their good fortune and taking it for himself.[91]

People of true moral character or those genuinely centering their actions in the common good were overwhelmed by Machiavellian actors displaying the amoral *virtù* of successful leaders.

Once we appreciate Machiavelli's "new species of republicanism, liberated from moral restraints . . . and bolstered by a peculiar mixture of savagery, ambitions and dread — what he calls *virtù*,"[92] then we can better understand the motivations for political leaders throughout time. In their world, virtue is measured only by success, and remains completely unencumbered by moral considerations.

War and Religion

For Machiavelli, war and religion were the main commodities of politics. These two forces allowed the leader to master *fortuna* as well as his own subjects. Of war, he said: "A prince must not have any objective, nor any thought, nor take up any art, other than the art of war.[93]

Religion became war's sibling, a power that could be fused with violence to bring God, war and the state together beneath the mantle of the prince's leadership.

> The unarmed prince . . . disposes of formidable weapons necessary to the art of war. The unarmed prophet becomes armed if he uses religion for his own purposes rather than God's; and because the prince cannot acquire glory for himself without bringing order to his principality, using religion for himself is using it to answer human necessity generally.[94]

More even than physical violence, Machiavelli respected fraud as the ultimate force. And for Machiavelli, religion represented the ultimate fraud. Machiavelli noted: "there is nothing more important than appearing to be religious."[95] Appearance was enough: "It is not necessary for the prince to have [moral qualities], but it is necessary to appear to have them."[96] This dovetailed with another central Machiavellian tenet: "Men are so simple and so obey present necessities that he who deceives will always find someone who will let themselves be deceived."[97]

Once the alliance was successfully proposed between the leader and religion, it merged the leader's desires, actions and laws with the Divine will. In Machiavelli's words:

> In truth, there never was any remarkable lawgiver amongst any peoples who did not resort to divine authority, as otherwise his laws would not have been accepted by the people; for there are many good laws, the importance of which are known to any sagacious lawgiver, but the reasons for which are not sufficiently evident to allow him to persuade others to submit to them; and therefore do wise men, for the purpose of removing this difficulty, resort to divine authority.[98]

Once the fusion between leader and religion was made, it was a short step to bring the whole machinery of the state into the equation, forming a seamless whole between leader, God and state. The state became the focus of religion, and the leader the de-facto Pope of the state creed.

The Language of Politics

> The illness of political language is characterized by double-talk, tautology, ambiguous cliché, self-righteous and doctrinaire pomposity and pseudoscientific jargon that mask a total callousness and moral insensitivity, indeed a basic contempt for man.[99]

If war and religion are the commodities of power, language is its currency. Language sells the image the prince wants to project. All of Machiavelli's non-violent methods of force center on the use of language. Professor Angelo Codevilla noted in "Words and Power":

> Language is the most powerful weapon in the struggle for primacy, and one particularly suited to the unarmed . . . [Machiavelli's] thesis is that languages are essentially particular articulations of the universal struggle for primacy . . . All speech is a form of rhetoric.

Morality, truth and reliability of action are irrelevant. Words alone can present the image that the prince wants to display. William B. Allen (professor of political philosophy at Michigan State University) noted in "Machiavelli and Modernity":

> For Machiavelli, the role of morals in politics (and one might almost say the role of words in general) is mainly to make useful impressions or, to put it starkly, to cultivate illusions. The only remaining question of principle is the extent to which "custom" (ethics) or "rule" (force) will enter into play for the sake of making the most effective impressions. It is the task of the ruler to decide clearly when it will be more useful to emphasize force and when to emphasize ethos. This, then, is the center of Machiavellian thought: it reduces ethos to useful illusions.[100]

Language, like religion and violent force, must be used judiciously, but always with a single goal: power. "For Machiavelli, the 'arts of peace' are those of nonviolent war by fraud."[101] In the god-less world of power politics, the successful prince will have no other objective against which to evaluate himself but one thing: did the subterfuge work?

MACHIAVELLI'S INFLUENCE ON LATER THINKERS

It is not too far a stretch to say that there has been no greater influence on post-Renaissance political thought than Niccolò Machiavelli, specifically with his two handbooks of power, *The Prince* and *Discourses on the First Ten Books of Titus Livius.*

As was earlier noted, by 1559 there were 15 editions of *The Prince* in print and 19 of the *Discourses on the First Ten Books of Titus Livius,* as well as French translations of each. And regardless of the Pope's attempt to suppress Machiavelli's work, the Florentine's ideas continued — and still continue — to influence political actors.

Inspiration on the Renaissance (c. 1350–1650) and the Enlightenment's (c. 1650–1800) greatest thinkers is not difficult to discern. *The Prince* was spoken of highly by Thomas Cromwell (executed in 1540; an English states-man who served as chief minister to King Henry VIII), as well as by Henry VIII himself (d. 1547), who executed Cromwell.[102]

The Holy Roman Emperor Charles V (d. 1558) possessed a copy of *The Prince,*[103] which undoubtedly aided him in his military campaigns in France, Spain, Italy, the Ottoman Empire and the Americas. In France, after an ini-tially mixed reaction, Machiavelli came to be associated with Catherine de' Medici (d. 1589; Queen consort of France from 1547 until 1559, as the wife of King Henry II of France). In the 16th century, Catholic writers "associated Machiavelli with the Protestants, whereas Protestant authors saw him as Italian and Catholic."[104] In point of fact, he was influencing both Catholic and Protestant kings.

Direct Machiavellian influence has been attributed to many of the 17th and 18th-centuries' most important political philosophers. In turn, these social theorists affected later thinkers, including America's Founding Fathers. Francis Bacon (d. 1626; served both as Attorney General and Lord Chancel-lor of England); René Descartes (d. 1650; considered the "Father of Modern Philosophy") and Montesquieu (d. 1755; a French social commentator and political thinker) all rehearsed Machiavellian themes in their work.

Additionally, Machiavelli's ideas influenced Algernon Sidney (d. 1683; an English politician and republican political theorist); John Harrington (d. 1677; English political theorist of classical-republicanism); John Milton (d. 1674; generally regarded "as one of the preeminent writers in the English lan-guage"); Baruch Spinoza (d. 1677; considered one of the great rationalists of 17th-century philosophy); Jean-Jacques Rousseau (d. 1778; his political philosophy influenced the French Revolution as well as the overall development of modern political, sociological and educational thought); David Hume (d. 1776; a Scottish philosopher considered one of the most important figures in the history of Western philosophy); Edward Gibbon (d. 1794; best known for authoring *The History of the Decline and Fall of the Roman Empire*) and Adam Smith (d. 1790; a Scottish social philosopher and a pioneer of political economy).

Other important political thinkers exhibited the Florentine's ideas, although Machiavelli was not always mentioned by name in their works. Scholars have pointed out similarities between Machiavelli and Michel Montaigne (d. 1592; one of the most influential writers of the French Renaissance), John Locke (d. 1704; widely known as the Father of Classical Liberalism) and Thomas Hobbes (d. 1679; his 1651 book *Leviathan* established the foundation for most of Western political philosophy from the perspective of social contract theory).

As Blair Worden (Emeritus Fellow at Oxford University) noted:

> In the seventeenth century it was in England that Machiavelli's ideas were most substantially developed and adapted, and that republicanism came once more to life; and out of seventeenth-century English republicanism there were to emerge in the next century not only a theme of English political and historical reflection, but a stimulus to the Enlightenment in Scotland, on the Continent and in America.[105]

Machiavelli had a major direct and indirect influence on the political thinking of principal American figures such as Benjamin Franklin, James Madison, Thomas Jefferson and Alexander Hamilton. John Adams commented profusely on the Italian's thought in his work, *A Defence of the Constitutions of Government of the United States of America*. The Machiavellian influence on America's Founding Fathers will be explored in more detail further along.

Closer to our era, the German philosopher Georg Wilhelm Friedrich Hegel (d. 1831; revolutionized European philosophy and was an important precursor to Marxism) "offered an emotional eulogy of Machiavelli, whose genius he celebrated against all the moralizing critics who belabored him."[106] A century later, Antonio Gramsci (d. 1937; founding member and a leader of the Communist Party of Italy) developed a conception of the "modern prince," which represented the mantle of Machiavellian power passing from a single exalted leader to the popular masses.[107]

Benito Mussolini (d. 1945; leader of Italy's National Fascist Party) encouraged the distribution of *The Prince* to demonstrate the need for a strong, central Italian leadership. A couple of decades later, in 1959 after Fidel Castro (b. 1926) overthrew the Batista government in Cuba, a newspaper reported that *The Prince* was on his revolutionary reading list.[108] And both Adolf Hitler (d.

1945) and Karl Christian Rove (b. 1950; central Republican political operative) kept the book as bedside reading.

> Machiavelli's inspirational legacy has lived on well into the twentieth century as a double-edged sword. The science fiction writer H.G. Wells wrote a political novel entitled *The New Machiavelli*, Antonio Gramsci attempted to update Machiavelli from a Marxian bent into *The Modern Prince*, feminist theorists have created *The Princess*, and the leaders of both Nazi and Soviet totalitarianism lifted their hats respectfully to the Italian master of realpolitik. In much more recent times the spin-masters of Tony Blair's New Labour Party might also be seen to owe something to Machiavelli's treatise on cunning guile.[109]

Machiavelli continues to be lauded by American scholars and politicians today. As Paul Grendler noted in *The European Renaissance in American Life*:

> Such books as *Power Rules: How Common Sense Can Rescue American Foreign Policy* (Leslie Gelb, 2009) are based on *The Prince*. Other recent titles including *Machiavelli on Modern Leadership* (Michael A. Ledeen, 1999), *What Would Machiavelli Do? The Ends Justify the Meanness* (Stanley Bing, 1999) and *The New Machiavelli: The Art of Politics in Business* (Alistair McAlpine, 1999) are testament to the ongoing fascination with the Renaissance thinker.

Lastly, to show that the appreciation for and resonance of Machiavellian thought is worldwide, a notice in the newspaper concerning the first presidential election (2012) in Egypt's history — a history dating back more than 5000 years —noted:

> Aboul Fotouh supporters have sought to disparage the [Muslim] Brotherhood. New billboards that have gone up around Cairo in support of Aboul Fotouh call the candidate's former [Muslim Brotherhood] group the "Machiavellian Brotherhood."[110]

Chapter Two: Machiavelli in America

> There is much to be grateful for in the vision of progress that
> Machiavelli launched. Those who should be most grateful are perhaps
> the beneficiaries who live in the most modern, and hence most
> Machiavellian, commercial society, the United States.[111]

Given the ubiquity of Machiavellian ideas in the 18th-century worlds of
arts and letters, it is not surprising that the Florentine had a deep influence
on the Founders and early American history. Even if they were not looking to
Machiavelli himself, the early American leaders were basing their concepts
on thinkers who had themselves taken much from the Renaissance political
philosopher.

As John Adams (d. 1826; American Founding Father, and the second
president of the United States) noted, Machiavelli "revived the ancient politics," thereby provoking the modern revolution in political thought. Adams
also assured that Machiavelli had directly influenced John Milton (d. 1674),
James Harrington (d. 1677), John Locke (d. 1704) and Montesquieu (d. 1755),
this last of whom, Adams claimed, "borrowed the best part of his book from
Machiavelli."[112]

Montesquieu in particular was an important bridge of Machiavellian
ideas for the early American thinkers. As Paul Carrese noted in *The Machiavellian Spirit of Montesquieu's Republic*:

> Montesquieu, and Machiavelli's influence upon him, should not be remote
> concerns in liberal democracies. Montesquieu's prominent place in the
> thought of the American Founders, especially at the time of the framing
> and establishment of the 1787 Constitution, is evident to any reader of *The
> Federalist*.[113]

America's subsequent inspiration on democracies near and far allowed Montesquieu to help make a distinctive Machiavellian imprint on world politics by advancing the "prominence of pluralism, faction, judicial power, federalism and globalization."[114]

Contemporary neo-Conservative thinker Michael Ledeen (b. 1941) noted the similarities between the beginnings of America and the Florentine's ideals: "There is much in Machiavelli that sounds like the American Founding Fathers . . . Machiavelli's notion of the good state calls to mind *The Federalist Papers*."[115]

Ledeen continued on to reference specific Machiavellian influence on Founding Fathers James Madison (d. 1836; fourth president of the United States), Alexander Hamilton (d. 1804; first United States secretary of the treasury) and Benjamin Franklin (d. 1790).

Franklin, the first United States Ambassador to France, channeled the far-off Renaissance thinker in his international politics:

> He [Franklin] had no inhibitions against treating weaker powers as pawns . . . his attitude toward Canada would be difficult to imagine outside this Machiavellian context . . . the wishes of the inhabitants scarcely entered into his, or anyone else's, calculations of power.[116]

George Washington

George Washington (d. 1799) remains the single most respected leader in the history of the United States. Not only is the American capital city named after him, but so also are one state, thirty counties, twenty-four cities, 241 townships, eleven colleges and universities and various mountains, islands and neighborhoods around the nation of which he is considered the "father."

Washington was the dominant military and political leader of the fledgling country from 1775 to 1799. He led America to victory in the Revolutionary War (1775–1783), presided over the writing of the United States Constitution in 1787 and then became the first president by unanimous choice of the 69 electors in the Electoral College (popular votes for president not being tallied until 1824). He oversaw the creation of a strong, well-financed national government that maintained neutrality in the wars raging in Europe, suppressed rebellion at home and won acceptance among Americans of all types.

One would be hard pressed to read a single negative thing about this man who "could not tell a lie." He was favorably compared in his lifetime to Cincinnatus (d. 430 B.C.E.), one of the heroes of early Rome who was considered a model of Roman virtue and simplicity.

However, the Father of the United States was not untarnished by his own Machiavellian actions. He undertook numerous measures that appeared to draw direct inspiration from the Florentine philosopher. Matthew Spalding (Director, B. Kenneth Simon Center for Principles and Politics at the Heritage Foundation) noted that Washington was granted virtually unlimited powers during the cold winters of 1776 and 1777, and he responded with Machiavellian efficiency. He commandeered all harvests from local farmers, proclaimed all persons not taking an oath of loyalty to him to be "enemies of the American states" and demanded complete and unthinking fealty from his subordinate officers.

Then, in a maneuver that Machiavelli would have particularly supported, he recommended that cowards be punished by death, and he encouraged swift executions of mutinous soldiers.[117] This last measure echoed Machiavelli's injunction that a few sensational and shocking executions will cause the prince's other subjects to come to his side,[118] which, as history shows, Washington's men most certainly did.

Later, as president, Washington continued to channel the Renaissance thinker. Michael Ledeen noted in *Machiavelli on Modern Leadership*:

> To be an effective leader, the most prudent method is to ensure that your people are afraid of you. To instill that fear, you must demonstrate that those who attack you will not survive. George Washington was well aware of the importance of decisive action against those who challenged his authority. In his first term as president he faced the Whiskey Insurrection, of citizens refusing to pay excise taxes on their liquor manufactures. His report to congress echoed the urgency of Machiavelli's advice . . . Washington called out the army and personally led it against the insurrection. No American president was ever so loved as George Washington, but he knew that fear was essential to his effective rule.[119]

In dealing with American expansionism and the Native American population, Washington also waxed Machiavellian. As the Florentine thinker stated: "Whoever becomes lord of a city and does not undo her, he may expect to be undone by her . . . if one does not disunite or disperse the inhabitants, suddenly in every accident, they come back."[120]

George Washington agreed. He wanted to be the father of the nation, not the moral lodestar around which some utopia may have been created. He stated: "The gradual extension of our settlement will as certainly cause the savage as the wolf to retire, both being beasts of prey, though they differ in shape."[121] The genocide of the Native Americans continued under Washington, and would do so for another hundred years, until the last vestiges of that once-proud nation were driven onto *Bantustans* in mostly un-tillable lands around the American Mid- and Southwest.

THOMAS JEFFERSON

Thomas Jefferson, another Founding Father whose name is synonymous with the best of the American spirit, is known as the principal author of the Declaration of Independence (1776). He served as the first United States Secretary of State (1790–1793) and third president of the country (1801–1809).

He is also remembered for purchasing the vast Louisiana Territory from France (1803), and for sending the Lewis and Clark Expedition (1804–1806) to explore the new West. In addition to his political activities, Jefferson was renowned as a Renaissance man, a leader in Enlightenment thinking, an international figure who spoke five languages and was deeply interested in science, invention, architecture, religion and philosophy — a basket of interests that led him to found the University of Virginia after his presidency. He has continually been rated by scholars as one of the greatest U.S. presidents.

However, once again we lift the smothering shroud of myth and historical narrative to find Niccolò Machiavelli lurking in the shadows of the accepted account. Paul Rahe (Charles O. Lee and Louise K. Lee Chair in Western Heritage, Hillsdale College) noted in "Thomas Jefferson's Machiavellian Political Science":

> In late July 1791 [Jefferson was Secretary of State at the time] the Chevalier de Pio wrote to his old friend from the midst of the French Revolution in Paris, remarking, "Actually, before my eyes, I have none but Locke, Sidney, Milton, J.J. Rousseau, Thomas Payne; that is my entire library; I have burned the rest, except for Machiavelli, whom all diplomats possess, though they dare not confess it, and whom free men ought to place alongside the Declaration of Rights" . . . [T]hat Jefferson was as deeply indebted to the Florentine as was the Chevalier de Pio we need not doubt.[122]

Given the influence of Machiavellian ideas in Jefferson's thinking, it is not difficult to discern specific inspiration of the one on the other. Like Washington just before him, Jefferson did believe that circumstances sometimes occurred which "made it a duty in officers of high trust, to assume authorities beyond the law." Jefferson continued — presaging the thinking of Dick Cheney (vice president, 2001–2009), George W. Bush (43rd president) and perhaps all American administrations: "A strict observance of the written law is doubtless *one* of the highest duties of a good citizen, but not the highest. The laws of necessity, of self-preservation, of saving our country when in danger, are of higher obligation."[123]

Jefferson also spoke in a Machiavellian vein when he noted that political turbulence is an "evil productive of good." In this he was indistinguishable from his Florentine predecessor, believing what Machiavelli had said: that every political community "ought to have modes by which people can vent their ambition."[124] As Jefferson commented: "What signify a few lives lost in a century or two? The Tree of Liberty must be refreshed from time to time with the blood of patriots and tyrants. It is its natural manure."[125]

As J.G.A. Pocock noted in *The Machiavellian Moment*, Jefferson's thought (as well as that of many other political thinkers of his era) "was based on premises entirely Machiavellian."[126]

John Adams

John Adams (d. 1826) was America's first vice president, serving two terms under George Washington. He served as the second president of the United States (1797–1801). Also a lawyer, statesman, diplomat, political theorist and leading champion of independence in 1776, Adams represented Enlightenment values promoting republicanism.

What is less well known about this Founding Father is his affection for Machiavelli's political program. Claiming the world was "much indebted to Machiavelli for the revival of reason in matters of government," he recommended the Florentine's political science to potential writers of the U.S. Constitution.

> Machiavelli was for Adams a kind of missing link, an important bridge between the political science of the ancient world and the empirical political tradition of the modern age. Adams thought that Machiavelli was the central figure in the resurrection of an empirico-inductive tradition of political science.[127]

Adams borrowed extensively from the Renaissance thinker in his *A Defence of the Constitutions of Government of the United States of America*, quoting from Machiavelli and openly acknowledging his debt to the earlier philosopher's ideas.[128] As Professor C. Bradley Thompson (Author of *John Adams and the Spirit of Liberty*) noted in "John Adam's Machiavellian Moment":

> Adams claimed to have been a "student of Machiavelli" . . . But even the most thoughtful reader of the *Defence of the Constitutions of Government of the United States of America* is hardly prepared when Adams advances on behalf of the Florentine a series of stunning claims. Adams refers to Machiavelli as "the great restorer of true politics." He also praised Machiavelli for having been the "first" to have "revived the ancient politics."[129]

James Madison

James Madison (d. 1836), the fourth president of the United States (1809–1817), was hailed as the "Father of the Constitution" for being instrumental in drafting that document. Also notable for composing the first ten amendments to the Constitution, he was designated "Father of the Bill of Rights," as well.

After the constitution had been written, Madison became one of the leaders in the movement to ratify it. His collaboration with Alexander Hamilton and John Jay produced the *Federalist Papers* (1788). Circulated only in New York at the time, they would come to be considered among the most important polemics in support of the Constitution.

Madison clearly evinced Machiavellian thinking. Gary Rosen (author of *American Compact: James Madison and the Problem of Founding*) noted that Madison was perhaps *the* outstanding example of Machiavellian prudence. Some of the specific views for which this Founding Father is renowned — "that government necessarily involves the spirit of faction and party, that neither moral nor religious motives can be relied on to control factious oppression and that a free constitution requires both the vigilance of the people and the mutual suspicion of the ambitious" — are borrowed directly from Machiavelli's writings. They represent the Americanization of Machiavelli's "effective truth" of politics: that men should govern themselves according to how they really are, and not how they wish they were.[130]

Madison also channeled the Florentine philosopher as he built support to usher the United States Constitution through the Constitutional Convention in 1787.[131] Madison was a chief proponent (along with another Machiavellian acolyte, Alexander Hamilton) of creating a new government rather than fixing the existing one. This fit directly in with Machiavelli's advice on "founding a new order." The Florentine philosopher's ideas were very helpful as Madison, Hamilton and the other Founding Fathers ushered the new governmental model into existence.

Alexander Hamilton

Alexander Hamilton (d. 1804) was the only one of these Founding Fathers who did not serve as president. However, as a Revolutionary War soldier, political philosopher, one of America's earliest constitutional lawyers and the first United States secretary of the treasury, he had a deep influence on the direction of the new republic.

Like his compatriots, his ideas displayed inspiration from the Florentine philosopher. As Karl-Friedrich Walling (author of *Republican Empire: Alexander Hamilton on War and Free Government*) noted in "Was Alexander Hamilton a Machiavellian Statesman?"

> Hamilton was arguably more like Machiavelli than any of the other American Founders because he devoted most of his career to this fundamental problem of political theory and practice [the challenge of waging war effectively and remaining free at the same time]. Like Machiavelli, he recognized that durable liberty required the kind of republic that could adapt to the changing necessities and fortunes of war. Energy, the central concept in Hamilton's political thought, was his means of endowing the American republic with some of the dynamic Machiavellian *virtù*.[132]

A book released in 2004 titled: *American Machiavelli: Alexander Hamilton and the Origins of U.S. Foreign Policy*, outlined the specific Machiavellian strategies of this signer of the Constitution. As the author John Lamberton (professor of foreign policy and European studies at the Johns Hopkins University Bologna Center) noted:

> For Hamilton, as for Machiavelli, "it was the test of a good political order to grow, to expand and to absorb other political societies, even to ward off decline for awhile" . . . Just as Machiavelli looked for inspiration to the quasi-miraculous rise of the Roman republic, Hamilton looked for lessons in the experience of the most remarkable and dynamic generator of *virtù*

(the bundle of qualities including steadfastness, guile, adaptability, bold-
ness and dexterity of arms) in his day . . . Hamilton's program for creating
a similar state in 18th-century America proved to be nearly as fabulous as
Machiavelli's vision for 16th-century Italy.

The kernel of Hamilton's system survived his political defeat in 1799-1800:
the kind of basic financial infrastructure with its monetized national debt,
secure federal revenues, and national bank, needed to promote economic
development and to mobilize wealth for military purposes. Hamilton's legacy also includes the kind of minimum standing forces, peacetime cultiva-
tion of the military arts and sciences, and defense-industrial preparedness
that would allow the United States not just to survive, but thrive, in war.[133]

Machiavelli in America Today

Machiavelli's influence hardly waned with the passing of those early
American leaders. The Florentine's inspiration on the contemporary American leadership ideal is not difficult to discern. It might even be stronger now
than it was on those American Enlightenment political thinkers. As Harvey
Mansfield noted in *Machiavelli's Virtue*, the seven most important facets of
the modern leader originated in Machiavelli:

> The political use of punishment, which demands an outsized executive; the
> primacy of war and foreign affairs over peace and domestic affairs, which
> greatly increases the occasions for emergency powers; the use of indirect
> government, when ruling is perceived to be executed by someone or some
> group other than the ruler; the erosion of differences among regimes as
> wholes, through the development of techniques of governing applicable
> to all regimes; the need for decisiveness, for government is best done sud-
> denly; the value of secrecy and the necessity of the single executive.[134]

Mansfield, writing in the *Wall Street Journal* toward the end of the George
W. Bush administration, rolled these ideas into the vision of a muscular,
Machiavellian chief executive, of which even George W. Bush, Dick Cheney,
Karl Rove and the rest of the Bush administration could only dream:

> Harvard political philosopher Harvey Mansfield's op-ed on executive pow-
> er in yesterday's *Wall Street Journal* [May 2, 2007] may be the best piece
> of Swiftian satire penned in recent memory. Or at any rate, it would be,
> if not for the terrifying probability that Mr. Mansfield is entirely serious.
> Machiavelli is transformed into a kind of patron saint of American political
> thought. *The Federalist Papers'* defense of a president with broad discretion
> within a carefully defined and narrowly circumscribed sphere is read as
> an unqualified endorsement of executive "energy." And past republics, Mr.
> Mansfield sweepingly asserts, were doomed by their own over-reliance on
> the rule of law.[135]

More than just Machiavellian scholar Harvey Mansfield acknowledges
the important role of the Florentine political advisor in today's America.
Machiavelli's presence at the center of American politics is often specifically

referenced, sometimes approvingly and sometimes simply journalistically, as if stating an obvious fact.

For instance, just after the midterm elections of 2010, an article ran with the headline: "Machiavelli Reigns: Dirty campaigns beg the question: 'Is everything fair game in American politics?'" The body of the piece treated the reader to a brief recitation of the importance of Machiavelli's "ends justify the means" politics from the earliest days of the American republic, in which character assassination replaced the Machiavellian corporeal assassination, though to the same effect:

> 1800: In the country's first contested presidential election, supporters of Thomas Jefferson claimed incumbent John Adams wanted to marry off his son to the daughter of King George III, creating an American dynasty under British rule. Jefferson supporters said: "John Adams is a blind, crippled, hermaphroditical character with neither the force and firmness of a man, nor the gentleness and sensibility of a woman, who secretly wants to start a war with France." Jefferson haters called [Jefferson] a fraud, a coward, a thief, and "a mean-spirited, low-lived fellow, the son of a half-breed Indian squaw, sired by a Virginia mulatto father."

> 1884: This race for the presidency produced two of the most infamous slogans in political history. One came from a Catholic-bashing Protestant minister who dubbed the Democrats the party of "Rum, Romanism, and Rebellion." The other one emerged after the Democrats' candidate, New York Governor Grover Cleveland, was accused of fathering an illegitimate child: Supporters of Republican James Blaine taunted, "Ma, ma, where's my pa? Gone to the White House, ha ha ha!"

> 1964: The Republican presidential candidate, Barry Goldwater, started the race with a reputation as a dangerous hawk. Lyndon Johnson's campaign leaped on that liability, creating what may be the most famous political ad ever. The film features a little girl pulling petals off a daisy until her game is interrupted by a nuclear holocaust.

> 1968: Richard Nixon had the last laugh over Hubert Humphrey in this race for the White House, but Humphrey's team fielded the most memorable ad. On the screen: the words "Agnew for Vice President?" On the soundtrack: a man laughing hysterically, louder and louder, until the laughs veer off into a groan.

> 1984: Incumbent Sen. Jesse Helms (R-N.C.) sensed early on that the state's moderate Democratic governor, Jim Hunt, posed a strong re-election threat. So Helms started running TV ads attacking Hunt a full 18 months ahead of Election Day, taunting him as a liberal flip-flopper with the tagline, "Where Do You Stand, Jim?" Hunt fired back with a graphic spot linking Helms to right-wing death squads in El Salvador.

> 2004: The venomous Kerry–Bush match-up got the headlines in 2004, but connoisseurs of political nastiness prefer a redistricting-induced Texas congressional race that pitted Rep. Pete Sessions, a Republican stalwart,

against Democratic Rep. Martin Frost, a member of his party's leadership. Late in the campaign, Frost aides gave the press a 1970s-era picture of college streakers, one of whom was Sessions. The Sessions campaign shot back by blasting Frost's planned fundraiser with Peter Yarrow of the folk trio Peter, Paul, and Mary, on the grounds that Yarrow had served three months in prison for taking "immoral and indecent liberties" with a 14-year-old fan.[136]

Machiavelli called for the literal assassination of political foes, while in contemporary America, character assassination is generally enough to insure electoral victory. The litany above of just such assassination attempts represents but a few examples of this favorite American electoral activity. Neo-Conservative writer Michael Ledeen noted:

> Nowadays we generally destroy men's reputations and careers rather than taking their lives, but the effect on the public is the same, especially as many of our most deadly modern executioners are journalists and broadcasters who provide the necessary stage and bring the drama to a large audience.[137]

MACHIAVELLIAN AMERICAN LEADERSHIP

> Even after half a millennium, Machiavelli's advice to leaders is as contemporary as tomorrow . . . Machiavelli's rules rest upon a clear-eyed view of human nature. If you think that people are basically good and, left to their own devices, will create loving communities and good governments, you've learned nothing from him. Machiavelli's world is populated by people more inclined to do evil than good, whose instincts are distinctly anti-social. The only way to dominate your foes and get your friends and allies to work together is to use power effectively.[138]

A republic is not a static project. It has a dynamism that forces it to change, grow and continue to found and re-found itself, in each new era and with each passing generation. Machiavelli's maxim: "A wise man will never censure anyone for having employed any extraordinary means for the purpose of establishing a kingdom or constituting a republic"[139] rings as true today as it did at the beginning of the American empire.

The reverberations of the long-ago Florentine political philosopher, writing alone in his study surrounded only by the shadows of past thinkers and rulers, continue to shake the foundations of American democracy. The reality of American politics turns away from the moral intentions of our Declaration of Independence and Constitution and toward a power-driven oligarchy, that is, rule by the few. Renaissance scholar Paul Grendler noted:

> Machiavelli has been a theme in American conservative political discussion since the 1940s. It is likely that the use of Machiavelli has contributed to the combative mentality that characterized American Cold War politics, the belligerency of American conservatism and the take-no-prisoners tactics and language employed against liberalism and the Democrats.[140]

This in spite of the country's self-image, captured by the great Machiavelli scholar Leo Strauss who declared: "The United States of America may be said to be the only country in the world which was founded in explicit opposition to Machiavellian principles."[141] Perhaps this political myopia — not shared, as has been shown, by the Founders themselves — is one of the problems the country must first overcome if it is to move beyond the spare realpolitik of Machiavellian leadership and into genuine opposition to Machiavellian principles.

WAR AND THE LANGUAGE OF POLITICS

> Language defines reality. It conditions us to believe that the way we think is the only way to think. To call something a "war" catalyzes human emotions . . . It creates a sense of battle — of hoped for victory for one side and hoped for defeat for the other . . . It rallies a country around its common identity, thereby engendering patriotism and the willingness to fight and/or make sacrifice for one's country. It creates a picture of a common enemy who must be stood up to.[142]

We live in an era where challenging a rival to a duel or simply assassinating an adversary is frowned upon. In contemporary political life, language represents the central Machiavellian tool for achieving and retaining power. Language is the most powerful implement for twisting facts into a reality that is supportive of an individual or political party.

The influence of Machiavellian reality-creating language is ubiquitous throughout the American public square. An op-ed in the *Washington Post* entitled "No More 'War,'" examined just how far-reaching is this language, with its binary formulation of winners and losers utilized to present issues as far-ranging as organic versus pesticide-soaked vegetables and tax equality concerns. In each case, the matter is presented as taking place between winners and losers (instead of defined by a common good for all), and war-like idiom comes to define virtually every aspect of shared reality:

> We have been waging "war on" this or that for decades. America is such a diverse and disputatious country that war, actual or metaphorical, has been one of the few causes capable of bringing together its various factions, regions and races . . . These metaphors attempt to recast an abstract threat as a particular enemy . . . For both parties, the goal is to encourage Americans to think of one another as enemies and, eventually, to hate and fear one another.[143]

The political sphere becomes combat, a Machiavellian free-for-all comprised only of winners and losers. This dualistic language — in which Americans are "encouraged to think of one another as enemies and, eventually, to hate and fear one another" — instigates responses from the lowest area of the human brain: the amygdala. It is here that Machiavellian politics takes root.

Virtually all successful politicians slip easily into this formulation in Machiavelli America. A small note in the magazine *Mother Jones* entitled: "The War President," explored the binary language applied to President Obama, the first sitting president to receive the Nobel Peace Prize. According to "conservative pundits, lazy headline writers and Google trawling," during his time in office, the president "declared war" on more than one hundred things, including religion, oil, coal, the Constitution, vegan shops, the American farmer, poor people, rich people, the Bowl Championship Football Series, success, fun and a host of other issues.[144]

While the brief reportage was poking fun at the "hyperventilating" language of the president's detractors, the more insidious dynamic must not be minimized, as opponents of the president thrive on this language, and the fact that if the President is at war with them, they must go to war with the president.

The purpose of this dualistic formulation is to create fear in the listener, and therefore more easily manipulate them into becoming a partisan to one's goals. Whether the war terminology is applied by friends of the president or his enemies, the effect is the same: to reduce the conversation to a "with us or against us" dynamic, as well as raise the stakes from the political to the life threatening. Due to this dynamic, the amygdala becomes primary (as opposed to the higher aspects of the brain structure) and the audience becomes more susceptible to the message. Even when talking about an opponent's "war" on Christmas trees![145]

The formulation hardly remains unremarked. As opinion writer Charles Lane wrote in the *Washington Post*:

> I don't know about you, but I am sick and tired of war. The Democratic National Committee accuses the GOP of a "Republican War on Women" to go along with its "war on working families" and "Paul Ryan's war on seniors." Various Republicans accuse President Obama of a "war on religious freedom" or even, in the words of Texas Governor Rick Perry, "a war on religion." According to the Republican National Committee, the president is also waging a "war on energy," the sequel, apparently to what the House Republican Leadership has called the "Democrats' war on American jobs." Progressive author Chris Mooney called his book "The Republican War on Science;" not to be outdone, conservatives Grover Norquist and John R. Lott Jr., have published "Debacle: Obama's War on Jobs and Growth" . . . And on and on and on — until you could almost lose sight of the fact that not one of these institutions or individuals is describing a physical conflict in which people fight, bleed and die.[146]

There is no shared goal of social or cultural health, only winners and losers. As the 20th-century philosopher Simone Weil stated: "Wherever there are political parties, democracy is dead."[147] 21st-century America represents a case in point.

Hardly hidden in the private thoughts of politicians, the idea that elections themselves represent "wars" is explicit. For instance, in the 2012 Republican primary in Florida, one of the two main candidates, Newt Gingrich was said to be a student of "Japanese samurai warlord Toranago, the Turkish revolutionary Kemal Ataturk and Chinese Military Strategist Sun Tzu" (c. 5th century B.C.E.; whose book *The Art of War* is still read by militaries around the world). Under a headline entitled: "Gingrich promises electoral brawl," an article noted: "One of the keys to Newt is that he's always seen politics as war."[148]

Hardly confined to Republicans, Sun Tzu's *The Art of War* also inspired one of America's allegedly most progressive politicians of the past four decades:

> Gov. Jerry Brown, a battle-scarred survivor in California politics who has vanquished well-armed opponents such as billionaire Meg Whitman, has said his strategic guidebook for decades has been a slim, 2,500-year-old volume: *The Art of War* by Chinese general Sun Tzu.[149]

At the same time as Gingrich was channeling the ancient, bipartisan political muse, his adversary, Mitt Romney, was "carpet-bombing" (Gingrich's words) the Florida airwaves with negative advertising against his foe. Romney and his cohorts were spending five times as much on advertising — upward toward $10 million — as the cash-strapped Gingrich. As the amoral propaganda took effect, the polls showed a rapid swing in fortunes. Romney caught and then surpassed Gingrich in popular support. The war had been won.

The ubiquity of war as the framework for social engagement and, more importantly for politics, was explained by Richard Eskow (Senior Fellow with the Campaign for America's Future):

> Our lives are defined by invisible wars, wars whose theater of combat is the human imagination. These economic and political wars are waged year in and year out, decade after decade, century after century. Words are the weapons of choice in these wars.[150]

The language of war, and therefore the shrinking of all social and political issues into a narrow, binary world of winners and losers, is reflected even in newspaper headlines. Here, the Machiavellian worldview suffuses the culture, screaming out from every newspaper box, magazine kiosk, Internet headline and vocally, from the radio and television airwaves. These few headlines culled from newspapers on a single day (January 2, 2012) show the unthinking ubiquity of this warlike world in which we live:

- GOP Readies its Plan of Attack (*Washington Post*)

- Democrats Become Target (*New York Times*)

- Gloves Off as GOP Candidates Battle for Support (*Fox News*)

- Romney Vows to Kill Dream Act (*Washington Monthly*)

- Attack Sparks 'Stop Whining' Pushback (*Huffington Post*)

- Romney Unleashes Attack On Obama, Evokes God (*Huffington Post*)

- Republicans Blitz Iowa (*Yahoo News*)

- 'There Will Be Blood' If Romney Wins Iowa and New Hampshire (*Yahoo News*)

- Newt Gingrich to Hit Mitt Romney 'Every Day' (*ABC News*)

- Chris Christie Threatens to Go 'Jersey-Style' on Iowa (*ABC News*)

- Bachmann attacks Santorum (*CBS News*)

- Romney Targets Obama (*Wall Street Journal*)

This conflation of war and social relationships permeates all aspects of society with Machiavellian choices. Win or lose. Kill or be killed. Realism is defined in terms that lead to Machiavellian actions, instead of a morally based social world:

> This is where realism begins - realism defined as "an approach to politics rooted in a cynical view of human motives and possibilities, and devoted to advancing the interests of a state without regard for moral or religious strictures." It is a view that lends itself to pithy formulations: "Might makes right", "Do or be done to", "It's a dog-eat-dog world", and Machiavelli's own contribution, "Men must either be caressed or extinguished."[151]

The Florentine's political calculus has become so pervasive that "it is difficult to gain the necessary perspective on the specific character and limitation of Machiavellian realism."[152] We can't see it, because it is everywhere around us. It suffuses human social interaction through language, media, history, education — and those who peek their heads out from underneath the smothering veil can do little more than stare wide-eyed with horror at the moral catastrophe of our public square, as every social subject from public transportation to farm subsidies becomes couched in war-like terms, fields of battle littered with winners and losers.

Meaning, in the end, that everyone suffers.

PROPAGANDA

> We humans seem to be attached to ideas based on human opinions, rather than those based on truth. This is so even when human opinions are contradictory. The reason that humans reject the truth is that it is morally strict and solemn.[153]

For Machiavelli, as for American politicians, words represent the ultimate weapon. As Diana Schaub (professor of political science at Loyola University Maryland) noted: "Machiavelli deployed words as a weapon . . . Machiavelli, the supposed champion of the force of arms, was in fact a practitioner of verbal fraud and distortion." To fight in the Machiavellian world of politics, one must be armed. As the Florentine himself noted, "all armed prophets won, and the unarmed came to ruin."[154] Because all social interaction is war, and corporeal violence is frowned upon within the borders of contemporary America, words and propaganda epitomize the most powerful political force.

Within the social and political realms, there is little difference between language and propaganda. Language mutates into propaganda as naturally as flour is baked into bread.

Frank Luntz (b. 1962; an American political consultant, pollster, and Republican Party strategist) is but a single opinion maker working in the field, yet his work stands out as a prototypical expression of this insidious dynamic. As the Republican propagandist noted on his website: "we are transforming mere words into an affective arsenal for the war of perception we all wage each and every day."[155] He is unabashed about the purpose of his work, allowing him to greasily assure:

> We have counseled Presidents and Prime Ministers, Fortune 100 CEOs and Hollywood creative teams in harnessing the power of language and visuals to change hearts, change minds and change behaviors.[156]

And Luntz is quite explicit about centering his messages in the amygdala, which provides a fertile cortical area for him to shape and control people's ideas: "80 percent of our life is emotion, and only 20 percent is intellect. I am much more interested in how you feel than how you think."[157] This central American figure went so far as to redefine the term "Orwellian" in a *positive* sense, stating: "To be 'Orwellian' is to speak with absolute clarity, to be succinct, to explain what the event is, to talk about what triggers something happening . . . and to do so without any pejorative whatsoever."

Although Luntz's description of "Orwellian" is considered to contradict both its popularly defined meaning as well as any connotation intended by George Orwell, Luntz understands that propaganda has more relevance to political reality than truth. "We know that words and emotion together are the most powerful force known to mankind."[158]

And as an example of how profound is our collective challenge in finding a moral and honest center for our social reality, far from being shunted to the side of American culture for his assurances that he can twist reality to the needs of his clients, he is a respected member of the pundit (expert commentator) class of opinion makers. Luntz is a frequent contributor to Fox News, a major media outlet. Voices such as Luntz's help eradicate morality from the center of our public conversations, replacing it with a Machiavellian jumble.

So it is with the vast majority of political speech, which becomes indistinguishable from advertising or propaganda. This is readily acknowledged, as politicians are packaged like toothpaste or cars, and sold to the public as two-dimensional versions of themselves, an image which the leader hopes will fool people into voting for him. In an article entitled: "Romney's Team Tries to Make Pitch-Perfect Ads," *Washington Post* journalist Philip Rucker noted:

> A colorful team of advertising gurus . . . try to apply what they've learned in careers marketing Colgate toothpaste, Big Macs, BMWs and Nationwide

Insurance to help pitch the American masses a product that lacks a dominant market share: Mitt Romney.[159]

PATRIOTISM AND RELIGION

Here I would also add one other important characteristic of neo-conservatism that is often overlooked — namely, the central belief in the importance of religion as a necessary social force and political instrument. While not particularly religious themselves, most of the neo-conservatives recognize the power of religious belief in maintaining social order and inspiring nationalist sentiment. As Irving Kristol has repeatedly argued, religion is the necessary glue that holds society together, without which it descends into vulgarity and chaos. At the same time, he also recognizes that religion, particularly in its most extreme fundamentalist forms, is a powerful political tool and a means to generate intense nationalist sentiment.[160]

Like the language of war, the alliance of the state's will with that of God — or patriotism, as it is known — becomes a bludgeon that opens up a wide field for the Machiavellian practitioner. With the most important arts of the leader being moral deception through language and war, bringing them together under the umbrella of patriotism is the highest form of Machiavelli's program. It offers a view of the world, its dangers and the leader's necessity that may appear unassailable.

Harvey Mansfield discussed Machiavelli's views concerning religion and the political leader at length:

> Religion is a weakness that can give strength, but only when it is well used by princes . . . In a republic, it is indispensable for the spirit of sacrifice [patriotism] that keeps the republic from becoming corrupted by the private interests of wealthy nobles . . . The necessity of using religion reveals the necessity of politicizing virtue, which means reducing and distorting it for the sake of its political consequences. It is in the context of his praise of religion that Machiavelli makes his deepest criticism of traditional moral virtue.[161]

In an elegant corruption of effect and cause, Mansfield goes on to note that regardless of the means that a prince uses to attain his objectives, if he is successful, the methods will always be judged not only in a favorable light, but if the leader has successfully suffused his actions with a religious patina, will actually be viewed as ordained by God. The contemporary neo-conservative thinker Michael Ledeen expanded on the explanation:

> "I believe," Machiavelli fervently pronounces, "that the greatest good one can do, and the most gratifying to God, is that which one does for his country." Since it is the highest good, the defense of one's country is one of those extreme situations in which a leader is justified in committing evil. If one's country is threatened, Machiavelli insists, "there should fall no consideration whatever of either just or the unjust, kind or cruel, praiseworthy of ignominious."[162]

The Ends Justify the Means

The manner in which this belief in eliminating morality from consideration when "protecting" the needs of the country permeates American society is not difficult to distinguish. During the decade of the 2000s, the United States employed a foreign policy that utilized torture as a central facet. Hardly hidden, it was declared permissible through a series of *ju-jitsu* legal rulings, and led American servicemen and woman to fervently believe in the justice of their actions. For example, an article in the *Washington Post* entitled "From an ex-CIA Official, a blunt defense of Harsh Interrogation" announced: "Jose A. Rodriguez Jr. has no regrets about decisions that he believes saves lives." It continued to note:

> Shortly after the 2001 attacks, the CIA set up secret prisons in Afghanistan, Thailand and several Eastern European countries for the explicit purpose of keeping detainees picked up on the battlefield or in other countries away from the U.S. justice system, which would grant them protections against, among other things, torture or otherwise harsh treatment . . . "I am certain, beyond any doubt, that these techniques, approved at the highest levels of the U.S. government, certified by the Department of Justice and briefed to and supported by bipartisan leadership of congressional intelligence oversight committees, shielded the people of the United States from harm." [163]

While it is impossible to know if the illegal (contrary to the Geneva Convention, of which the United States is a signatory) and harsh techniques did save lives — the article noted that people both inside and outside of the government have argued that they were unnecessary — it is certain that Jose A. Rodriguez Jr., who personally approved of them, suffered no lasting damage to his person or career. Rodriguez Jr. retired in 2007 and wrote a book about his experiences (glossing over more difficult aspects of his time at the agency) in 2012. His book *Hard Measures* became a New York Times bestseller.

Rodriguez Jr. did not discuss the relationship of God and the United States, but he didn't have to. The fusion of the state and religion is made at higher levels, situating the actions of people like Rodriguez in the realm of the Giver of All Life. For instance, Rodriguez Jr.'s commander-in-chief at the time of the torture, President George W. Bush, had invoked Jesus as his most important political mentor (in a 1999 debate) and continued through two presidential terms appealing to religion and God to justify his policies. Enough people in the country bought into the Machiavellian fraud to provide him eight years of support, though at this writing he is the most unpopular living former president.[164]

We can see this conflation of God, state and political actions in many, if not most successful American leaders. The use of religious language to speak of war and the state — thereby situating the leader within the religious and even eternal pantheon — is a time-honored American tradition, one that I treated in detail in my book *A Fatal Addiction: War in the Name of God* (Algora Publishing, 2012). However, in the context of America's Machiavellian political system, it bears a brief review.

The basic aspect of patriotism demands that citizens be willing to sacrifice their lives for the desires of the prince. This is Machiavelli's rendering of it, and it is difficult to argue that it has any other meaning. In the United States, this often concerns young men (and more recently women) being willing to fight and die in wars, usually in far-away lands against people of non-Caucasian descent.

Here is one example of the "indispensable spirit of sacrifice" proposed by an American leader, the 2008 Republican presidential candidate, Senator John McCain (R-AZ), in talking of a fallen soldier:

> He loved his country, and the values that make us exceptional among nations, and good . . . Love and honor oblige us. We are obliged to value our blessings, and to pay our debts to those who sacrificed to secure them for us. They are blood debts
>
> . . . The loss of every fallen soldier should hurt us lest we ever forget the terrible costs of war, and the sublime love of those who sacrifice everything on our behalf.[165]

"Sublime love" — a sentiment that we often think of in religious and even mystical terms — applied to a warrior who gave himself to patriotism represents the perfect Machiavellian twist. Patriotism is based in particularism, and in this case the bellicose desires of a single leader, the Republican George W. Bush. As Leo Tolstoy noted concerning this fusion of God and state:

> How can patriotism be a virtue in these days when it requires of men an ideal exactly opposite to that of our religion and morality — an admission, not of the equality and fraternity of all men, but of the dominance of one country or nation over all others?[166]

But we live in Machiavelli's world, not Tolstoy's. Sublime love, sacrifice, the state and, most importantly, the *virtù* of the individual leader come together to help secure power for those agile in Machiavellian fraud. When George W. Bush referred to his wartime Secretary of Defense Donald Rumsfeld as "Rumstud," he was not referring to the three sleepy years Rumsfeld had spent in the Navy in the 1950s. He referenced the septuagenarian "Rumstud's" ability to send other Americans to fight, kill and die in Afghanistan and Iraq at Bush's whim.

For the political voice, situating war and state within the highest human spiritual ideals makes good sense. And sometimes, as might be true in the case of Senator McCain — himself a war hero — perhaps the politician believes his or her words. It is much easier to fool the general population if one has fooled oneself first . . .

The political language of spirituality and war repackages even the grossest violations of Godly commandments to give them the necessary religious patina. For as Machiavelli noted: "The great majority of humans are satisfied with appearances, as though they were realities, and are often more influenced by the things that seems than those that are."[167]

> On the basis of the Biblical teaching, love of God becomes fervent zeal for the glory of God; it becomes a passion that, in Machiavelli's eyes, is not distinguishable from the passions of partisanship or fanatical loyalty to a leader whose cause is not identical with the common good of a particular state.[168]

This leads politicians to present even the most egregious violations of human and spiritual rights in religious terminology — and influence the American public and political square with such language. Here is how President George W. Bush framed the American "War on Terror" and his actions in the religious sphere, stating:

> I'm driven with a mission from God. God would tell me, "George, go and fight those terrorists in Afghanistan." And I did, and then God would tell me, "George, go and end the tyranny in Iraq ..." And I did. And now, again, I feel God's words coming to me, "Go get the Palestinians their state and get the Israelis their security, and get peace in the Middle East." And by God I'm gonna do it.[169]

The appearance is of a deeply committed religious man, following only the word of God. But the Machiavellian reality? Here is one fact illustrating what happened beneath the veil of religious double-speak during the Bush years:

> The International Committee of the Red Cross has charged in confidential reports that the American military has intentionally used psychological and sometimes physical coercion "tantamount to torture" on prisoners at Guantanamo Bay, Cuba. Some doctors and other medical workers were participating in planning for the interrogations in "a flagrant violation of medical ethics." Investigators found a system devised to break the will of the prisoners and make them wholly dependent on their interrogators through "humiliating acts, solitary confinement, temperature extremes and use of forced positions." The methods used were increasingly "more refined and repressive."[170]

These actions took place under the umbrella of Bush's conversations with God, and were approved by the religious American public (see below). As British journalist Nick Spencer noted in *The Guardian*:

> Machiavelli genuinely does speak to us today. Some of *The Prince*'s observations are painfully acute. The advice to a political leader that "there is nothing more important than appearing to be religious," could well serve as a motto for US politics.[171]

Senator John McCain, perhaps even more than George W. Bush, took Machiavellian ideals of subjugating God to the state to its natural conclusion. As Kathryn Lofton, a fellow at Princeton's Center for the Study of Religion, noted:

> The higher being McCain believes in is not God or Christ. "That higher being is America," Lofton writes. "Someone once called atheism an undetectable God. McCain's God can be detected, it can be found: his God is the country for whom McCain survived."[172]

Or, as Eric Drummond Smith (professor of Political Science, University of Virginia) stated:

> One type of propaganda is that of state religion, according to Machiavelli. If religion is properly used than it not only becomes a motivation for the people of the state to act in a moral and just fashion, but also to support the state as they would support God. The use of religion as a tool of statecraft is thus the manipulation of the very core of the human character. Furthermore, religion can be used to instill a sense of loyalty and militancy in the citizens' militia without parallel.[173]

POLITICAL PARTIES

Good people fear all political parties.[174]

The political party in modern democracies attempts to ally its own interests with that of the state, and through that association, with God. The political party sets itself up against other citizens of the same country, claiming the mantle of the Almighty for itself, damning half of the country to a god-less hell.

Harvey Mansfield, in *Machiavelli's Virtue*, traced the genesis of the modern two-party system into pre-Renaissance Italy, where the dispute between Pope Alexander II (d. 1073) and the Holy Roman Emperor Henry IV (d. 1106) caused the citizenry of Italy to fracture along sectarian lines, ushering in an era of "you're either with us or against us" that still influences political activity to this day. As Mansfield stated: "The dispute between the pope and the emperor was the prototype, as well as the origin, of the modern parties . . . and though unnatural, it continues; the system, as we say today, was in equilibrium."[175]

The dynamic of splitting into two parties, and then having each claiming the mantle as true purveyor of domestic serenity, can be readily seen in America. In this empire, the two parties are forever claiming responsibility for genuine "American values," while implying — or outrightly stating — that the other party is "less American," or even un-American. Of course, "American values" implicitly implies, and sometimes explicitly states, that God is on "our" side, and that the other political party is not only in error, but also blasphemers.

The language of partisan rancor dominates American political campaigns. For instance, as the 2012 Presidential campaign began to heat up in the early summer, Republican candidate Mitt Romney intoned: "We're a united nation, he [Obama] divides us. He tries to divide America, tear America apart."[176] Republican mouthpiece Rush Limbaugh bleated: "I think it can now be said, without equivocation — without equivocation — that this man [President Obama] hates this country. He is trying — Barack Obama is trying — to dismantle, brick by brick, the American dream."[177]

And an article in the *American Thinker*, a daily conservative online magazine, entitled "Evil Democrat Paradigms" noted:

> Here are two paradigms which evil, divisive Democrats have shamefully promoted and exploited for years: one, white men are burning the midnight oil thinking of ways to keep blacks down; and two, all rich white people are selfish, evil, and deserving of punishment . . . Democrats are masters at creating a hated "bad guy" to further their agenda.[178]

Going even further to link God, country and a specific political party, the Cornerstone Church (one of hundreds operating in similar style around the country) in San Antonio, Texas, held an annual "God and Country" church service in which more than 60 political hopefuls came to "press the flesh with the evangelical congregation." In keeping with Texas politics, of the potential elected leaders, only a few were Democrats. To underscore that God was most definitely on the Republican side of the ledger, the pastor of the mega-church, John Hagee, said:

> "Unfortunately, this [Obama] administration has made America a laughingstock," he thundered from the pulpit. "Our enemies no longer fear us, and our friends no longer trust us." The election of 2012 is about "freedom of religion being under fire," he said. He criticized President Barack Obama's health care reform and his attempts to make Catholic employers provide birth control insurance coverage to female employees.

To underscore the atmosphere, "rousing songs celebrated the military and Jesus. A group of high school seniors received new Bibles."[179]

And in an article entitled "One Nation Under God" appearing in *Newsweek Magazine*, Lisa Miller, *Newsweek's* religion editor, noted:

> Powerful new rhetoric on the religious right pits Obama and big government against "God's America" — and promises to galvanize Christians in 2012. "The marriage between evangelicalism and patriotic nationalism is so strong that anybody who is raising questions about loyalty to the old, laissez-faire capitalist system is ex post facto unpatriotic, un-American, and by association non-Christian." Support for Obama, in other words, equals an abandonment of American principles [and] godlessness.[180]

Going further still, the televangelist and one-time Republican candidate for president Pat Robertson spoke directly with God to discover that President Barack Obama was, indeed, un-American and his policies were contrary to the Almighty's wishes. An article entitled "God Tells Robertson that 'Radical' Obama will Bring Down America" explained:

Last year, Robertson claimed God told him that America's future will be bleak because of debt and divisions, and today on *The 700 Club* said that God again communicated to him that financial problems and partisan politics are going to bring America into decline. Unsurprisingly, Robertson said God is no fan of President Obama: "Your president holds a radical view of the direction of your country which is at odds with the majority, expect chaos and paralysis." Robertson claimed that the country would be devastated by an "economic collapse" and "the country will begin disintegrating." He also claimed that God revealed to him who the next president will be, but that he is "not supposed to talk about that." [181]

Aligning the good of the country with a political party is not the sole purview of the Republicans, however. Although they are certainly better and more insistent in this arena, the Democrats — after getting pummeled with God and the flag throughout the 1980s — learned how they might, as well, claim the mantle of true American values, while denigrating those of the other side.

President Barack Obama and his Democratic surrogates resort to the same kind of language, situating their politics on the side of patriotism, and the other's on the side of the enemy. As journalist Carl Cannon noted in his article "Patriot Games":

> Media outlets and commentators openly sympathetic to Obama's policy aims often parroted his language: *Daily Beast* columnist Michael Tomansky attacked the Senate Republican leadership in a 2011 piece headlined, "Mitch McConnell: Putting Party Ahead of Country Every Time." Last month, *Newsweek*, *Daily Beast*'s sister publication, carried a column by Democratic Party operative Paul Begala: "The GOP Puts Party Ahead of Country Every Time." Last week, *Chicago Sun-Times* columnist Neil Steinberg celebrated Independence Day in a column condemning Republicans headlined, "Happy Fourth of July to the Treason Party." [182]

Questioning the patriotism of rivals has been a salient approach to smearing the opposition since the beginning of the Republic. And over the past generation, it has been a staple for Republicans officeholders. On one hand, journalistic ethics would demand that I cite as many Democratic examples of this particular brand of party politics as Republican efforts, but the truth is that the Republicans are both more adept and more grotesque about fusing God with their party politics than those on the American left.

In the Machiavellian world of party politics, truth is easily shunted out of view. For instance, in addition to enlisting the partisan God, Republican leaders have imputed the patriotism of Americans who have served and/or fought for the country, while holding that their (Republican) officeholders — who often shirked this same duty — were the more patriotic candidates.

In 2004, President George W. Bush (a draft-dodger during the Vietnam War) accused Senator John Kerry (who won a Bronze Star, a Silver Star and three Purple Hearts in Vietnam after volunteering for the military) of being un-American. During the Republican National Convention, conventioneers passed out Band-Aids to mock the war wounds that Kerry had received in combat. As for the more politically pro-military Bush, he had (like many of his co-generational neo-conservatives) not served in the armed forces, spending only a brief and unverifiable stint in the Texas National Guard.

As if to prove Machiavelli's assurances that people are more convinced by appearances than reality, a recent article entitled "Fundamentalism at the U.S.'s Corps" noted, concerning neo-conservative voices advocating American military engagements around the world:

> Neo-conservatism has a long connection to the US military. This may be initially puzzling, as most neo-conservatives skillfully avoided military service during the Vietnam War and their newer followers have only a somewhat closer connection to actual service.[183]

Like the medieval Catholic Church, these Republican leaders propose that American citizens do as they say, not as they do. The America they want others to protect is their America. How can they fully enjoy it if they are risking their lives to protect it? But this is Machiavelli's America, and only the appearance of their *virtù* matters, not proving it through action.

The litany of hypocritical and successful character assassinations of this sort continues. Saxby Chambliss (R-GA; another Republican draft dodger) excoriated Senator Max Cleland (D-GA) — another Democratic Vietnam War veteran, who lost three of his four limbs in combat in Southeast Asia — for not being appropriately patriotic:

> Cleland, 60, is still livid over a now-infamous TV commercial that Republican challenger Saxby Chambliss ran against him. It opened with pictures of Osama bin Laden and Saddam Hussein, and then attacked Cleland for voting against President Bush's Homeland Security bill.[184]

In the American political landscape, there is no shame. In this case, even Republican senators Chuck Hagel (R-NE) and John McCain (R-AZ), themselves Vietnam War veterans, expressed strong disgust with Chambliss's methods. The Machiavellian tactics were successful, however. Although Cleland was running ahead in the polls up until election night, Chambliss eked out a victory and then, when questioned, assured that he had nothing to add in regards the advertisement or Cleland's service to his country.

Chambliss was hardly sanctioned, for as Machiavelli assured, the outcome of the action, if successful, is all that is remembered. Chambliss rose to become the Senior Senator from Georgia, the Vice Chairman of the Senate Select Committee on Intelligence and was considered one of the moderate and mature voices of the Republican Party until his retirement.

George Orwell assured: "Political language is designed to make lies sound truthful and murder respectable."[185] Virtually every single politician in any office anywhere will jettison his or her deepest held principles for the cause of "party unity." Political parties, God, state fuse together into the amoral center of American politics.

FREEDOM AND VIOLENCE

Even concepts of freedom — those upon which our country was allegedly founded — may take a destructive turn in American culture, as "freedom" is used to justify everything from an individual or corporation's right to destroy environmentally sensitive areas for private gain to torture in the name of protecting freedom. However, in the culture of the United States, the ideal of freedom, combined with the ubiquity of guns and violence, represents one American political subtext of which the Florentine would certainly have approved.

J. G. A. Pocock noted in *The Machiavellian Moment* that for Machiavelli "freedom, civic virtue and military discipline seem to exist in close relation to each other."[186] This fusion of freedom, civic virtue and military discipline is most clearly seen in American's attitudes toward gun ownership. And American attitudes fit neatly in with Machiavellian political ideals.

While estimates range for gun ownership in America — those who own them often being too paranoid to admit it — at least one gun per citizen circulates in the country, and some estimates range upward to two per resident. This puts the tally to at least 300 million guns owned by United States citizens, with each individual gun-owning household possessing an average of seven firearms.

Leo Strauss discussed the importance of individual ownership of weapons in Machiavelli's writing, noting in *Thoughts on Machiavelli*:

> Just as a tyrant comes to power by exploiting the division between the great and the people, he maintains himself in power by creating a division within the people. In some cases, he does not have to create such a division; he can arm the peasantry and with its help keep down the urban populace.[187]

This is not to say that Americans are taking up arms against each other. However, studies have indicated that rural homes on average have a gun more than homes in urban neighborhoods,[188] mimicking the Machiavellian dynamic of "arming the peasantry." The wedge of "gun rights" v. "gun control" plays the same role as a bloody confrontation in separating the population into two warring camps, and helping to "keep down the urban populace."

This dynamic is not difficult to discern in American presidential elections, as evidenced by this quote by the Republican nominee for president in 2012, Mitt Romney, in a speech that he gave to the National Rifle Association just after securing the Republican presidential nomination in April of that year:

> In his first major speech to conservatives since his Republican rival Rick Santorum quit the presidential race, Mitt Romney turned his sights on the general election and accused President Barack Obama of waging "an

assault on our freedoms." Romney addressed the Annual Meeting of the National Rifle Association, which drew more than 60,000 gun enthusiasts to St. Louis to inspect the latest in personal weaponry and feast on tough political attacks against the White House.[189]

Coupled with ideals of freedom and the reality of guns come "guts" for the American people — with "guts" echoing Machiavelli's ideal of *virtù*. For Machiavelli, this distinctive characteristic represented a "species of republicanism liberated from moral restraints . . . and bolstered by a peculiar mixture of savagery, ambitions and dread."[190] This concept can be seen in the American *zeitgeist*, represented by one American blogger who noted:

> "God, Guts and Guns made America great." In this case, much of America's greatness is summed up in just seven words . . . As Patrick Henry said of Americans in whom I share his utmost faith, we the " . . . people, armed in the holy cause of liberty . . . are invincible by any force which our enemy can send against us." Soldier on my friends.[191]

The above writing is hardly representative of a tiny, fringe minority in America. The views seen in the above blog piece represent a strong current of mainstream American thought, as evidenced by voting patterns and gun ownership tallies. A note on *Fox News* stated:

> Sales of handguns and ammunition are booming across the country, and retailers say it's all about the November election. Gun shop owners around the nation told *FoxNews.com* that sales, brisk ever since President Obama was elected, have spiked upward in recent months. This year's uptick comes on top of a record 2011, when nearly 11 million firearms were sold in the U.S.[192]

American "God, guns and guts" based politics goes beyond the right of individual gun ownership. As Machiavelli noted: "A Prince must not have any objective nor any thought, nor take up any art, other than the art of war."[193] It is in this art that Machiavellian virtue is hewn and the American *zeitgeist* is forged. The institutionalization of violence, coupled with the sacralization of the State, brings the Machiavellian power dynamic to full fruition.

AMERICA, MACHIAVELLI AND FRAUD

> If you only notice human proceedings, you may observe that all who attain great power and riches, make use of either force or fraud; and what they have acquired either by deceit or violence, in order to conceal the disgraceful methods of attainment, they endeavor to sanctify with the false title of honest gains . . . God and nature have thrown all human fortunes into the midst of mankind; and they are thus attainable rather by rapine than by industry, by wicked actions rather than by good. Hence it is that men feed upon each other, and those who cannot defend themselves must be worried.[194]

More powerful even than arms, fraud is the ultimate Machiavellian currency of power. And like all other Machiavellian strategies, this one is not hard to uncover in American politics, as religion, constant war talk, personal threats, character assassinations and the full basket of the Florentine's delights are parroted, though rarely exposed by the compliant media.

Fraud in America is a huge industry, perhaps second only to the military. As Machiavelli noted, people judge more from appearances than from reality, and with upward to three billion dollars dedicated to advertising in the 2012 election, the plaintive tweets of those who might want to insert truth and morality into the American political spectrum are about as successful as a butterfly trying to bring down a jet plane.

Even more so when the mainstream press takes pride in the fact that it isn't truth based, expanding the audience for any number of lies and fraud, in the name of objectivity! As *Washington Post* journalist Melinda Henneberger noted, concerning her profession's (lack of) attachment to truth in reporting: "Newspapers hardly ever haul off and say a public figure lied, and I like that about us."[195]

American politicians are well aware of the media and public's aversion to the truth, making easier their rise to positions of power through the use of fraud. They will generally stop at nothing to continue using it, at least until they are caught in a lie of personal sexual or fiscal weakness, which, for some reason, our political system holds to be outside the pale, while blatant falsehoods about war, the economy, health care, taxes and other policy issues are simply presented as politics as usual.

The litany of flagrant lies told by politicians could fill a tome much larger than this study, but a few recent examples must suffice. At the Republican Convention in 2012, the Vice Presidential nominee, Paul Ryan, stood before the nation and lied through his teeth (to put it colloquially):

> Paul Ryan's speech was well-written, well-delivered, and well-received. All of that was evident to anyone watching on TV. It had a number of nice smilingly vicious hit lines — starting with the masterful "staring up at the faded Obama posters" riff — plus a note of encouraging uplift at the end. It was also profoundly dishonest in ways large and small . . . a major party's nominee for national office apparently just doesn't care that he is standing in front of millions and telling *easily catchable* lies.[196]

This is but one example of an ongoing facet of American politics: lies are a vital weapon for the unarmed politician. After all, Ryan's speech as "well-received" by his partisan followers. It is unfair, and even absurd, however, to single out this politician as somehow extreme in his representations. As was noted in an article entitled "Lying in American Politics" in *USA Today*:

> Geoffrey R. Stone got to the heart of modern lying. He's a distinguished professor of law at the University of Chicago. Writing for *The Huffington Post*, Stone said about lying politicians: "An essential element of this strategy is that the perpetrators of the lie will insist, no matter what, that the lie is true. Confronted with the facts, the perpetrators will reiterate

the falsehood. The key to this strategy is the willingness to lie, and to lie repeatedly."[197]

A central reason that it works is that the press, wedded to objectivity, will repeat the lie as one point of view, offering the truth as the opposing point of view. Even more disturbing is the general public's disinterest in the truth, adding to the downward spiral of this pernicious dynamic. As Melinda Henneberger continued, in her article "Truth Seldom Yields Applause Lines":

> Only rarely is a politician made to pay full fare for even the most full-blown flight from reality. Instead, we punish those moments when we're made to hear the truth . . . candidates would surely try harder to get it right if they weren't rewarded for getting it wrong. And regularly made to regret those occasions when the truth does trickle out.[198]

The mauling of reality becomes the most powerful tool in the politician's arsenal.

As Henneberger observed, in this atmosphere truth represents a *faux pas* — something to be avoided. Politicians cannot tell the truth; they would be unmasked if they did. As one well-known statement holds, the definition of a gaffe (verbal blunder) is when a politician tells the truth. Or, as Cardinal Richelieu (d. 1642; King Louis XIII of France's chief minister) said: "If you give me six lines written by the most honest man, I will find something in them to hang him."[199]

Better to lie than risk being hanged.

FRAUD AND THE AMERICAN VOTER

It's not the people who vote that count; it's the people who count the votes.[200]

Fraud in American politics takes more than just verbal form. In recent years, Republicans have tried to control the voting tallies, instead of just influence them. In 2004, about half of the votes of that year's electorate (70 million Americans) were cast on electronic voting machines that left no paper trail, and which were collated and counted by four companies all of which were owned by major Republican donors.

> It turns out that Diebold Election Systems' CEO is Bob Urosevich. His brother Todd founded "rival" ES&S. Together, these two companies will tally around 80% of votes cast [electronically] next November.

> Howard Ahmanson bankrolled the Urosevich brothers in the vote-counting business. Ahmanson is also a member of the Council for National Policy, a right-wing "steering group" that whispers into Dubya's [President George W. Bush] other ear.

> The publicity shy Ahmanson is also a major financial backer behind the extremist "Christian Reconstructionist" movement. The *St. Petersburg Times* reveals that this group "openly advocates a theocratic takeover of American democracy, placing all Americans under the 'dominion' of 'Christ the King'"

— personified by God's chosen representative in Washington, holy warrior G. W. Bush.[201]

The specific, potentially election-changing nature of this behavior was not difficult to uncover, yet still made no difference in the anti-democratic behavior. In the 2004 election, Governor Jeb Bush (R-FL; President George W. Bush's brother, and Governor of one of the most important swing states) refused to allow independent audits of the electronic voting machines, assuring that the tally reported from the Republican-leaning companies would stand as reported.

> Imagine that you could subvert the voting process in ways that would allow you to steal elections without anyone knowing. This is an accurate description of the voting system that will determine the next leader of the most [morally] bankrupt and militarily powerful nation on the planet — regardless of how Americans actually vote.[202]

In 2012, 25% of the nation's registered voters used paperless electronic voting machines,[203] but other methods of voter fraud were devised and implemented. Howard L. Simon, executive director of the American Civil Liberties Union of Florida, examined how a new system of election malfeasance was being perpetrated around the country for the 2012 election season:

> What is happening in more than two-dozen states is that the claim of widespread voter fraud has been used as an excuse to make it more difficult to register to vote, to cast your vote, and to have your vote counted. That — rather than the chimera of widespread voting fraud — is the real threat to democracy. These laws are not intended to apply evenly. The voting restrictions enacted in Florida disproportionately impact minority groups, recently naturalized citizens, students, and people who need to get time off from their jobs to vote.[204]

Another article in the *Washington Post*, "Laws May Cut Latino Voting," noted that the new legislation might prevent up to ten million Hispanics from voting in November 2012 — coincidentally, a population that was previewed to overwhelmingly support the Democratic candidate for president.[205] Republican state legislatures passed *all* of the new laws restricting access to the polls, and the legislation targeted historically Democratic voting populations.

The irony, of course, is that if some of these exact same voter fraud methods were utilized in countries such as Iraq, Vietnam or Venezuela, Colin Powell, Jimmy Carter and the U.S. government would be sternly warning that the veracity of the vote would be called into question, and stating that to fully trust the results, the United States needed greater assurance of election credibility.

But when it happens here on the home soil, these laws are simply presented as "safeguarding" our vote. An article in August 2012 about a voter "protection" law in Pennsylvania exhibited a selection of Machiavellian strategies:

> In the wake of a judge's decision not to block Pennsylvania's controversial voter ID law, Mike Turzai, the Republican legislator who made headlines in June when he said the law would help Mitt Romney win the state in November, repeated the falsehood that the state has a history of election fraud. "The many election reforms enacted, including voter ID, are aimed to ensure citizens and registered voters have the right to vote and have their vote counted," Turzai said in a statement. "It's about one person, one vote, and each instance of fraud dilutes legitimate votes." . . . As they fought to defend the law in court, state officials conceded that no one had ever been prosecuted for in-person voter ID fraud and that there was no evidence that it had ever occurred in the state. In-person election fraud, which the state's ID law is supposed to prevent, is extremely rare: a study of in-person voter fraud in presidential elections going back to 2000 found just 10 cases of voter fraud during a period when more than 600 million votes were cast.[206]

Turzai followed strictly Machiavellian dictates. As the Florentine philosopher stated: "One should never show one's intentions, but endeavor to obtain one's desires anyhow."[207] And so Turzai, who had stated (in a private gathering) that the law would help elect a Republican president (his desire), continued publicly in his dissimulation by assuring that the new laws "aimed to ensure citizens and registered voters have the right to vote and have their vote counted."

This history of this type of voter fraud in America goes back longer than the 2012 election season and runs deeper than presidential elections. Journalist Thom Hartmann noted in "If You Want To Win An Election, Just Control The Voting Machines":

> Maybe Nebraska Republican Chuck Hagel honestly won two US Senate elections. Maybe it's true that the citizens of Georgia simply decided that incumbent Democratic Senator Max Cleland, a wildly popular war veteran who lost three limbs in Vietnam, was, as his successful Republican challenger suggested in his campaign ads, too unpatriotic to remain in the Senate. Maybe George W. Bush, Alabama's new Republican governor Bob Riley, and a small but congressionally decisive handful of other long-shot Republican candidates really did win those states where conventional wisdom and straw polls showed them losing in the last few election cycles.

> Perhaps, after a half-century of fine-tuning exit polling to such a science that it's now sometimes used to verify how clean elections are in Third World countries, it really did suddenly become inaccurate in the United States in the past six years and just won't work here anymore. Perhaps it's just a coincidence that the sudden rise of inaccurate exit polls happened around the same time corporate-programmed, computer-controlled, modem-capable voting machines began recording and tabulating ballots.

> The respected Washington D.C. publication *The Hill* has confirmed that former conservative radio talk-show host and now Republican U.S. Sena-

tor Chuck Hagel (R-NE) was the head of, and continues to own part interest in, the company that owns the company that installed, programmed, and largely ran the voting machines that were used by most of the citizens of Nebraska . . . When Bev Harris (a citizen activist of *blackboxvoting.org*) and *The Hill's* Alexander Bolton pressed the Chief Counsel and Director of the Senate Ethics Committee, the man responsible for ensuring that FEC disclosures are complete, asking him why he'd not questioned Hagel's 1995, 1996, and 2001 failures to disclose the details of his ownership in the company that owned the voting machine company when he ran for the Senate, the Director reportedly met with Hagel's office on Friday, January 25, 2003 and Monday, January 27, 2003. After the second meeting, on the afternoon of January 27th, the Director of the Senate Ethics Committee resigned his job.

Meanwhile, back in Nebraska, Charlie Matulka had requested a hand count of the vote in the election he lost to Hagel. He just learned his request was denied because, he said, Nebraska has a just-passed law that prohibits government-employee election workers from looking at the ballots, even in a recount. The only machines permitted to count votes in Nebraska, he said, are those made and programmed by the corporation formerly run by Hagel.[208]

Machiavelli would be proud.

MACHIAVELLI: BECAUSE IT WORKS

[Machiavelli] displays a bias in favor of the impetuous, the quick, the partisan, the spectacular and the bloody over and against the deliberate, the slow, the neutral, the silent and the gentle.[209]

Fear, lies, fraud, war — they are employed decade after decade, century after century because there are no more successful strategies for coming to and retaining power. Even Adolph Hitler had a 90% approval rating in 1934,[210] *after* he had attained power, dissolved the opposition and begun to implement his fascist reforms!

The Nazis proved beyond a doubt that the big lie theory does work. Millions of Germans had religious devotion for Hitler. In 1934, after Hitler had consolidated his hold on Germany, Hitler had a 90% approval rating by his people. In the 1930s, if Germans saw Hitler step out of a car, many times people were breathless with adulation, fainting dead away in the street.[211]

While it is facile to use Hitler to support any political argument, the fact remains that he was simply the most extreme measure of an endemic human predicament. The difference between Hitler's language and method for attaining and retaining power and that of other world leaders — even today — is one of degree, not method. Regardless of the system, all governments are beholden to Machiavellian rules.

Machiavelli wrote his grammar of power and came close to setting down the imperatives by which men govern and are governed in political communities, whatever the epoch and whatever the governmental structure.[212]

The specific similarities between the various political structures are not difficult to uncover. As former *Wall Street Journal* reporter Russell Drake noted in a disturbing article entitled, "Bush-Hitler: Hypnotizing the Masses:"

> Of all the labels hung on George W. Bush, the hardest to shake may be the comparison with Hitler. Perhaps the clearest likeness between the two men lies in their use of emotionally induced hypnosis to plant in the mass consciousness an image of themselves as protectors of their subjects from threats to national survival both inside and outside the fatherland. In a June 2003 article written for *The Nation* about Bush's "mastery of emotional language, especially negatively charged emotional language," clinical psychologist Reanna Brooks observed that "Bush creates and maintains negative frameworks in his listeners' minds with a number of linguistic techniques borrowed from hypnosis and advertising to instill the image of a dark and evil world around us."
>
> Writing in *The New Yorker* of July 12 & 19, David Greenberg tells how Bush speech writer Michael Gerson, "himself an evangelical, laces the President's addresses with seemingly innocuous terms that the devout recognize as laden with meaning: 'whirlwind,' 'work of mercy,' 'safely home,' 'wonderworking power.'" Aspiring political hypnotists would do well to study Hitler as an introduction to Bush.[213]

I am not conflating the actions of these two leaders, but I am suggesting that their methods are disturbingly similar, and fit in with Machiavellian techniques.

George W. Bush: An American Prince

> The Bush administration's worldview is a form of politically institutionalized religious fundamentalism that has little in common with a model of democracy based on checks and balances, separation of church and state, and government transparency ... while it may have little in common with democracy, such a worldview does fit quite well with neo-Machiavellian "iron rules," which demand both a sense of divine mandate and a willingness to enter into evil.[214]

Machiavellian inspiration runs deeply through the American political world, both historically as well as in the contemporary world. However, in my lifetime, no politician so quintessentially embodied the Florentine's methodology as George W. Bush (b. 1946). While virtually all other successful American politicians have employed some Machiavellian means in their march to power, none was so clear about it, nor as successful, as the 43rd president of the United States.

Though George W. Bush has eased away from the national stage, his legacy lingers in a strengthened military industrial complex; a heightened domestic surveillance state; a degraded environment; a shattered economy; and other aspects of pure Machiavellian rule that work for the moneyed few while working against the shared interests of the country and, indeed, the world.

It is for this reason that I am centering this study of Machiavelli in America on the presidency of George W. Bush, as well as his reelection campaign of 2004. By examining his words, actions and power grabs, we can better appreciate how Machiavellian ideas are implemented in contemporary American politics, and begin to understand the underlying illness not only of our political system, but also of many aspects of our public square (including business, religion, popular culture, media and other shared facets), as these are affected by the Machiavellian dictates of Social Darwinism.

THE ENDS JUSTIFIES THE MEANS

> Machiavelli holds that there is no other way to look at virtue than politically, that is, for what it gets you. For Machiavelli, virtue is defined in politics. The consequence is that he is forced to abandon justice as a virtue, for when virtue is political, the only political virtue, the one that would restrain politics, disappears.[215]

We should be thankful of George W. Bush because he showed us just how far America will go as a society in the direction of the Florentine philosopher. How quickly and easily the United States may give in to fear and turn its collective back on its own professed values and even Constitution, caving to the power politics defined by the amoral Renaissance thinker.

Leo Strauss said in *Thoughts on Machiavelli*:

> Once one realizes the power of that necessity which is the natural necessity to sin, and therewith the inseparable connection between sinning and everything noble and high, one will cease to deplore the necessity.[216]

And Bush did just this, by using any violation of common decency and morality to further his own interests, in the name of the state. "Republics fall under the doctrine of *raison d'état*, which holds that rulers must commit deeds that violate traditional morality, for the purpose of providing such political goods as security, prosperity, empire and greatness."[217]

In so doing, he showed the American citizenry quite explicitly that it believed in torture (waterboarding; 58% for, in a 2009 poll[218]); that it believed in singling out people due to their religion (nearly 50% of Americans believed that "the values of Islam are at odds with American values"[219]); that it believed that money should be taken from the poor and given to the rich (Bush tax cuts[220]); that climate change was either not happening or not urgent;[221] that the government did not have a moral obligation to help those in need (only 35% of respondents felt that the federal government should do more to help people[222]); that international treaties should be abrogated[223] and that politics should revolve around partisan warfare and not the good of the country. As Professor Richard Skinner (Williams College) noted in "George W. Bush and the Partisan Presidency":

> George W. Bush is the epitome of a partisan president, owing his electoral and legislative victories to overwhelming support from his fellow Repub-

licans, showing little regard for neutral competence in administration or policymaking, and cultivating a new partisan press.[224]

Just to make clear how literal was Bush's Machiavellian inspiration, I cite this article exploring George W. Bush's 2004 budget, which was proposed during his re-election campaign:

> While seeking an unprecedented $1.5 trillion in new tax cuts, largely benefiting the richest Americans, the Bush administration has used its 2004 budget plan to propose a wide array of attacks on the poorest sections of the working class, with outright cuts in some programs, tightened eligibility requirements for others, and the shifting of much of the remaining social welfare system from federal to state responsibility.[225]

The end — Bush's hold on power — excused any means. And what's more, Bush convinced himself and enough Americans that he was expressing God's will through his policies. He not only claimed that his greatest political mentor was Jesus Christ, but that God spoke directly to him, asking him to undertake various military campaigns for the good of the world (see above). But as Max Lerner noted in his introduction to a volume including both *The Prince* and *The Discourses on the First Ten Books of Titus Livius*:

> The most destructive imperialisms in the world have been those of men who have elevated their preferences to the pinnacle of moral imperatives and who have then confidently proceeded to impose those imperatives on others.[226]

However, this also represents the best manner of implementing a Machiavellian program of power. And indeed, it might stand as one definition of it.

APPEARANCE V. REALITY

> The aide [to President Bush] said that guys like me [*New York Times* journalist Ron Suskind] were "in what we call the reality-based community," which he defined as people who "believe that solutions emerge from your judicious study of discernible reality. That's not the way the world really works anymore. We're an empire now and when we act, we create our own reality. And while you're studying that reality — judiciously, as you will — we'll act again, creating other new realities, which you can study too, and that's how things will sort out. We're history's actors — and you, all of you, will be left to just study what we do."[227]

Reality is not a static panorama interpreted by opinion makers and the media. Through using language as an "effective arsenal for the war of perception" (Frank Luntz), reality itself is shaped by the mass marketing propaganda organs of media, advertising and political speech. And as the above quote notes, leaders can shape not only the perception of reality, but also its actuality, through action.

Machiavelli said: "The great majority of humans are satisfied with appearances, as though they were realities, and are often more influenced by the things that seem than by those that are."[228] Creating appearances — or fraud, with the use of language and, more recently, the amplifying force of the media — is the best tactic for regulating *fortuna*.

For eight years, George W. Bush was *de facto* the most powerful man on Earth. And Bush, well aware of his Machiavellian teacher, made no bones about it. As Machiavelli noted: "The right of the stronger is to be unimpeded by the minds of the weaker."[229] Bush never allowed his way to be impeded by the "minds of the weaker." As the 43rd President stated:

> I'm the commander in chief, see — I don't need to explain; I do not need to explain why I say things. That's the interesting thing about being the president. Maybe somebody needs to explain to me why they say something, but I don't feel like I owe anybody an explanation.[230]

George W. Bush created a world that enough people wanted to live in, and then crushed the rest with Machiavellian power. Let others judiciously study reality all they wanted; Bush and his minions were the unbridled masters of the world.

An excerpt from a book by David Corn (b. 1959; chief of the Washington bureau for *Mother Jones*) a truth-based journalist who is about as relevant to the mainstream press as a can of corn, noted:

> George W. Bush is a liar. He has lied large and small, directly and by omission. His Iraq lies have loomed the largest. In the run-up to the invasion, Bush based his case for war on a variety of unfounded claims . . . He said that Saddam Hussein possessed a 'massive stockpile' of unconventional weapons and was directly 'dealing' with al-Qaeda — two suppositions unsupported (then or now) by the available evidence. He said the International Atomic Energy Agency had produced a report in 1998 noting that Iraq was six months from developing a nuclear weapon; no such report existed (and the IAEA had actually reported then that there was no indication Iraq had the ability to produce weapons-grade material) . . . Lying has been one of the essential tools of this presidency.[231]

Corn went even further, saying things in the alternative press that would never be allowed in the mainstream (though often factually inaccurate) outlets that help define America's social reality:

> With his misrepresentations and false assertions, Bush has dramatically changed the nation and the world. Relying on deceptions, he turned the United States into an occupying power. Using lies, he pushed through tax cuts that will profoundly reshape the US budget for years to come, most likely insuring a long stretch of deficits that will make it difficult, perhaps impossible, for the federal government to fund existing programs or contemplate new ones . . . The future of the United States remains in the hands of a dishonest man.[232]

If truth is not relevant to the perception of reality, than perhaps George W. Bush was right about a faith-based presidency. As long as people have faith in the president, then the leader can undertake any Machiavellian strategy to lie and steal, cheat and commit institutional murder (war) as he so desires — and his partisans, at least, won't even perceive it as such. He is acting behind an invisible veil provided by a compliant media that blocks the truth from view — only letting out that which the faithful choose to perceive and believe.

No matter what the rest of us might think, this is exactly how a leader who wants to master *fortuna* should behave.

> A man of supreme virtue, of ancient virtue, should and can regulate fortune so that she has no cause to show her power all the time. Fortune is changeable and hence unreliable: to trust in her and put one's hope in her is madness.[233]

And so Bush did beat back fortune with fraud and lies. According to his narrative, Bush's wars were about "spreading freedom," not the slaughter of tens of thousands of innocent civilians. They were about Truth and Beauty and protection of the American Dream — and not about turning a generation of America's youth into torturers and murderers.

Reality? George W. Bush decided what the social and political reality was — and citizens could either go along for the ride, or stew impotently in the corner somewhere. George W. Bush was a have-your-cake-and-eat-it-too kind of leader:

> George W. Bush is one of history's great confidence men . . . I mean it in the sense that he's a believer in the power of confidence. At a time when constituents are uneasy and enemies are probing for weaknesses, he clearly feels that unflinching confidence has an almost mystical power. It can all but create a reality.[234]

Perhaps a very instructive psychological examination of George W. Bush could be done, but it probably wouldn't look any different from that of other leaders throughout the ages who robbed from the poor to give to the rich; who used religion as a political bludgeon and who were willing to do as much as they could get away with to achieve and retain power. Why worry about the personal psychological health of one or another world leader, when all we need do is to read Machiavelli's handbook of power?

Ultimately, the problem is not with the leader, but with the followers. Any leader, from the most powerful tyrant to the gentlest democratic president, must have some level of popular support. And all citizens are beholden to that leader's Machiavellian philosophy of power. As the Florentine noted:

> When a people goes so far as to commit the error of giving power to one man so that he may defeat those whom they hate, and if this man be shrewd, it will always end with his becoming their tyrant.[235]

George W. Bush's behavior while in office was simply a representation of a collective human illness, one that was codified in the clearest possible way by the far-off Florentine political philosopher.

The fraud of Bush's faith was so profound, and his personal psychology so insecure, that he demanded fealty to himself in the manner of any of the great dictators of the past. It was entirely within the realm of possibility that his fraud extended even to himself, and he believed the Machiavellian world-view that he proposed to the American people for nearly a decade. As Ron Suskind (Pulitzer Prize winning journalist) noted in an article about Bush:

> The president has demanded unquestioning faith from his followers, his staff, his senior aides and his kindred in the Republican Party. Once he makes a decision, often swiftly, based on a creed, or moral position — he expects a complete faith in its rightness.[236]

And as another long-time politico, Bruce Bartlett, who was a domestic policy advisor to Ronald Reagan, put it:

> I think a light has gone off for people who've spent time up close to Bush: That this "instinct" that he is always talking about is this sort of weird, Messianic idea of what he thinks God has told him to do. This is why George W. Bush is so clear-eyed about al-Qaeda and the Islamic funda-mentalist enemy . . . He understands them because he's just like them. He dispenses with people who confront him with inconvenient facts.[237]

That Bush believed in his own myth, in his own fraud and use of religion for his purposes in creating reality, so much the better. It is the natural end of the Machiavellian political philosophy, that the leader himself should be fooled by his own apparent religiosity.

> Religion makes men faithful to the gods and hence to the men the gods recommend . . . the first necessity of ruling is for rulers to hide their own nature [arrogant mastery] by means of religion, or in the Machiavellian equivalent, fraud.[238]

If George Bush was able to hide his own "nature" even from himself, it would make no difference in terms of his political life. And if 50.1% of the voting public signed on, who cared what might have been the psycho-pathology, or the truth? Reality was the only thing that mattered — and a successful leader might control that through action, fraud and religios-ity. Truth, after all, only represents *fortuna* — and she can be mastered by a leader of exceptional Machiavellian *virtù*.

In a liberal democracy, the majority of the voting public represents the only legitimate force,[239] and can define reality as it sees fit. And this general voting public is, as Rumi noted, held hostage to the single leader, and the single leader to his own delusion of religious grander — Machiavelli's fraud — bringing the whole society together under the horrible fantasy of a single, powerful actor.

RELIGIOUS, BUT NO MYSTIC

> A certain present day prince, whom it is not good to name, never preaches anything but peace and faith and is the greatest enemy of the one and of the other, and one as well as the other if he had observed them, would many times have taken from him either his reputation or his state. Through using

both pious cruelty and faithlessness, [this leader] became out of a weak king the first king of the Christians in fame and glory.[240]

As much as it might seem that this quote applied to George W. Bush, it actually referenced an earlier leader, King Ferdinand of Spain (d. 1516), who evicted his Jewish and Muslim citizens from that country in 1492 and then, under the guise of piety and peace, hunted the *Marranos* (converted Jews) and drove them from the Iberian Peninsula, as well.

Echoing the medieval Spanish rule, George W. Bush utilized his "Christian fervor" to paint the American reaction to the World Trade Center attacks (September 11, 2001) as a "crusade" against Muslims.[241] On the home front, reprising King Ferdinand's mopping-up work against the Jewish converts, Bush undertook a similar program:

> The "national security" measures undertaken since fall 2001 by the Justice Department have targeted almost exclusively people from the Middle East and South Asia, and led to the incarceration, deportation and interrogation of numerous individuals who had nothing to do with September 11.[242]

At the same time, like the Spanish king, all of George W. Bush's actions were slathered with religion's schmaltz. Machiavelli noted:

> A prince must have great care that nothing ever leave his mouth that is not full of pious, faithful, humane, integral and religious qualities, and that he appear all piety, all faith, all integrity, all humaneness, all religion . . . but while keeping one's spirit predisposed so that, needing not to be those things, you might know how to change to be the contrary . . . Everyone sees what you appear, few feel what you are . . . the vulgar are taken by what seems and the outcome of the thing.[243]

George W. Bush mastered this advice, a skill that sickened the few while satisfying the vulgar multitudes. As was noted in an article in the *Christian Science Monitor* in 2003, Bush infused his public persona with religion and God:

> President Bush has never been shy about injecting his faith into the public arena — his campaign remark that Jesus Christ was his "favorite political philosopher" was an early signal. In this year's State of the Union address, for example, Bush quoted an evangelical hymn that refers to the power of Christ. "'There's power, wonder-working power,' in the goodness and idealism and faith of the American people," he said . . . The infusion of religious conviction into presidential speeches warms many hearts. To one of his most vocal supporters, Bush is simply using the language of American civil religion.

"George Bush is standing squarely in a tradition as old as the country," says Richard Land, head of the Southern Baptist Convention's Ethics and Religious Liberty Commission.

Others applaud Bush's clarity in a time of national crisis. "He has reintroduced into the culture the language of morality and moral distinctions," says Richard Mouw, president of Fuller Theological Seminary, in Pasadena, Calif.[244]

For the few who judged President Bush on his actions, his words rang hollow, and even frighteningly hypocritical. But, as Machiavelli made clear, "in the world there are only the vulgar; and the few don't stand a chance against them."[245]

As was noted above, the highest Machiavellian dictum of leadership is to bring religion and war together, and ally them both with the desires of the prince. George W. Bush's policies, antithetical to spiritual and moral values, were nonetheless always couched in a religious frame. Here is a quote from the third presidential debate (Bush v. John Kerry) in autumn 2004:

> When I make decisions I stand on principle. And the principles are derived from who I am. I believe we ought to love our neighbor like we love ourself. That's manifested in public policy through the faith-based initiative where we've unleashed the armies of compassion to help heal people who hurt. I believe that God wants everybody to be free. That's what I believe. And that's one part of my foreign policy. And so my principles that I make decisions on are a part of me. And religion is a part of me.[246]

The reality of his policies, however, was hardly representative of the above stated position. He advocated a domestic policy that took money from the poor to give to the rich; based his foreign policy in mass murder; actively utilized torture as an interrogation method; lied repeatedly and knowingly about issues great and small, and then covered it up by destroying evidence thereof (more than 22 million missing emails[247]) and undertook a series of other actions that *no* religion would claim as its own.

But it worked. As Machiavelli said: "in the actions of all men, and especially princes, one looks to the results."[248] Bush won two presidential elections, began two wars, got a huge number of bills passed, helped his party take over the Congress and left office with his life and wealth intact.

We are left with the impression that George W. Bush's religiosity seemed more aligned with the Machiavellian posture: "It is not necessary for a leader to have [moral] qualities, but it is very necessary to *seem* to have them," rather than that of his stated political mentor (Jesus).

God and War

> What Machiavelli is saying to us is that it remains open to us as a civilization (or to some enterprising innovator within our civilization) to *reinterpret* Christianity in such a way that it secures the political advantages that the Romans were so adept at exploiting through a judicious manipulation of religious beliefs and practices.[249]

Bush did just this to motivate the American population for his wars. And in fighting wars, he was able to unify the citizens behind his governance. As journalist Tom Carver noted in his article "Bush Puts God on his Side":

Bush became convinced that God was calling him to engage the forces of evil in battle, and this one time baseball-team owner from Texas did not shrink from the task. "We are in a conflict between good and evil. And America will call evil by its name," Mr. Bush told West Point graduates in a speech last year. Mr. Bush's rhetoric does have a huge audience. One in three American Christians call themselves evangelicals and many evangelicals believe the second coming of Christ will occur in the Middle East after a titanic battle with the anti-Christ.

Does the president believe he is playing a part in the final events of Armageddon?

If true, it is an alarming thought. But he would not be alone, as 59% of all Americans believe that what is written in the Bible's Book of Revelation will come to pass.[250]

George W. Bush's religiosity, shorn of all moral precepts such as "turn the other cheek," "do unto others as you would have them do unto you" and "if you want to be perfect, go, sell your possessions and give to the poor" (all maxims of Bush's most important political philosopher: Jesus), allowed him to utilize the fiction of his faith to further his personal leadership goals. His doublespeak was worthy of an Orwellian novel. Here was a man who "tied the confrontation with Iraq to the ongoing campaign in Afghanistan, and placed both in what he described as an American tradition of benign foreign interventions."[251]

President Bush certainly did not invent this interrelationship between America, God and the military. The dynamic weaves itself deep into the fabric of the historical narrative of American values. But he was adept at tying his military-religious worldview in with his actions. Here are the words of President George W. Bush, uttered in the run up to the Iraq War in November of 2002, just after having used the specter of war to crush the Democrats in the midterm elections:

The president outlined a far-reaching moral-mission for his presidency: "I will seize the opportunity to achieve big goals — there is nothing bigger than to achieve world peace. We're never going to get people all in agreement about the use of force, but action — confident action that will yield positive results — provides kind of a slipstream into which reluctant nations and leaders can get behind and show themselves that there has been — you know, something positive has happened towards peace."[252]

He spoke these words in advocating a unilateral, unprovoked attack on a sovereign nation. The country he attacked (Iraq) remains destabilized as I write this more than ten years later. Hundreds of thousands of people, both Americans and Iraqis, were killed, displaced or permanently psychologically maimed. Yet it was, as Machiavelli assured, good politics. It helped Bush consolidate power in the 2002-midterm elections, and then win reelection in 2004.

This "war is peace" construction was framed within Bush's prophetic self-image as a national and even world leader, as was explicitly noted in the *Independent* (U.K.):

> President George Bush has claimed he was told by God to invade Iraq and attack Osama bin Laden's stronghold of Afghanistan as part of a divine mission to bring peace to the Middle East, security for Israel, and a state for the Palestinians.[253]

This quote sounds remarkably like one from Machiavelli's *Discourses on the First Ten Books of Titus Livius*, which concerned the founding of a republic:

> Numa (the founder of Rome's religion and its lawgiver) pretended to have private conferences with a nymph who advised him about the advice he should give to the people. This was because he wanted to introduce new institutions to which the city was unaccustomed, and doubted whether his own authority would suffice.[254]

Leaving aside whether he was a fool who was fooling himself, or a Machiavellian actor who understood that people were far more convinced by appearance than reality, for George W. Bush, pre-emptive bombs were the new face of a muscular Christianity. And also good politics.

FEAR

> Love is held by a chain of obligation that, men being selfish, is broken whenever it serves their purpose; but fear is maintained by a dread of punishment which never fails.[255]

As Machiavelli oft noted, there is no better tactic for spurring humans on to action than fear. Fear stems from the center of our being — injected into our consciousness from the amygdala — where it overwhelms self-critical and rational thinking, turning us into little more than reactive animals. For a politician, there is no quicker or surer way to bring people together around his own campaign or ideas than to inspire fear, and promise to alleviate it through his program.

We are, due to our cortical structure, always prepared for "fear" to overcome any higher thought processes. As Doug Holt noted in "The Role of the Amygdala in Fear and Panic":

> The amygdala is specialized for reacting to stimuli and triggering a physiological response, a process that would be described as the "emotion" of fear. After this, the stimuli of the activation of the amygdala is transmitted to the cortex. In the cortex the frightening stimulus is analyzed in detail, using information from many parts of the brain . . . Unfortunately the neural connections from the cortex down to the amygdala are less well developed than are connections from the amygdala back up to the cortex. Thus, the amygdala exerts a greater influence on the cortex than vice versa. Once an emotion has been turned on, it is difficult for the cortex to turn it off.[256]

Politically, fear works — and in the Machiavellian construction, the only way to alleviate fear within is to project it without. We witness this dynamic time and again, as politicians utilize fear of everything from Socialism to terrorism to the end of "Medicare as we know it" to garner votes and demonize the "other," in the continuous political battle known as democracy.

It is easy to see why politicians run political campaigns based in fear instead of hope. How George W. Bush could spend eight years at war, watch his popularity rating shrink, yet still pass many of his legislative priorities up until his final days in office. As late as July 2008, at a time when his approval rating stood at around 33% and the Democrats controlled both the House of Representatives and the Senate, he was still able to have passed a bill (Foreign Intelligence Surveillance Act of 1978 Amendments Act of 2008, H.R. 6304) expanding the government's surveillance authority and granting legal amnesty to telecommunications companies that had facilitated his (illegal) warrantless surveillance program.

He did this by driving his message deep into the heart of the limbic system, utilizing fear as a motivator. As CBS News noted:

> President Bush, in remarks meant to spur House Democrats into accepting a controversial new bill that would expand the government's ability to spy on Americans, warned that the country faced terror strikes that would make September 11 "pale by comparison." In response, critics of the new bill accused Mr. Bush of "fear-mongering," and of trying to deflect attention from the bill itself. Mr. Bush also raised the specter of what would happen if telecom immunity is not accepted by the House, by recalling the crime scene on 9/11:

> "At this moment, somewhere in the world, terrorists are planning new attacks on our country. Their goal is to bring destruction to our shores that will make September the 11th pale by comparison."[257]

Holt also noted that there is an antidote to this primal response to external stimulus, but it is one that neither Machiavelli nor contemporary politicians wish to inspire.

> There are methods of reducing fear and inhibiting the fear response. It has been determined that when attention is shifted away from the anxiety-provoking stimulus, less fear is observed.[258]

It is for this reason that politicians will continually talk about what is most fearful — so that attention will *not* be shifted away from the fear provoking stimuli. It not only elects politicians, it sells newspapers and attracts TV viewers and has become central to our national *zeitgeist*.

> We have to become aware of the poisonous effect of the mass media that keep violence, cruelty and sadism constantly present to the minds of unformed and irresponsible people . . . We have to consider that the hate propaganda, and the consistent heckling of one government by another, has always inevitably led to violent conflict. We have to recognize the implications of voting for politicians who promote policies of hate.[259]

Not to say that truly horrible things don't happen here, but in the general scheme of things worldwide, the U.S. is a pretty safe, sanguine place. However, fear and violence have become endemic to our national culture because they are powerful selling points. They bypass the conscious, reasoning thought process of the prefrontal cortex and make a beeline for the amygdala, providing compelling selling motivation for everything from an SUV to a public figure.

American culture and politics follows the Machiavellian dictum that "the political man would have to summon passions of a primordial, animal nature, not modulated or restrained by scruples of a more human nature."[260]

> A society such as ours which allows films of unremitting violence to be beamed down 24 hours a day to television screens of adults, who have nothing better to do with their lives, and children who haven't formed their power of judgment, is bound to engender moral confusion and despair.[261]

Compare this with a statement by the 20th century prophet, Thomas Merton, who thought about these same matters from a very different perspective:

> The real focus of American violence is in the very culture itself, its mass media, its extreme individualism and competitiveness; its inflated myths of virility and toughness and its overwhelming preoccupation with the power of nuclear, chemical, bacteriological and psychological overkill.[262]

Things are so extreme in America that even peripheral cultural commentators have noticed. This came out in the sports page of the *Washington Post*, offering wisdom and perspective from a sportswriter:

> Howard Cosell (d. 1995) once said, "Sports is a microcosm of life." Lately, it's not a microcosm of life; it's larger than life. Either way, we're going to hell in a hand basket, sponsored by Coors Light . . . It's a deterioration of civilized thought and behavior, and it's played out daily in more than just the sporting arenas. I mean, I don't know if you've noticed, but there's a lot of anger out there. So you have people cutting each other off on the highway and parents fighting each other at youth soccer games and voters screaming at each other at polling booths. And while sports fans aren't necessarily more belligerent than they were generations ago, the means of belligerence — talk radio and the internet — have become more pervasive . . . What we really need is a massive re-socialization.[263]

Yet, politicians do everything they can to keep driving the social conversation into the lowest reaches of the human "primordial" experience, where fear and anger, violence and retribution rule. Here is a single statement, of an almost infinite number that could be culled from our public square over the last couple of decades, from one of the most powerful men in the United States at the time he spoke, doing all he could to *not* allow the attention to be shifted away from the anxiety-provoking stimulus. Vice President Dick Cheney sowed dread in September 2004, in the heat of the election season:

A November win by Democratic presidential candidate John Kerry would put the United States at risk of another "devastating" terrorist attack, Vice President Dick Cheney told supporters Tuesday. Cheney told Republican supporters at a town hall meeting in Des Moines that they needed to make "the right choice" in the November 2 election. "If we make the wrong choice, then the danger is that we'll get hit again — that we'll be hit in a way that will be devastating from the standpoint of the United States," Cheney said.[264]

Each paroxysm of fear can be momentarily effaced from the amygdala by checking "Destroy" in the ballot box and dropping another 2000-pound bomb on some people, far away. And who better to undertake this action than the politician promising to "annihilate" fear in the most obvious and muscular way?

AMERICA'S DARK ARTISTS: OTHER POLITICIANS

George W. Bush's presidency receded into the rear view mirror of American history some time ago, and grows dimmer with every passing month. Soon, the National Archives will begin disgorging emails and papers from that sad era, and historians and journalists will paint a truer version of what took place under his dominion. That will be but an academic exercise.

However, the Machiavellian influence on American politics hardly waned with the passing of Bush's presidency. In America, Machiavellian dictates continue to inform winning politics. The struggle for truth and morality to become central to our public square is lost. Politician after politician utilizes the same political playbook, some with more success than others.

In the 2012 election season, public figures continued to claim that God was on their side, which allowed them to provide the appearance of morality, not through actions, but words. For instance, Rick Santorum (b. 1958; former Republican senator from Pennsylvania), who ran in the Republican presidential primaries, won several state victories by claiming to have the "God" vote:

> Its [Santorum's victory speech in Louisiana on March 13, 2012] inescapably churchy overtones, with thanks to God and references to prayer at the very beginning and the biggest applause line invoking the "integrity of the family and the centrality of faith in our lives." [Santorum's] campaign transmogrifies into a holy crusade for the "centrality of faith in our lives," with Republicans in open opposition to contraception, university education and the separation of church and state.[265]

And Newt Gingrich (R-GA; Speaker of the House of Representatives from 1995-1998) a serial philanderer, liar, thrice-married self-aggrandizing political animal who was central in American political life from the late 1980s through the 2012 presidential election, had the audacity to intone: "There is no attack on American culture more deadly and more historically dishonest than the secular effort to drive God out of America's public life."[266]

As columnist E. J. Dionne noted in the *Washington Post* about Gingrich's brief rise to the top of the Republican primary field in late 2011:

> Gingrich's rise is the revenge of a Republican base that takes seriously the intense hostility to President Obama, the incendiary accusations against liberals and the Manichaean division of the world between an "us" and a "them" that his party has been peddling in the interest of electoral success. The right-wing faithful knows Gingrich pioneered this style of politics.
>
> [As Gingrich said:] "One of the great problems we have had in the Republican Party is that we ... encourage you to be neat, obedient, and loyal and faithful, and all those Boy Scout words which would be great around the campfire but are lousy in politics ... You're fighting a war. It is a war for power ... What is the primary purpose of a political leader? To build a majority."[267]

Ironically, this same politician was done in by the very methods that he espoused. After all, Machiavelli is not partisan to any individual or political party — he simply offers the clearest strategy for getting elected. The person who best marshals his amoral ideals wins:

> Republican presidential candidate Newt Gingrich attacked negative advertising — and those who use it — at a campaign stop in Waterloo [Iowa] Sunday. "I said from the very beginning we would run a positive campaign," he said. "We would talk about positive ideas, and we would offer positive solutions. Some of my opponents have taken a very different tack, partly because they couldn't defend their record ... "[268]

As a reader noted in the comment section to the online article: "The unmitigated gall of Gingrich to complain when patented 'Gingrich Tactics' are used against him!"[269]

Writing in the article "Cruelty Well Used: Machiavelli, [Scott] Walker [Governor of Wisconsin], and Romney?" Carson Holloway (professor of Political Science at the University of Nebraska), a Republican sympathizer, offered advice for the 2012 Republican nominee for President: "Machiavelli's advice to princes holds important lessons for Mitt Romney if he is elected president."[270]

He stated that, as Machiavelli assured, "cruelty well used" will be the most efficient tactic for a potential Romney administration "not to shrink from imposing this pain [the gutting of social programs] but to enact such reforms as quickly as possible after taking office so that, once accomplished, the voters will have plenty of time to forget the pain before the next election."[271] Holloway contended that by slashing such programs as Social Security and Medicare, Romney would be siding with the "people" over the "great" — a contention that is in itself of such dubious worth that itself seems to follow the Machiavellian dictates that people will believe more in what appears (that slashing the social safety net is in their interest) instead of what is (it simply frees up more money for tax cuts for the wealthy).

President Obama's Machiavellian Foreign Policy

> The White House report and the National Security Strategy
> . . . draw heavily from Machiavelli's formula for the combination of
> propaganda [portraying the Third World as a threat to the U.S.] with
> the need for violence and domination in order to stay atop of the global
> power hierarchy. Machiavelli's propaganda prescription has been the
> necessary medium through which U.S. political leaders have convinced
> the American public of the veracity and necessity of their imperial
> actions.[272]

Even Barack Obama, the left's most recent "savior," is proving no more morally superior than past Machiavellian American actors. Under his administration, illegal drone (pilotless attack aircraft) attacks around the world have more than tripled from the Bush years. Additionally, his administration has killed hundreds of people in extra-judicial assassinations (including American citizens), all without the press or public having the ability of ascertaining whether the victims were "innocent" of the crimes that his administration imagined they had or would commit.

As journalist Glenn Greenwald noted:

> Attorney General Eric Holder provided the most detailed explanation yet
> for why the Obama administration believes it has the authority to secretly
> target U.S. citizens for execution by the CIA without even charging them
> with a crime, notifying them of the accusations, or affording them an op-
> portunity to respond, instead condemning them to death without a shred
> of transparency or judicial oversight. The administration continues to con-
> ceal the legal memorandum it obtained to justify these killings.[273]

Indeed, these executions represent a verbatim Machiavellian tactic for retaining power. As Harvey Mansfield noted in *Machiavelli's Virtue*:

> Machiavelli . . . pronounces that sects, republics and kingdoms need pe-
> riodic "executions" to return them toward their beginnings . . . These ex-
> ecutions are praised for their "good effects" and not for their accuracy in
> retribution. It does not seem important that a formal law has been broken,
> still less that procedural regularity has been preserved . . . "A memorable
> execution of the enemies of the present condition is necessary." The execu-
> tion may as well be tyrannical as legal, provided that it be memorable.[274]

Pilotless drones perform Obama's Machiavellian executions in the far-off lands of Yemen, Pakistan, Somalia and other locales. The Democratic president has personally authorized more than 300 such attacks, which "essentially has charged, tried and executed suspects, including at least one American citizen, without a hearing, a trial or official conviction."[275] Here is Machiavelli's advice in such matters:

> A prince, therefore, must not mind incurring the charge of cruelty for the
> purpose of keeping his subjects united and confident; for, with a very few
> examples, he will be more merciful than those who, from excess of tender-
> ness, allow disorders to arise, from whence spring murders and rapine; for
> these as a rule injure the whole community, while the executions carried

out by the prince injure only one individual. And among all princes, it is impossible for the new prince to escape the name of cruel, since new states are full of dangers.[276]

The highlight of these extralegal executions was that of Osama Bin Laden (May 1, 2011), which continued to be trumpeted by the administration right through the next election, and showed how "tough" and "resolute" the Democratic president was, referencing, of course, Machiavelli's perverse version of *virtù*.

Additionally, Obama's assassinations helped bring the country together under the leadership of the prince by pointing the murders outside of the country, on an "other" that clarified the delineations of "us" and "them." An *ABC-Washington Post* poll found that an overwhelming 83 percent of Americans approved of Obama's drone policy.[277]

However, the reality of the drone attacks is quite different than the appearances provided by reports of the surgical strikes killing only militants in the assaults. As was noted in an article in the *Chicago Tribune*:

> The most infamous example of a tragic drone error came in March of last year when more than 40 civilians attending a tribal gathering in the Pakistani region of North Waziristan were killed. The region is reported to have received more drone attacks than any other area.
>
> "The community is now plagued with fear," said one survivor, in testimony reprinted in the current *Harpers Magazine* from a lawsuit by the British human rights group Reprieve. "The tribal elders are afraid to gather together . . . People in the same family now sleep apart because they do not want their togetherness to be viewed suspiciously through the eye of the drone."[278]

Of course, like all successful politicians, Obama couched all of this in his own "vessel of faith," the Machiavellian fraud used to conceal amoral political actions in the frame of religion. An article in *Newsweek Magazine* explored Obama's religious creed:

> "It's hard for me to imagine being true to my faith — and not thinking beyond myself, and not thinking about what's good for other people, and not acting in a moral and ethical way," [Obama] says. When these ideas merged with his more emotional search for belonging, he was able to arrive at the foot of the cross. He "felt God's spirit beckoning me," he writes in *The Audacity of Hope*. "I submitted myself to His will, and dedicated myself to discovering His truth."[279]

No doubt, Obama like Bush has a vision of himself that is centered in his own morality and goodness. However, judging a person by their actions leads to a very different conclusion: that one cannot lead in America without tacking far closer to Machiavelli's vision of power than any spiritually based version of working humbly for the common good of all. As Machiavelli noted:

> Men in general judge more by their eyes than by their hands, because seeing is given to everyone, touching to few. Everyone sees how you appear, few

touch what you are; and these few dare not oppose the opinion of many, who have the majesty of the state to defend them.[280]

AMERICA'S DARK ARTISTS: POLITICAL OPERATIVES

Today, Machiavelli's influence on political policy may be greater than at any time since he served the Florentine government. Machiavelli has become an American.[281]

According to Renaissance scholar Paul F. Grendler, Machiavelli has been important to American political advisors — specifically conservative and neo-conservative thinkers — since 1943. At that time, James Burnham (d. 1987; an American philosopher and political theorist, who began his career as a Trotskyite, but finished it as a leader of the American conservative movement) proposed a contemporary political science based on the Florentine thinker. He began by rehabilitating Machiavelli, assuring that British and American thinkers had a low opinion of the Renaissance philosopher because Anglo-Saxon politics is characterized by hypocrisy and an avoidance of truth.

Burnham was awarded a Presidential Medal of Freedom by Ronald Reagan in 1983.

Burnham drew an important social distinction, based on Machiavelli's teachings, which can be seen in clear evidence in the politics of 21st-century America:

> The most important division in society is between the ruling class and the ruled, the elite and the non-elite. The elites rule through a political formula containing myths, ideology and/or religion. Nevertheless, the interests of the elite and non-elite do sometimes coincide. And understanding this is the key to achieving partial — but not complete — liberty and democracy.[282]

Machiavelli's — and the Presidential Medal of Freedom winner Burnham's — council inspires many of our contemporary political advisors. Granted, for the most part in our American political system, Machiavellian means stay loosely within the law. Most political assassinations are of the character, and personal armed militias are frowned upon. But these are differences of degree, not philosophy.

Politicians and political operatives consciously foment the Machiavellian, winner-take-all dynamic as the surest method of achieving victory, seeding the public square with the negative energy that poisons the political conversation.

Lee Atwater (d. 1991) might be the first of our era to give himself completely to the Florentine's worldview, presaging the successful and ongoing work of his protégé, Karl Christian Rove (b. 1950). Atwater was an advisor of U.S. Presidents Ronald Reagan and George H. W. Bush, as well as Chairman of the Republican National Committee. However, as the *New York*

Times noted, his mentor was definitely not Republican Party luminaries from Abraham Lincoln to Dwight D. Eisenhower:

> The political Magus who ushered in our new muddier era was Lee Atwater, best known for engineering George H.W. Bush's win in 1988. Mr. Atwater became such a mythic figure in American politics that he was praised at his funeral in 1991 for being Machiavellian "in the very best sense of the word." As many Democratic victims could attest, Mr. Atwater was Machiavellian in the actual sense of the word.[283]

The article continued on to note the pervasive influence of this Machiavellian actor on subsequent political campaigns, as well as on today's "dark artists." For starters, and in today's cultural climate, most importantly, Atwater knew how to play the news media. He would drop a fake story on the best of journalists and then watch the effect unfold. As one writer recalled after he had been hoodwinked by Atwater: "Lee laughed and said, 'Bandy, you got used.'"[284]

Atwater also clearly stated how he utilized language, in addition to the amplifier of the supine media, to appeal to racists in elections. In 1981, political scientist Alexander P. Lamis interviewed Atwater for his book, *Two-Party South*. In the interview, Atwater explained how the GOP, in its appeal to Southern voters starting with Richard Nixon's Southern Strategy, reconfigured overtly racist policies from the Jim Crow era into Reagan-era economic policies, including specific budget cuts targeting the poor.

He said that Republicans utilized "coded-language to appeal to the racists in their base." This cynical use of language could still be seen in 2012, when both Newt Gingrich and Rick Santorum exploited this verbal strategy during the presidential primaries, with Newt Gingrich claiming that President Obama was a "food stamp president" and Rick Santorum asserting that he didn't "want to make black people's lives better by giving them someone else's money." The veiled (and not-so-veiled) racism continued into the 2012 presidential campaign, as noted in an article entitled "Romney's Welfare Attack Ads Are Racist, Desperate":

> In 1976, Ronald Reagan campaigned for the Republican nomination for president by citing an anecdote of a woman in Chicago living the high life on public assistance, thus the term "welfare queen" was born. Those attacks by Ronald Reagan were a political ploy to exploit racial animosity among working-class whites.
>
> Over 36 years have passed since Ronald Reagan promoted the image of the "welfare queen," and yet the power of using social programs as a tool of political and racial division is still widely used. During a primary debate in January, former presidential candidate Newt Gingrich called President Obama the "food stamp president." Now the Romney campaign is resorting to these same attacks in an attempt to stir working-class animosity toward the president.[285]

Atwater perfected this racially divisive tactic in the 1988 campaign to elect President George H. W. Bush, when he used a racist and factually inaccurate ad about a furloughed African-American inmate's rape of a white woman to destroy the campaign of the Democratic nominee, Michael Dukakis. The *Christian Science Monitor* considered it the top political attack ad over the past 50 years:

> The ad, sponsored by the National Security PAC, a group informally allied with the Bush campaign, highlighted a Dukakis policy on prison furloughs for some criminals while he was governor of Massachusetts. The spot wiped out Dukakis's double-digit lead over Vice President Bush and gained lasting notoriety for its use of a racially inflammatory photograph of convicted murderer Willie Horton. Bush went on to win the race by a landslide.[286]

Today, Willie Horton's face is the only thing some voters remember about the 1988 Democratic nominee.

Perhaps the most frightening aspect of America's attack politics is how completely unrepentant are these dark arts operators. As noted above, Atwater was *praised* at his funeral for being Machiavellian "in the very best sense of the word."

National Public Radio produced a segment entitled *An Inside Look At The 'Dark Art' Of Politics*, in which the "invisible hand of opposition research" is referred to as the "dark art of politics."[287] Here, political operatives on both sides of the aisle (Democrat Chris Lehane is mentioned along with Joe Rodota, a Republican political consultant) concur that character assassination of this sort is central to American democracy. And as Lehane noted, there is also delicate strategy in how the assassination is carried out:

> If you get some information, what do you do with it? You don't just send out a press release, Lehane says. You may have a relationship with a particular reporter, or maybe a particular show or newspaper might be the right platform, he says. "And then you want to have different elements of it, so it's not just merely a one-day story; you want to extend this and make it a multiple-day story," Lehane says. "And so you think of all the other pieces that you will drop out there, so that you take the initial issue and create all sorts of subsequent problems."[288]

Specific examples of this dark art are easy to uncover in American politics. One need only pick up a newspaper within two years of an election to find them. However, I will discuss a few incidents, each of which could be replaced by any of hundreds of others over the past several elections seasons.

In the 2000 Republican primary, Senator John McCain surprised George W. Bush with a victory in New Hampshire and then pivoted to South Carolina, looking strong. Immediately, Karl Christian Rove, "the minister of the dark arts for the last Texas president"[289] swung into action:

A "push poll"[290] was part of a smear campaign against John McCain in 2000. According to McCain's campaign manager, Richard Davies: "It didn't take much research to turn up a seemingly innocuous fact about the McCains: John and his wife, Cindy, have an adopted daughter named Bridget. Cindy found Bridget at Mother Teresa's orphanage in Bangladesh, brought her to the United States for medical treatment, and the family ultimately adopted her. Bridget has dark skin.

"Anonymous opponents used 'push polling' to suggest that McCain's Bangladeshi-born daughter was his own, illegitimate black child. The 'pollsters' asked McCain supporters if they would be more or less likely to vote for McCain if they knew he had fathered an illegitimate child who was black. In the conservative, race-conscious South, that's not a minor charge. We had no idea who made the phone calls, who paid for them, or how many calls were made. Effective and anonymous: the perfect smear campaign."[291]

The amazing thing about this particular anecdote is that the political operative took values that we allegedly hold dear in our culture — charity, adoption, caring that goes beyond color of the skin or provenance of the child — and turned them into a liability for the opposition candidate. As Machiavelli averred: "The great majority of humans are more influenced by the things that seem than by those that are."[292] Bush rolled to victory in South Carolina, in the general election and then ran roughshod over the Democratic opposition, the Afghanis, the Iraqis and the United States Constitution.

It should be noted that South Carolina, as one of the most important early primary states — a place where presidential campaigns can be won or lost — focuses the Machiavellian energies to a searing point. "The fight is rough here, that's for sure,"[293] intoned one South Carolina resident as the state prepared for the 2012 Republican primary. An article in the *Washington Post* noted:

Voters and political operatives are girding for the kind of whisper campaigns, viral innuendo and dubious personal attacks that have made South Carolina a state where the politics are as harsh as the tea is sweet. Already, a blitz of negative ads is expected to hit the airwaves, funded by outside groups that have no intention of using their inside voices . . . [In the past] candidates have been ambushed with accusations that have ranged from distorted to invented . . . In 2008, a state Senate campaign allegedly paid an undocumented immigrant to infiltrate a crew painting the house of an opposing candidate, and then accused him of hiring illegal workers. Two years later, then-candidate Nikki Haley was hit with two charges of adultery in the days before her runoff race for the Republican gubernatorial nomination. Several other critics also raised questions about her sincerity as a Christian.[294]

This character assassination is the equivalent of the midnight knife thrust of a Shakespearean play or by a Medici partisan. McCain's "black child" successfully ended his presidential bid, though his life continued on. Neutered of political *kudos* (glory), McCain was sent back to the Senate, where he lived out his life in the relative anonymity (and irrelevance) of the country's legislative branch.

The dynamic is hidden in plain view, explained away as simply politics as usual. Time and again, the Machiavellian dark arts political operative is explicitly noted in the press. A March 2011 headline bleated: "Mitch Daniels' Marriage Fodder For Opposition's Dark Artists." (*Huffington Post*) An article in *Mother Jones* (2008) had a piece about a political operative named Fred Karger, who was "One of the GOP's Top Dark-Arts Operators."

And this note appeared in *Politico*:

> Opposition research, long vilified and romanticized as a kind of political dark art, has stepped out of the closet for the 2012 presidential campaign, in which current and former opposition researchers are taking prominent roles, the self-described "high road" candidate has an extensive research operation and the climate couldn't be better for dropping negative stories small and large.

> [Journalist Ben] Smith also makes it clear how ubiquitous are the "dark arts" in American politics: "Oppo is like pot: Everybody has tried it, but it used to be [that] nobody admitted it," said one prominent Democratic research consultant who, like many oppo hands of the old school, asked that his name not be used and spoke with some regret of the changes in the field. "Oppo is finally out front."[295]

Time and again we see explicit mention of this Machiavellian approach to our democracy. An article about the GOP political "playbook" detailed hundreds of potential "targets" to help bring President Obama down in the 2012 election. The article noted: "The book's primary author [is] Joe Pounder, a 28-year-old specialist in the dark arts and the Republican National Committee's Research Director."[296]

Of course, adopting the cool and detached journalistic voice of contemporary society, the author of the article gives no clue as to whether he, personally, approves or disapproves of the political "dark arts." However, as the young man is the Research Director of the national political party, we are left with the impression that his "dark arts" are highly regarded.

It must be noted, as well, how much pure, unmitigated joy it gives the participants. It offers all the adrenaline of war, without the actual life-threatening experience:

> Mark McKinnon, a smooth, energetic and fast-talking 49-year-old Texan, can't wait for the final frenzied fortnight of the battle for the White House. As President George W Bush's chief media strategist, he is about to unleash a multi-million dollar advertising blitz to undermine John Kerry, the Democrat challenger.

> "There's no adrenaline rush like it. It's a great time to be involved in a campaign. This is the biggest sandpit in the world and it comes with the best toys. The two sides are going to spend at least $50 million between

now and Election Day on ads. Fifty million dollars! People are going to be bombarded."[297]

Machiavellian politics is not only good fun, but it also makes good theater. An article in the *New York Times* discussed two different movies made about Democratic political operatives, self-deprecating fellows who had but wanted to serve their country and their president:

> Mr. Lehane and Mr. Carson are, at least in Washington, well-known products of a notoriously tough school of political campaigning, whose currency is quick and aggressive efforts to discredit opponents and critics; both served Bill Clinton.
>
> But these days, Mr. Lehane and Mr. Carson are enjoying a new kind of fame. They are models for characters in movies that go beyond the usual Hollywood glorification of political consultants, offering dark and at times unsettling accounts of what is done in the name of winning elections.[298]

No need to worry about the "new round of debates over the troubling ends-versus-means questions that have always hovered over politics,"[299] as these doubts are being snowed under by *billions* of dollars of negative, character assassination advertisements this campaign season (2012), fueled by a Supreme Court decision (*Citizens United v. Federal Election Commission*; see below) which opened the floodgates for unlimited corporate and private money to help fuel the conflagration.

Hardly confined to electoral politics, the Machiavellian dynamic bleeds into the economic sphere as well. Although the subject is outside of the scope of this study, it is important to note how pervasive is this illness and how ultimately destructive it is for American society. Every aspect of the public square is reduced to a win or lose dynamic, regardless of the long-term effects on our society, the moral degeneration it represents and any sense of a shared community that it destroys.

As neo-Conservative thinker Michael Ledeen noted: "We need Machiavellian wisdom and leadership. Without it, our fine political, religious, economic and athletic institutions will go to ruin."[300] Climate Change issues, universal healthcare, economic fairness, religion — all are swallowed up in the black-and-white world of "dark arts" political persuasion.

An article in the *Los Angeles Times* entitled "Using the dark arts of land-use politics to defeat NIMBYs" discussed a book detailing methods for overcoming opposition by community groups trying to stave off destructive infiltration by multi-national corporations:

> The authors have produced what amounts to an introductory promotional handbook to the dark arts of land-use politics, which argues that this is a job that requires an expert professional approach. It is a good example of the local political shenanigans and Machiavellian manipulation . . .[301]

KARL ROVE

Machiavelli said that a prince who is not wise himself cannot be well advised unless by chance he gives himself over to "one alone" to govern him in everything.[302]

Our era's prototypical Machiavellian operator has been at the center of elections since the late 1990s, though his study of the dark arts goes back into the 1970s. Regardless of the tactics or accomplishments of other operatives and politicians, there are none more successful or seemingly without moral qualms than Republican operative Karl Christian Rove (b. 1950).

Unabashedly influenced by the Renaissance Florentine political theorist, Rove was George W. Bush's political guru from 1999-2006. More recently, he has been in charge of hundreds of millions of dollars, as head of the Super PAC, *American Crossroads*. As he noted on his website, the most recent book he had read (at the beginning of 2012) was *Machiavelli: A Biography* by Miles Unger which, assured Mr. Rove, "makes it easier to understand *The Prince*."[303]

And as Paul Anderson shared in *Machiavelli's Shadow: The Rise and Fall of Karl Rove*: "For years Rove had told people the book he had read regularly, perhaps as much as once a year, was *The Prince*, by Niccolò Machiavelli ... 'Rove's political bible is *The Prince* by Machiavelli,' according to Tom Paulken, the Chairman of the Republican Party in Texas in the 1990s."[304]

A passage about "The Architect" (as Rove is known) in *What Would Machiavelli Do?* cast some light on this dark artist's influences and actions:

> Rove's Machiavellian tactics have helped him achieve a well-deserved reputation as a master of dirty tricks. In fact, Rove's tricks go back to 1970, when the nineteen-year-old stole campaign letterhead from Alan Dixon, a Democrat running for state treasurer in Illinois, and forged an invitation for "free beer, free food, girls and a good time for nothing" at Dixon's campaign headquarters.

> Since Karl Rove began working for George W. Bush, Bush opponents Ann Richards and John McCain have been smeared in the signature Rove style: other people do the dirty work, the candidate appears uninvolved, and Rove himself leaves no fingerprints.[305]

Rove's Machiavellian work cuts a wide swath through the first decade of America's 21st century. He undertook character assassination campaigns against two American war heroes, Senator Max Cleland (D-GA; in 2002) and Senator John Kerry (D-MA, in 2004). Clelend's case was detailed above, though Rove's involvement was not highlighted.

In Kerry's case (which will be explored in depth below), Rove's shadow group started a campaign implying that the decorated war veteran who had volunteered for duty during the Vietnam War (while Rove's boss, George W. Bush, had shirked his duty, hidden somewhere in the Texas National Guard) was a "whiner."

"Swift Boat Veterans for Truth" was a Rove-sponsored PAC that challenged the legitimacy of each of the combat medals awarded to Kerry by the U.S. Navy. Although the claims were called patently "false" by the *Los Angeles Times* editorial page (August 24, 2004), the group's calumny was credited with swinging the very close 2004 election to Bush. About the Swift Boat Veterans for Truth, the *New York Times* stated: "A series of interviews and a review of documents show a web of connections to the Bush family, high-profile Texas political figures and President Bush's chief political aide, Karl Rove."[306]

These are just two examples of a litany of lies, slander, subterranean machinations and other Machiavellian tactics that Rove has applied over the course of his three-decade long career as a political savant. However, his Machiavellian actions have been so extensive that journalist Paul Alexander, a former reporter for *Time* magazine who has also written for *Rolling Stone*, *The New York Times Magazine*, *The Nation*, *The Village Voice* and *The Guardian*, penned a book entitled: *Machiavelli's Shadow: The Rise and Fall of Karl Rove*. In it, he outlined the career (up until publication of the book, in 2008) of the Machiavellian mastermind of contemporary Republican politics:

> Karl Rove has come to personify scorched earth political tactics and merciless, win-at-any-cost trickery. His status as the so-called architect behind Bush's election victories has elevated him to a mythic kingmaker in the national imagination. Not since Mark Hanna, special assistant to President William McKinley, has someone not elected to public office played such a vital role in the governance of our nation. In *Machiavelli's Shadow*, the full, unvarnished truth about the mastermind of the Bush administration is revealed.[307]

ROVE'S WISDOM

> A wise man will never censure anyone for having employed any extraordinary means for the purpose of establishing a kingdom or constituting a republic.[308]

Karl Rove undoubtedly considers himself just such a wise man. And he is hardly alone in his high self-regard. In late 2004, after he had masterminded the reelection of a president who had little positive record to run on, Reuters news service announced: "White House adviser Karl Rove topped the unofficial list of contenders for *Time's* 2004 Person of the Year, according to a panel assembled by the magazine on Tuesday to debate the question."[309] In the end his charge, George W. Bush, was named to the honor, leaving Rove to pontificate on his boss's attributes instead of humbly accepting the tribute for himself.

Not everyone is so positive about the Machiavellian bent to American politics, and its most successful practitioner, however. Wayne Madsen (a Washington, D.C.-based author, columnist, and investigative journalist specializing in intelligence and international affairs) denoted him "America's Joseph Goebbels."[310] Madsen was a lonely voice, however, as the American media, following Machiavelli's dictum, lauded the winner of the 2004 election, regardless of the means used to secure the victory.

Rove has hardly faded from the scene. As recently as the election of 2012, he was leading a shadowy Super PAC group practicing the Machiavellian dark arts in support of the Republican nominee for president, as well as senatorial and congressional candidates around the country. An article in *USA Today* entitled: "Karl Rove-affiliated groups target President Obama" elaborated:

> Two conservative groups Karl Rove helped create announced plans today to raise $120 million to challenge President Obama and Democrats in next year's election.[311]

Another article noted the reach of Rove's group: "A conservative Super PAC co-founded by Republican political strategist Karl Rove is picking apart Democratic Senate candidates across five states in a series of ads portraying them as liberals out of step with the country."[312]

The legacy of America's Machiavelli continues to grow.

Swift Boat Veterans for Truth

> The ads are filled with lies, distortions and conflicting statements. But remember, truth and fairness were never issues for Rove and his fellow vermin.[313]

Perhaps no single episode so defines Rove's work — or Machiavelli America — as the Swift Boat Veterans for Truth, which helped turn the 2004 election for Rove's boss. The shadowy Bush support group, well connected to George W. Bush, Dick Cheney and Karl Rove, stands out as one of the most baldly misleading, and wildly successful, character assassinations of recent political history.

The group issued a series of lies about Democratic challenger John Kerry's Vietnam war service. Despite the fact that these were essentially fabrications cooked up by Karl Christian Rove and various Republican funders and operatives, the press, hewing tightly to its obligation to ignore the truth in service to objectivity, not only dutifully reported the charges, but compounded the damage by playing and replaying aspects of the false accusations, reporting these lies as news.

In covering the libelous story, the media noted that the material represented one position concerning Kerry's military service, while the truth of the matter was offered as the opposing political party's point of view. The differences were portrayed as a disagreement between two versions of the events.

Swift Boat Veterans for Truth ran an attack ad in which former Swift Boat (attack boats used during the Vietnam War, upon one of which Kerry had been a captain) veterans claimed Senator Kerry lied to get one of his two decorations for bravery and two of his three purple hearts. But the veterans who accused Kerry were contradicted by Kerry's former crewmen, as well as by Navy records.

However, the insinuations took root in the minds of the American public as the media, in the early days of the ad campaign, simply parroted the information without clearly stating that it in no way reflected any recorded truth of the incidents and medals. Steve Hayes, an early member of the group, stated that he had come to believe that the group was twisting Kerry's record. He broke with the Swift Boat Veterans and voted for Kerry. Hayes told the *New York Times*:

> The mantra was just, "We want to set the record straight," Mr. Hayes said this month. "It became clear to me that it was morphing from an organization to set the record straight into a highly political vendetta. They knew it was not the truth."[314]

And John Kerry himself said: "They lied and lied and lied about everything. How many lies do you get to tell before someone calls you a liar?"[315] The unwillingness of the media to simply and forcefully call a lie a "lie," allowed the falsehoods to take hold in the minds of the American voter, even though some later articles and editorials debunked the slanderous material.

The alternative news magazine *Media Matters for America* recounted the series of events:

> On September 22 [2004], the discredited anti-Kerry group Swift Boat Veterans for Truth released for television a spurious new attack ad. FOX News Channel's *Hannity & Colmes* (on September 21) and *FOX & Friends First* (on September 22) both aired the ad, but neither reported on the ad's inaccuracies. The new ad claims that Senator John Kerry "secretly met with enemy leaders in Paris," and it repeats the group's previous false charge that Kerry "accused American troops of committing war crimes on a daily basis." But as *Media Matters for America* has noted, the meeting cited in the ad was not a secret; Kerry spoke about the meeting in public Senate testimony. After *The Washington Post* reported on the ad's inaccuracy, FOX News Channel's general assignment reporter Major Garrett and CNN senior political analyst and American Enterprise Institute resident fellow Bill Schneider then reported, without challenge, claims by the defenders of the ad that Kerry met with communists in Paris a second time.[316]

It is interesting to note that members of the Swift Boat Veterans for Truth and Karl Rove continued (as late as the election of 2012) to work together, simply morphing into a different entity to continue their work as Machiavellian masters of the American political landscape:

> Now he [Bob Perry, who financed the Swift Boat Veterans for Truth] and his Swift Boat Veterans for Truth buddies are financing Karl Rove's very creepy group called American Crossroads. A trio of wealthy Texans have donated more than half of the money the pro-Republican Super PAC

American Crossroads has received, according to a new study by the Center for Public Integrity. Bob Perry, Harold Simmons and Robert Rowling have combined to donate $30.5 million to the group, more than half of the $56 million the total the group has raised since its creation.[317]

ROVE'S BRAIN

Your conscience ought not "dismay you, because those who win, in whatever mode they win, never receive shame from it."[318]

Neo-conservative thinker Michael Ledeen is lesser known, but no less important for offering a philosophical underpinning for Machiavelli America. Ledeen (b. 1941), a Svengali-like character in the American political panorama, has been present in Republican back rooms for nearly 40 years. He was a former consultant to the National Security Council, the State Department and the Defense Department.

He was implicated in the Iran–Contra Affair, helping convince then Vice President George H. W. Bush to appoint Iranian arms merchant and Iranian/Israeli double agent Manucher Ghorbanifar as a middleman in the scandalous matter in 1984.[319] Additionally, he was central to the "yellowcake" (nuclear material) allegations against Saddam Hussein that were used as part of the justification for the 2003 invasion of Iraq. He ushered a forged document on stolen letterhead by a discredited Italian SISMI (analogous to the CIA) agent through back channels to George W. Bush's White House.

This work led directly to the famous "16-word" utterance by President Bush during his January, 2003 State of the Union Address: "The British Government has learned that Saddam Hussein recently sought significant quantities of uranium from Africa."[320]

More recently, Ledeen has advocated for an attack on Iran, proposed a theory that France and Germany struck a deal with "radical Islam" in an attempt to bring down the American empire and has undertaken a host of other dubious acts to thrust America to the fore of the international community, utilizing whatever Machiavellian means he could muster. As Ledeen noted: "To achieve victory, the first step is to see the world plain, to accept the facts about human nature and to act vigorously to dominate, lest we be dominated by others."[321]

Ledeen has worked intimately with this generation's Richelieu. He served as Karl Rove's only full-time foreign policy advisor during the George W. Bush administration. The *Washington Post* quoted Ledeen as saying that Rove told him, "Anytime you have a good idea, tell me."[322] Ledeen has been referred to as Rove's "brain," the very same epithet that many applied to Rove *vis-à-vis* George W. Bush.

Hardly coy about his inspiration, Ledeen penned a book (1999) just before the George W. Bush presidency entitled *Machiavelli on Modern Leadership: Why Machiavelli's Iron Rules Are As Timely and Important Today as Five Centuries Ago*. In it, he laid out quite specifically how Machiavellian ideals could and should be implemented in the United States — ideas that in many instances turned into actions under the administration of George W. Bush and *his* Svengali, Karl Christian Rove.

Ledeen stated quite clearly that the goal in politics was power, which equated to the domination over others. Winning was everything, allowing the victor to savor what Machiavelli called "the sweetness of domination."[323]

Ledeen's fingerprints could be found all over Bush era doctrine, perhaps stemming from his not very well written treatise on Machiavellian leadership. For instance, although he wrote before the terrorist attacks of September 11, 2001, he presaged them in a manner which might give cause to reconsider the various conspiracy theorists who assured (and still assure) that these attacks were either the work of the U.S. government, or tacitly accepted as "necessary" and therefore allowed to take place.

Writing in 1999, Ledeen stated:

> Stunning events from the outside can providentially awaken the enterprise from its growing torpor, and demonstrate the need for renewal, as the devastating Japanese attack on Pearl Harbor so effectively aroused the United States from its soothing dreams . . .[324]

I am not a conspiracy theorist and do not, personally, believe that the United States government either perpetrated or knew of beforehand the attacks on the World Trade Center. But there are many who do believe this. And Ledeen's writings certainly were circulating at the highest levels of government prior to the attack. As Ledeen was a confidant of Karl Rove, it is not too far a stretch to at least see the possibility of this Machiavellian strategy for "renewal." Ledeen noted:

> Peace increases our peril by making discipline less urgent, encouraging some of our worst instincts and depriving us of some of our best leaders . . . War is a necessary part of God's arrangement of the world. Without war, the world would deteriorate into materialism.[325]

Ledeen, who studied Italian Fascism at the beginning of his career and proclaimed "the rightness of the fascist cause"[326] in 1972, certainly had much influence on the Bush administration's muscular executive, which took America as far in the direction of fascism as we have seen in the past half-century. "In the final analysis, Ledeen's advocacy of strong leadership and militarism based on Machiavellian principles has eerie echoes of the rhetoric and actions of Benito Mussolini."[327] Ledeen proposed a strong unitary power, a kind of American fascism that could be hidden beneath the patina of democracy.

> Any state, any organization, even the freest and most democratic, requires strong leadership, because only such leaders can restrain the ruinous impulses that drive human actions, and force men to act for the common good. We must *not* be left to our own ruinous devices, but instead be made to do the right thing . . . The usual Machiavellian paradox: compulsion — or

necessity, as he terms it — makes men noble and enables them to remain free, while abundant choice is dangerous.[328]

This "compulsion" was to be applied using specific Machiavellian strategies. In Ledeen's words:

> The tools of discipline — arms, laws and religion — are common to all well-constituted states . . . All three compel men to repress their dangerous instincts and act virtuously. This is accomplished by fear. Without fear of God, no state can last very long, for the dread of eternal damnation keeps men in line, and inspires them to risk their lives for the common good.[329]

It is important to remember that Ledeen wrote this in 1999, just before George W. Bush's dubious election victory, and that he was respected within those halls of power to the point of being called "Rove's Brain." Ergo, it is not difficult to draw a direct line from Ledeen's Machiavellian thinking to George W. Bush's conception of executive power.

Professor Hugh Urban (Ohio State University) is quoted in *The Secrets of the Kingdom: Religion and Concealment in the Bush Administration*:

> There is a name for a system of government that wages aggressive war, deceives its citizens, violates their rights, abuses power and breaks the law, rejects judicial and legislative checks on itself, claims power without limit, tortures prisoners and acts in secret. It is dictatorship. The administration of George W. Bush is not a dictatorship, but it does manifest the characteristics of one in embryonic form.[330]

Ledeen, God and the USA

In other fundamental ways, Ledeen presaged Bush and Rove's implementation of their program. As Urban also noted, Ledeen felt that religion and faith were central to a "healthy" state. But not the religion of peace, love and harmony that exists in the *words* of religious leaders, but that of Machiavelli: a muscular, virile religion that, when brought together with the national interest, creates a religion of the state. Worship of God and state intermingled.[331] Ledeen noted:

> Good religion teaches men that politics is the most important enterprise in the eyes of God. Like Moses, Machiavelli wants the law of his state to be seen, and therefore obeyed, as divinely ordained. The combination of God and fear of punishment.[332]

He continued on to state that American evangelical Christianity is the kind of religion that Machiavelli demanded, as it does not "quietly accept" its destiny, but feels called upon to fight within the social and political realms to reestablish virtue.[333] And by "virtue," Ledeen meant the Machiavellian variety, not that of Jesus, Gandhi, Merton or any of the other religious thinkers whose virtue was based in humility and love.

This dynamic was easy to perceive under Bush and his minions. As Jeet Heer and Dave Wagner noted in "Man of the World: Michael Ledeen's adventures in history":

> Ledeen displayed an activist's interest in deploying sacred nationalist mythology for contemporary political purposes. For Ledeen, early 20th-century European mass politics, rooted in a half-millennium-old cultural legacy, could serve as a wellspring for reinvigorating contemporary middle-class nationalism, particularly in the United States.[334]

Exactly this form of religious nationalism was well documented in the wake of the September 11, 2001 attacks on America, as an outpouring of flags, "God Bless America's" and President Bush's constant invocation of "God Almighty," "good" (us), "evil" (them) and a divinely ordained "Crusade" overwhelmed all frank discussions of the geopolitical issues that might have led nineteen stateless individuals to attack the American homeland.

The Bush White House's cynical use of religion as a Machiavellian tool was documented in the *Guardian* (U.K.) in a 2006 article entitled "Aide says White House mocked evangelicals":

> A former senior presidential aide has accused the Bush administration of using evangelical Christians to win votes but then privately ridiculing them once in office.

> David Kuo (the former deputy director of the White House office of faith-based initiatives) portrays the Bush White House's commitment to evangelical causes as little more than a cynical facade designed to win votes.

> "National Christian leaders received hugs and smiles in person and then were dismissed behind their backs and described as ridiculous, out of control, and just plain goofy," Mr Kuo wrote, according to MSNBC television, which obtained an early copy of the book. In particular, he quotes Karl Rove, the president's long-serving political adviser and mentor, as describing evangelical Christians as "nuts."[335]

As Ledeen had stated, Evangelical Christianity was the perfect state religion as it did not "quietly accept" its destiny but brought God and State together. But Ledeen, a Jew, certainly doesn't believe in the spiritual and religious principles of Christian Evangelism. Like Rove, he undoubtedly viewed them as a necessary tool of power — and little more.

An American Oligarchy

> There is no essential difference between the motives of the prince and the motives of the ruling class [for Machiavelli]. The excellent ruling class . . . is not dedicated to the common good as the common good is primarily understood. It identifies the common interest with its own particular interest.[336]

In the contemporary American social panorama, where literal assassinations and individual mercenary armies are frowned upon, the weapons of the successful prince are of a subtler, though no less successful variety. As we have seen, religion, fraud and a never-ending series of wars, leading to a massive and disciplined national army, are all variations of contemporary Machiavellian arms.

Perhaps even more important, however — especially given the American media climate — is money. "Money, power's master key, is means at its purest."[337] With money, leaders can control the news and through the news, control reality, turning nuanced issues into binary questions, and the social responses into a primal "us" v. "them" formulation. As John P. McCormick noted in *Machiavellian Democracy*:

> The aristocratic effect and the privileged access to resources and information enjoyed by magistrates in modern republics render elections inadequate mechanisms of elite accountability and responsiveness; moreover, a socio-political definition of "the people" that includes wealthy citizens, rather than one that sets the latter apart from or even opposed to the people, allows the wealthy to dominate common citizens in quasi-anonymous and largely uncontested ways.[338]

This exact dynamic can be seen quite clearly in the recent Supreme Court ruling *Citizens United v. Federal Election Commission* (2010 — see below for more discussion of the ruling and its ramifications), which concluded that the First Amendment of the United States Constitution prohibited the government from restricting independent political expenditures by individuals, corporations and unions, terming all of these entities "people" having the right to a political voice. Due to this ruling, there has been a massive influx of money from very few supporters, exacerbating American Machiavellianism, and allowing a small handful of wealthy citizens to dominate the political landscape.

> It's no secret that some very rich people support the Super PAC's and other groups that have inundated the 2012 campaign with unlimited sums of cash. According to Harvard law professor Lawrence Lessig . . . in the current presidential election, 0.000063% of Americans — fewer than 200 of the country's 310 million residents — have contributed 80% of all Super PAC donations. "A relatively few wealthy individuals and interests are dominating our public square, drowning out the rest of us."[339]

Through money, not only are political victories won, but also the common good is conflated with the desires of a tiny sliver of the electorate. American democracy suffers, and the country is left with a de-facto oligarchy, a power structure in which power effectively rests with a tiny number of people — "0.000063% of the population," according to the recent article in the *Washington Post*.

As Machiavelli noted, "One who deceives will always find those who allow themselves to be deceived,"[340] and it is through money and its pervasive control of the media and advertising that this formulation plays out in contemporary America. Advertising becomes one of the most important tactics for creating political reality, and actors are hired to represent "real" Americans with "real" concerns. Money, power's master key, fuels the creation of a public reality that has little to do with truth, but everything with electing a leader who will serve the greedy interests of the few.

As was noted in the *Washington Post* concerning Mitt Romney's (Republican nominee for president in 2012) "strongest assets":

> One of Mitt Romney's strongest assets as the GOP presidential front-runner . . . is a small group of millionaires and billionaires . . . Some of Romney's biggest supporters include executives at Bain Capital, his former firm; bankers at Goldman Sachs and a hedge fund mogul who made billions betting on the housing crash.[341]

The same article notes that President Obama has plenty of wealthy benefactors, as well, including 445 "bundlers" (who raised $50,000 each or more), though centered more in the technology and entertainment sectors than in banking.

The total amount of money being raised and spent — the vast majority of which funds negative adds meant to assassinate the character of the adversary, as well as suppress interest among voters who might remain undecided (and therefore might potentially vote against the correct candidate) — is astronomical, totaling nearly two billion dollars for all presidential candidates in the 2012 election cycle, and another billion for down ballot candidates. Three billion dollars is more than the annual revenue of nearly 100 countries and territories in the world![342]

> The greater freedom of action enjoyed by both political and socio-economic elites . . . is a threat to the liberty of other citizens and to the stability of the regime itself.[343]

This threat is not hard to discern. As the *Los Angeles Times* noted, the interests of the moneyed few do, indeed, receive special preference — despite the absurd protestations of the politicians themselves:

> "People give money because of whatever reasons motivate them, and we evaluate legislation regardless. I know that that's a hard concept for some people.... I cannot think of anything they've asked me to do," said Speaker [of the California State Legislature] John A. Pérez (D-Los Angeles).

> "Whatever reasons motivate them"? They're motivated by sound investment practices. That's what corporations do. And it pays off, or they wouldn't continue to invest. In this case, they're laying money on legislators who make policy decisions that affect the corporation's bottom line.

> The American way — like it or not, and most moneyed special interests do like it

> . . . But perhaps we should grant Pérez the benefit of doubt. He might actually believe that political money is benign. Conceivably he's in denial.

"I'm sure Pérez believes that," says longtime lobbyist George Steffes, whose first Capitol gig was as Governor Ronald Reagan's legislative liaison. "He has to believe it for his own good. A legislator who isn't saying to himself, 'OK, I'm a crook,' has to say, 'It doesn't affect me.' Otherwise, he probably couldn't sleep at night."[344]

Machiavellian fraud begins in the politician's head, where deception finds one who is "easy to deceive" — the politician himself.

The necessity of money to successful politicians is crystal clear. In the 2004 general elections, 95% of House races and 91% of senate races were won by the candidates who spent the most on their campaigns.[345] Money is the most potent weapon of the 21st-century prince.

An article in the U.K.'s *Guardian* entitled: "US elections: no matter who you vote for, money always wins" laid out the American oligarchy clearly:

> The trend towards oligarchy in the polity is already clear. There are 250 millionaires in Congress. As a whole, the polity's median net worth is $891,506, nine times the typical US household. Around 11% are in the nation's top 1%, including 34 Republicans and 23 Democrats. And that's before you get to Romney, whose personal wealth is double that of the last eight presidents combined. All of this would be problematic at the best of times, but in a period of rising inequality it is obscene.
>
> The issue here is not class envy, hating rich people because they are rich, but class interests — cementing the advantages of the privileged over the rest. The problem is not personal, it's systemic. In the current climate, it means a group of wealthy people in business will decide which wealthy people in Congress they would like to tell poor people what they can't have because times are hard.[346]

Unfortunately, it takes a foreign newspaper to highlight the American oligarchy. As the German magazine *Der Spiegel* asserted, "Those who follow this race daily may have long since lost perspective on how absurd it is."[347] And perspective is one thing that is desperately needed in American politics . . .

AMERICAN OLIGARCHY: THE SUPER PAC

> We have a society in which money is increasingly concentrated in the hands of a few people, and in which that concentration of income and wealth threatens to make us a democracy in name only.[348]

The Merriam-Webster Dictionary defines "oligarchy" thusly: "a government in which a small group exercises control especially for corrupt and selfish purposes."[349] Contrast this with a quote by David Donnelly, director at the Public Campaign Action Fund, an advocacy group favoring limits on political spending:

> There are probably fewer than 100 people who are fueling 90 percent of this outside money right now. When you think about the amazing impact that this small number of people have on deciding the election, on the information that people will have on who to vote for, it's mind-boggling.[350]

The 2010 Supreme Court decision *Citizens United v. FEC* opened the floodgates for unregulated money from wealthy individuals and corporations to flood into the political system. With this ruling, the Supreme Court deepened the role of money in American elections, creating a cascade of lower-court rulings which allowed individuals to blow past the $2500 per individual limit on political donations, with a few wealthy citizens writing checks over $1 million,[351] and with one brave soul (Las Vegas casino owner Sheldon Adelson) pledging to spend as much as $100 million to help elect Republican presidential candidates in 2012.[352]

Within the Machiavellian world of politics, it should come as no surprise that even the Supreme Court becomes a tool for the wealthy:

> Elite dominated, counter-majoritarian institutions such as supreme courts, despite being charged with the protection of minorities, nevertheless have proven notoriously susceptible to capture by or collusion with entrenched, highly resourced interest groups.[353]

Columnist Ruth Marcus noted in the *Washington Post*:

> The barrage of commercials tells the story: This is a presidential election [2012] without meaningful contribution limits or timely disclosure, outsourced to political action committees whose spending often dwarfs that of the candidates they support. The PAC's benign, intentionally uninformative names belie the brutal nature of their attack ads and the closeness of their relationships with the candidates . . . The emergence of these entities is the logical outgrowth of the Supreme Court's ruling in *Citizens United v. FEC*.[354]

Spending on television ads by these "independent groups" in the first two Republican primaries (Iowa and New Hampshire) was already five times what it was during the entire Republican primary four years ago.[355] Another A-section article explored the impact of this Supreme Court ruling on the election:

> Iowans were inundated with millions of dollars in negative advertising in the final weeks before Tuesday's caucuses, most of it paid for by a new breed of organization, called "Super PAC's," which don't have to play by the same rules as candidates . . . The trend marks a major shift away from the 2008 election cycle, when outside groups were subject to more legal restrictions and played a relatively minor role in the presidential contest.[356]

Even Machiavelli might have blanched at the effect of this legal ruling, as he noted: "He who comes to the principality with the help of the great maintains himself with greater difficulty than the one who becomes prince with the help of the people."[357] America, so long channeling the far-off Florentine political philosopher, has outpaced even the master himself!

WORKING AGAINST THE COMMON GOOD

As astounding are the numbers (the vast amount of money pumped into the political system coupled with the shrinking number of donors), the political, social and environmental positions of the people and corporations behind those figures are even more terrifying. The common good becomes submerged in the narcissistic greed of a few unthinking Mayberry Machiavelli's[358] who want nothing more but a de-regulated world in which they may take their massive amounts of money and double it, often leading to profound social and environmental degradation.

Specific examples of the dynamic are not hard to unearth. Dallas billionaire Harold Simmons gave $13 million to the *American Crossroads PAC* early in the 2012 election cycle.[359] As was noted in an article entitled: "Harold Simmons Is Dallas' Most Evil Genius," the Republican donor planned to make his "next billion" by burying hazardous waste in West Texas.[360]

Another Texan, house builder Bob Perry of Houston came in second for GOP-related campaign contributions. Perry gave $2.5 million to *American Crossroads* and $4 million to *Restore Our Future*.[361] Perry also gave nearly $5 million to the so-called Swift Boat Veterans for Truth in 2004 (see above); $5 million to the Economic Freedom Fund in 2006 (which primarily paid for negative advertisements targeting Democratic Party candidates) and at this writing, he funneled further millions into the campaign of the 2012 Republican presidential candidate, Mitt Romney.

Perry has been a member of the Council for National Policy for more than thirty years. The group has been described by the *New York Times* as a "little-known group of a few hundred of the most powerful conservatives in the country."[362] The group describes its members as "united in their belief in a free enterprise system, a strong national defense, and support for traditional western values."[363] "Free enterprise system" is often code for a de-regulated business world wherein the rich can do as they please, and the rest need suffer what they must.

Four other million-dollar donors to Mitt Romney supporting Super PACs were hedge fund managers, one of who made $5 billion in one year by betting on the mortgage crisis.[364] In general, hedge fund managers represent the worst of Machiavellian energy, as hedge funds — though lucrative for their managers — pose systemic risks to the financial sector. They were shown to have played a substantial role in the financial crisis of 2008. However, as hedge funds are built to make money in either a rising or falling market — through various obscure trading tactics — in many instances, the funds themselves did not suffer from the economic crisis they helped create.

These donors are not giving millions to promote income equality, shelter the homeless, cut back on military expenditures or rein in Wall Street. A CNN report noted that the top eight Super PAC donors were all "conservatives,"[365] supporting Republican officials. One after another Super PAC funder used their money to further Machiavellian goals, while eschewing the needs of the greater population, and Mother Earth herself.

Hedge-fund king John Paulson, who donated $1 million to a group back-ing former Massachusetts governor Mitt Romney, would very much like to see President Obama's financial reforms repealed. Paulson made much of his money betting on the housing market's collapse. The Marriott broth-ers, who also gave $1 million to a pro-Romney super PAC, have lobbied Washington for favorable tax policies. And casino magnate Sheldon Adel-son recently dashed off a $5 million check to a group backing former House speaker Newt Gingrich . . . Adelson is well known for supporting hard line policies favoring Israel while also advocating measures that would benefit the gambling industry.[366]

These few funders use negative advertising to roll back protecting regu-lations; break open the financial system like a private piggy-bank; make the already dangerously low taxes on the rich even smaller; remove environmen-tal protections that might stand between them and their monetary goals; disseminate a world view often independent of reality (no human-caused cli-mate change, for instance) and remake the world into a barren place where a few winners sit atop a massive collection of powerless individuals.

An article noted, quantifying this American Oligarchy (without calling it such):

Super PAC mega-donors continued to dominate the independent spend-ing playing field in May [2012] as their percentage of total giving to Super PACs increased.

There are now ninety-five donors or collections of related donors that have given more than $500,000 to Super PACs. Those donors had given $153.6 million through the end of May . . . Wealthy donors giving $500,000-plus provide the vast majority of contributions to Super PAC's.[367]

And the "vast majority" of this money is poured into negative advertis-ing. As the *Washington Post* noted, an average of 77 percent of the ads run by the Super PACs supporting the four GOP candidates during the Republican primaries were negative.[368]

The politics of George W. Bush and Karl Rove, or Lee Atwater before them, has not changed or mellowed. In the post-George W. Bush era, this new practice of wielding Machiavellian power has emerged that allows even greater access to the creation of an American oligarchy, utilizing time-hon-ored Machiavellian means.

Adding to the insidious dynamic, the Super PACs needn't disclose in a timely manner from whom they receive their massive cash influxes. *American Crossroads* and other Super PACs are allowed to raise and spend unlimited sums, providing disclosure of all donations only every six months or so, often long after the electoral races have been affected.

This fact is freely admitted as central to the Super PACs' mission. *Ameri-can Crossroads* was formed because "some donors didn't want to be disclosed" and were "more comfortable" giving to an entity that keeps donors' names secret. *American Crossroads* steadfastly refused to disclose any information about who gives to it.[369] Machiavelli would be proud.

THE MEDIA

Through the media, frank lies and emotionally charged language can be disseminated without concern of being unmasked, as many members of the press have already *explicitly* stated that they will not call a lie a lie.

As Melinda Henneberger (she who proudly noted that she "liked" the fact journalists will not call politicians "liars" — see above) stated, concerning some mainstream media outlets which prominently tagged a number of points Vice Presidential nominee Paul Ryan made in his Republican National Conventions speech (August 29, 2012) as "flatly inconsistent with the facts": "of course, each of these pieces is analysis or opinion rather than a straight news story."[370] And this "opinion" (i.e. the truth) has less impact on the shared reality of the public square than a "straight news story" (i.e., one that does not separate fact from fiction).

The campaigns themselves agree — that facts can be presented as "spin" by the partisans, and therefore falls under the rubric of "opinion." An article in the *Washington Post* noted:

> Jon Cassidy, writing on the website *Human Events*, said one fact-checking outfit declares conservatives inaccurate three times as often as it does liberals. "You might reasonably conclude that PolitiFact is biased," he wrote [as opposed to the fact that Republicans simply lie more often]. Brooks Johnson, executive director of FactCheck.org, said he fears that the campaigns have come to see running afoul of fact checkers as something of a badge of honor.[371]

As if lying for partisan gain represented the highest form of politics. So even when peripheral members of the media do point out the variance between political claims and the truth, it hardly matters. As was noted during the 2012 Presidential election, concerning an explicitly false ad being run by the Mitt Romney (Republican) campaign:

> There has been no dispute among fact checkers on this question, with PolitiFact awarding the GOP claim "Pants on Fire" and FactCheck.org also saying it was incorrect. Interestingly, Romney pollster Neal Newhouse dismissed the complaints of fact-checking organizations after a Romney ad executive said that an ad based on this assertion was "our most effective ad."

> "Fact checkers come to this with their own sets of thoughts and beliefs, and we're not going to let our campaign be dictated by fact checkers."[372]

The political dark arts operator dismisses "fact checkers" as having their own "sets of thoughts and beliefs." Regardless of whether these "thoughts and beliefs" represent the truth, the ad-meisters are not beholden to them.

Within the public square, truth can be successfully dismissed as just another opinion.

With more than one billion dollars to spend on bleating any message it so pleases, each presidential campaign can ignore the annoyance of the truth, as well as the few media outlets that are peddling it, and concentrate on getting their story into the public square. And as journalist Melinda Henneberger of the *Washington Post* noted, even calling out political claims as flatly inconsistent with the facts is represented by journalists as analysis or opinion (see above).

THE MEDIA AND REALITY

Nelson Mandela noted that newspapers are poor shadows of reality.[373] However, through its massive size and ubiquitous nature, the media creates an impression that is accepted as objective reality, and even, at times, mistaken for the truth. And this overwhelming megaphone becomes fused with the wishes and needs of the ruling class. As Mandela noted: "[Newspapers'] information is important because it discloses the biases and perceptions of both those who produce the paper and those who read it."[374]

And as Harvey Mansfield said in *Machiavelli's Virtue*:

> Since the ruling part of every society is the most powerful part of the society, it is the most visible part. It is the public, for the public is what shows, and what shows is the power that does not need to hide.[375]

The tactic by which the powerful control reality through the media is not difficult to perceive. An article in the *Washington Post* discussed media coverage of the Obama health care overhaul (Affordable Care Act, which was upheld in a Supreme Court vote in June 2012), stating that the media aided the Republicans in "winning" the fight over this bill, regardless of the outcome of the legal wrangling:

> A new study from the Pew Research Center makes it abundantly clear that the political fight over health care is over. And the Republicans won. The media coverage (from June 1, 2009, through March 31, 2010) focused heavily on the politics and strategy of the measure, as opposed to the guts of the actual package. That focus on the politics and strategy clearly benefitted the Republicans. "Opponents of the reform won the so-called 'messaging war' in the coverage," according to a Pew memo analyzing the coverage . . . . People made up their minds because of how the legislative fight was covered in 2009 and 2010.[376]

Utilizing the media — a post-Renaissance invention that only shifted and expanded the mouthpiece for lies, fraud and character assassination from the church or the military to the more "genteel" diffusion of public propaganda — remains central for decision makers. This hardly goes unremarked by the politicians themselves. A few years after he left office in 1969, President Lyndon Johnson was asked by a TV news producer what had changed in American politics since the 1930s when he came to Washington as a young Texas congressman.

> "You guys," [Johnson replied] without even reflecting. "All of politics has changed because of you. You've broken all the [party] machines and the ties between us in the Congress and the city machines. You've given us a new kind of people." A certain disdain passed over his face. "Teddy, Tunney. They're your creations, your puppets. No machine could ever create a Teddy Kennedy. Only you guys. They're all yours. Your product."[377]

This new era of media politics was nicely quantified by John Zaller (professor of political science at the University of California, Berkeley), who stated in his book *A Theory of Media Politics* that it was "a system of politics in which individual politicians seek to gain office, and to conduct politics while in office, through communications which reach the citizens through the mass media."[378] And in so doing, they are able to *control* the message (and reality) as well as launch their political attacks.

We are left with a press which merely responds to the most grating stimulus, dutifully echoing whatever messages are sent its way. And for the few journalists who *are* deeply concerned with the disconnect between truth and reality, there is little recourse but to write ineffectual columns in the alternative media, which do little to change the narrative of power.

And the powerful are well aware of this.

Bill Moyers (b. 1934; well known as a trenchant critic of the U.S. media) noted in his 2007 reportage *Buying the War*, a 90-minute documentary that explored the role of the press in the lead-up to the invasion of Iraq:

> In the run-up to war, skepticism was a rarity among journalists inside the Beltway . . . [There was a] stream of unchecked information from administration sources and Iraqi defectors to the mainstream print and broadcast press, which was then seized upon and amplified by an army of pundits. While almost all the claims would eventually prove to be false, the drumbeat of misinformation about WMDs [Weapons of Mass Destruction] went virtually unchallenged by the media . . . throughout the media landscape, stories challenging the official view were often pushed aside while the administration's claims were given prominence.

> "From August 2002 until the war was launched in March of 2003 there were about 140 front page pieces in the *Washington Post* making the administration's case for war," says Howard Kurtz, the *Post*'s media critic. "But there was only a handful of stories that ran on the front page that made the opposite case. Or, if not making the opposite case, raised questions." The *Washington Post*'s Walter Pincus notes: "We've sort of given up being independent on our own."[379]

With the press unwilling to make a stand for the truth on the most important aspects (politics, war etc.) of our shared reality, then politicians become unleashed to utilize its megaphone as they see fit, whether to undertake Machiavelli's most important art (war), or to assassinate political opponents, as in the case of the Swift Boat Veterans for Truth, or with the swarm of advertisements by the Super PACs.

All Things Not Being Equal

It must be noted that one party, more than the other, has perfected this dynamic of using the media as a megaphone for lies and fraud. Two very well-respected Washington insiders, Thomas Mann (Senior Fellow at the Brookings Institution) and Norman Ornstein (Resident Scholar at the American Enterprise Institute) noted in an article entitled: "Let's Just Say It: The Republicans are the Problem":

> The GOP has become an insurgent outlier in American politics. It is ideologically extreme; scornful of compromise; unmoved by conventional understanding of facts, evidence and science; and dismissive of the legitimacy of its political opposition . . . "Both sides do it" or "There is plenty of blame to go around" are the traditional refuges for an American news media intent on proving its lack of bias . . . But a balanced treatment of an unbalanced phenomena distorts reality. If the political dynamics of Washington are unlikely to change anytime soon, at least we could change the way that reality is portrayed to the public. Our advice to the press: don't seek professional safety through the even-handed, unfiltered presentation of opposing views. Which politician is telling the truth?[380]

It should be noted that the two writers were essentially ostracized for their bi-partisan, truthful article! As the alternative news outlet *Media Matters* noted a couple of weeks after the publication of the article, "their [Mann and Ornstein] recent conclusion that Republicans are responsible for political dysfunction has been largely ignored, with the top five national newspapers writing a total of zero news articles on their thesis."[381]

I'm not talking about philosophical or existential issues, mind you — just the facts. If the facts don't drive news — and one could argue that the media drives the facts *away* from the news — how can America ever expect to have a reality-based political system? Machiavelli must be smugly rubbing his hands together, sitting at his writing desk in the sky.

Media Fragmentation

The fracturing of the American media panorama constitutes another insidious, though not often remarked, facet of Machiavelli America. While a proliferation of news outlets obviously offers some benefits — in that it has become more difficult for a single entity or person to control the news — the downside is that American voters may choose whatever reality most clearly fits in with their pre-conceived notions, wiped clean of any pesky objective truths.

A pre-2004 election poll by the PIPA/Knowledge Networks of the University of Maryland, entitled "The Separate Realities of Bush and Kerry Voters," gave a clear example of how this dynamic plays out. According to this poll, just prior to the Iraq War, 72% of Bush voters believed that Iraq either had weapons of mass destruction (WMD) or a major program headed in that direction; 26% of Kerry voters believed the same thing. Additionally, after the war, 56% of Bush voters, though only 18% of Kerry voters, believed that Iraq *had* had WMD. For the record, Iraq had neither weapons of mass destruction nor a major program leading to them. All the experts agreed that there were *no* WMD there prior to the war.

Additionally, 75% of Bush voters believed that Iraq was either directly involved with or gave substantial support to al-Qaeda for the September 11, 2001, attacks; only 30% of Kerry supporters believed this. The truth of the matter is that Iraq had no material relationship whatsoever with al Qaeda prior to the war. Saddam Hussein did not like or trust the Islamic fundamentalists.

The *New York Times* noted this disconnect, and how insidious it is to creating a shared sense of reality based in the truth:

> Partisan fragmentation throughout America's news media and their audiences has grown significantly . . . Press critics worry that the rise of media polarization threatens the foundation of credible, common information that American politics needs to thrive. Mark Mellman, a strategist for the Democratic presidential nominee, John Kerry, said that the current media environment was a hothouse for political misinformation.[382]

THE MEDIA AND THE LANGUAGE OF WAR

> A prince must not have any objective, nor any thought, nor take up any art, other than the art of war, and its ordering and discipline; because it is only the art of war that pertains to him who commands.[383]

War, the media and American leadership wrap together into an unbreakable bind. As was earlier shown, not only is war language often the idiom of the press, but as Machiavelli variously noted, war and successful leadership are uniquely suited to each other. Leaders utilize the press to disseminate the binary view encapsulated in war, as well as to garner support for their leadership and literal wars.

Nothing galvanizes and unifies a population behind a leader like the threat of combat. Additionally the language of conflict helps the media express a black and white, binary version of the world that reduces nuance and reflection, and paints an objective reality that is clear and easy to comprehend. As neoconservative thinker Michael Ledeen noted: "Good leaders recognize that conflict is omnipresent, and they rightly prepare to fight and win."[384]

A quote from Howard Kurtz (b. 1953), a journalist covering the media, clarified the malignant influence of conflict on the news corps:

> Journalists often use military terminology in describing [political] campaigns. We talk about the air war, the bombshells, targeting politicians,

knocking them off, candidates returning fire or being out of ammunition. So we shouldn't act shocked when politicians do the same thing.[385]

A Machiavellian politician would want it no other way. A black and white tableau in which there are clear winners and losers. The amygdala engages; the higher functions of the brain quiet, or are simply put in service to the primal emotional drivers.

Additionally, the laws of politics can track those of war: anything goes. Confident that the media will not expose them for lying, they can employ the Florentine's maxim to the fullest: "The role of morals in politics is to cultivate illusions."[386] Bringing the idiom of war and the media together is the perfect way in which to do this.

> The language of escalation is the language of naked power, a language that is all the more persuasive because it is proud of being ethically illiterate and because it accepts, as realistic, the basic irrationality of its own tactics . . . The language itself is given universal currency by the mass media. It can quickly contaminate the thinking of everybody.[387]

The only point I disagree with here in Thomas Merton's contention is that the language of raw power is "irrational." It is highly rational, focus group tested and based in the extensive Machiavellian program that has proven efficacious for more than six centuries. Perhaps those who don't give in to this program are irrational, believing against all proof to the contrary that a different style of successful leadership is feasible.

The ubiquity of bellicose language in American politics goes much deeper than just a series of newspaper headlines. Journalist John Pitney noted in the *National Review*, in his short but telling article, "Military Language in Politics Proves Resilient":

> Right after the Tucson shootings [January 8, 2011, of U.S. Representative Gabrielle Giffords, D-AZ], some called for a halt to the use of military language in politics. At the *Huffington Post*, Gary Hart wrote: "The degree to which violent words and phrases are considered commonplace is striking. Candidates are 'targeted.' An opponent is 'in the crosshairs.' Liberals have to be 'eliminated.' Opponents are 'enemies'" . . . at *Politico*, Ben Smith reports: "The liberal group *Media Matters* has quietly transformed itself in preparation for what its founder, David Brock, described in an interview as an all-out campaign of 'guerrilla warfare and sabotage' aimed at the Fox News Channel."

> Exhortations to "de-militarize" political rhetoric were never practical to begin with. Although actual incitement to violence is wrong, it would be impossible to purge battlefield language from politics. Years ago, the manager of a presidential campaign wrote: "Other campaigns, John Kennedy in 1960, McCarthy in 1968, Robert Kennedy in 1968, had relied heavily on the classic insurgency technique of rousing the countryside — the volunteers — to beat the entrenched powers. Like most political techniques, this one

is based on military principles; it is New England citizens with pitchforks and muskets against George III's troops."[388]

THE MEDIA AND REAL WAR

I had a couple of friends once, journalists. The three of us happened to find ourselves together in a trendy little bar off DuPont Circle in Washington D.C. during the run up to the Iraq War (late 2002). The bar was one of those places where even the tap water comes in a martini glass.

I was beside myself not only with grief at the compliant nature of both the American public (behaving as if the declaration of war would somehow provide personal emotional catharsis) and the press (operating as a propaganda arm of the Bush administration), but also at the facts of war itself, war's destruction, murder, devastation, psychic maiming; a soul-numbing reality. And a war with Iraq, which had nothing to do with the attacks on the World Trade Center, a war that I viewed as unnecessary and most probably illegal.

So there I sat with two journalist friends who had learned earlier in the day that they would both be "embedding" (covering the war from within) with two different army battalions as the Americans blasted their way to Baghdad. And these two adults — a man and a woman — were acting as if they were kids about to go to summer camp.

I have rarely seen two grown-ups more excited about anything other than money itself. Their eyes sparkled and their movements were animated. Small beads of spittle gathered in the corners of their mouths as they asked each other excitedly how many pairs of underwear and what kind of satellite hook-up, the quality of their sleeping bag and how to keep sand out of the hair and away from a laptop computer.

My disgust grew until I could stand this macabre frenzy no longer. I attempted to cut into the absurdity of their joy with a sliver of reality — or at least with a reminder of the murders that they would surely witness. "Do you both realize where exactly you're going?"

"Of course!" After all, they were journalists, not children.

"And doesn't it disturb you at all? An illegal aggression that is surely to slaughter thousands of innocent children, kill hundreds of our warriors and turn a slice of our youngest generation into murderers. Did you know that 90% of the casualties in modern wars are civilians?! And you're going to witness it? And be part of the American propaganda machine?! Don't you care?"

Silence.

Then one said: "Hey, what's bad for the world is good for my career."

As I write this in 2012, one of these journalists currently writes front-page articles for the *Washington Post* and the other writes for *USA Today*.

Regardless of some personal successes for individual journalists, after the Iraq War the mainstream outlets went through a period of self-examination. The *Washington Post*, *New York Times* and other media organs that had breathlessly backed the war throughout 2002 and into 2003 were later forced to apologize for their jingoistic and lockstep (with the administration claims) approach to their coverage. As was noted by the *Agence France Presse* (and it should be noted that this, like so many objective articles on American politics and culture, appeared first in a foreign news outlet):

> The *Washington Post* became the latest prestigious US newspaper to question its own coverage of Iraq leading up to the US-led war, saying it underplayed stories questioning White House claims that Saddam Hussein had weapons of mass destruction. In retrospect, said Executive Editor Leonard Downie Jr., "we were so focused on trying to figure out what the administration was doing that we were not giving the same play to people who said it wouldn't be a good idea to go to war and were questioning the administration's rationale." In May, the *New York Times* issued a similar critique of its coverage in the run-up to the war, saying administration claims were published with insufficient doubt.
>
> "Some of the *Times's* coverage in the months leading up to the invasion of Iraq was credulous; much of it was inappropriately italicized by lavish front-page display and heavy-breathing headlines," Public Editor Daniel Okrent said at the time. Okrent's column came four days after the *Times's* editors printed their own mea culpa, admitting the newspaper was taken in by spurious information from Iraqi exiles — especially over the issue of weapons of mass destruction — with their own agenda to oust Saddam Hussein.[389]

While it was nice to see this kind of soul-searching *after* the fact, at the time when it was most important, the media played the role of compliant concubine, offering all of the steely insistence on the facts that a wet noodle might. The book *The War in Iraq and Why the Media Failed Us* (David Dadge, 2006) explored how the media is sometimes little more than a propaganda arm for the political and corporate oligarchy in the United States:

> Many [Americans] based their support for the war on misinformation. [Author David] Dadge explores why the media did not aggressively investigate the claims made by the administration and intelligence agencies; in short, why they did not do their job: to fully inform the citizenry to the best of their ability. He examines pressures from the Bush administration, pressures from corporate consolidation of media ownership, patriotism, self-censorship, and other factors.[390]

The media has become but another facet of Machiavelli America, and not the free and independent voice that some of the Founding Fathers had once envisioned. And with war being the prince's most important art, it is with great consequence that the media falls into line so easily in this vital area.

THE ROLE OF THE MEDIA

The opposite of good is not evil. It is indifference.[391]

Amoral and too-often proud of it, the media represents a central and pernicious aspect of our collective Machiavellian situation. Operating in a world beyond truth, the news too-often offers little more than a recitation of whatever emits from the mouths of politicians and opinion makers. The media and its presentation of actuality represent a high hurdle to leap for a society desperately in search of a moral center.

We have ingrained in our psyche the notion that the press is an impartial and fair judge of what goes on in our public square. The legislating solemnity of the media — who refer to themselves as "fair, balanced and free," offering the only allegedly objective force that commands any respect within the public square — is chimerical.

Although the perception of media objectivity has begun to fracture over the past decade or so, due to the proliferation of partisan websites, e-zines, cable TV shows, screaming talk radio hosts and other obviously slanted reportage, there is still a vague, almost subconscious belief that the mainstream media plays the role of an impartial referee, sifting through various claims and pointing out which are correct and which factually inaccurate (lies).

Sadly, this is not the case. In point of fact, journalists often see their obligation as reporting the news (whatever any partisan actor tells them), remaining indifferent to whether the statements have any relation to reality or truth. In the journalistic code of ethics, this impartiality represents the highest code of honor.

> Objectivity in journalism has nothing to do with seeking out the truth, except in so much as truth is a matter of accurately reporting what others have said. This contrasts with the concept of scientific objectivity where views are supposed to be verified with empirical evidence in a search for the truth. Ironically, journalistic objectivity discourages a search for evidence; the balancing of opinions often replaces journalistic investigation altogether.[392]

This media's moral flaccidity, coupled with politicians' flagellation of language until it becomes little more than meaningless tautology, a propagandistic tool, creates a public square that is a Machiavellian dream come true. Journalists, often going out of their way to appear dispassionate and objective, help to create the muddle.

As has been variously shown, politicians, consultants such as Frank Luntz and party elders *know* that if they peddle any lie, however egregious, the media will not uncover the truth so much as present both sides of the issue (i.e., the lie and the truth) as if they both have competing claims to veracity.

Some journalists do point this problem out, though they are always in a minority. Ironically, they are simply viewed as offering a differing "point of view." Katrina vanden Heuvel (b. 1959; publisher and part owner of the magazine *The Nation*) noted in the *Washington Post*:

> The media [is] obsessed with false equivalence: How the election is covered will almost certainly have a measurable impact on its outcome. The *New York Times'* Paul Krugman describes what he's witnessing as "post-truth politics," in which right-leaning candidates can feel free to say whatever they want without being held accountable by the press.
>
> There may be instances in which a candidate is called out for saying something outright misleading; but, as Krugman notes, "if past experience is any guide, most of the news media will feel as though their reporting must be 'balanced'."
>
> For too many journalists, calling out a Republican for lying requires criticizing a Democrat too, making for a media age where false equivalence — what Eric Alterman has called the mainstream media's "deepest ideological commitment" — is confused, again and again, with objectivity.
>
> In that world, candidates can continue to say things that are "flatly, grossly, and shamefully untrue," as he *Washington Post's* E.J. Dionne described it, without fear of retribution.[393]

Paul Krugman (b. 1953; 2008 Nobel Prize in Economics), who wrote the original article for the *New York Times* ("The Post Truth Campaign," December 22, 2011), noted that his editors at the paper "barred him from using the word 'lying' when writing about George W. Bush"[394] during the 2000 campaign. This same article stated:

> *New York Times* public editor Arthur Brisbane has a new column wondering if the readers of the Paper of Record want to know if the politicians the paper covers are telling the truth. He writes: "I'm looking for reader input on whether and when *New York Times* news reporters should challenge 'facts' that are asserted by newsmakers they write about."[395]

We're not talking about a subterranean conspiracy of which only a privileged few are aware. It is a dynamic that is openly discussed, and it has the editor at one of the most important mass media newspapers in the country wringing his hands and wondering aloud if the American public is even interested in being presented with the truth.

As has been noted, the media members themselves are often aware of their own equivalency over truth journalistic paradigm. But the dynamic is so destructive to democracy, as well as so completely in keeping with the Machiavellian paradigm, that it warrants a bit more attention. In an editorial by the *Los Angeles Times* calling the 2004 Swift Boat Veterans for Truth allegations against John Kerry fictitious, the editors stated:

> The technique President Bush is using against John F. Kerry was perfected by his father against Michael Dukakis in 1988, though its roots go back at least to Senator Joseph McCarthy [d. 1957; R-WI, whose demagogic, reckless, and unsubstantiated accusations of anti-Communist activities with-

in the U.S. government spawned the term "McCarthyism"]. It is: Bring a charge, however bogus. Make the charge simple: Dukakis "vetoed the Pledge of Allegiance;" Bill Clinton "raised taxes 128 times;" "there are (pick a number of) Communists in the State Department." But make sure the supporting details are complicated and blurry enough to prevent easy refutation.

Then sit back and let the media do your work for you. Journalists have to report the charges, usually feel obliged to report the rebuttal, and often even attempt an analysis or assessment. But the canons of the profession prevent most journalists from saying outright: These charges are false. As a result, the voters are left with a general sense that there is some controversy over Dukakis' patriotism or Kerry's service in Vietnam. And they have been distracted from thinking about real issues (like the war going on now) by these laboratory concoctions.

Not limited by the conventions of our colleagues in the newsroom, we can say it outright: These charges against John Kerry are false. Or at least, there is no good evidence that they are true. George Bush, if he were a man of principle, would say the same thing.[396]

The most disturbing line in this editorial is: "The canons of the profession prevent most journalists from saying outright: These charges are false." Why is this so? Although I have seen many instances of this overt self-awareness by journalists of the fact that truth has no place in their profession, I am still left with the mouth-agape question: *why not?* While Niccolò Machiavelli would certainly approve, *why* do the "canons of the profession" prohibit calling a liar a "liar"? What is the difference between a fact — which are forever being checked and re-checked in press rooms around the country — and truth?

Matt Taibbi (b. 1970; a journalist reporting on politics, media and finance for *Rolling Stone* and other outlets) noted:

> Though we're tempted to blame the politicians, it's time to dig deeper. It's time to blame the press corps that daily brings us this unrelenting symphony of buncombe, and never comes within a thousand miles of an apology for any of it. And it's time to blame the press not only as a class of people, but also as individuals.[397]

This lack of accountability in the media presents one of the greatest threats to democracy and the American republic, of the many existential threats that we face. Greater than climate change, greater than the terrorist menace, greater even than a frontal attack by a nuclear China, the media's unwillingness to base their reporting in the truth, opting instead for a mushy and moving center point between whatever the members of the two political parties are saying, reduces the public conversation on any matter to a debate over points of view (one often factually inaccurate) instead of an exploration of the unassailable truth of any issue.

CHAPTER THREE: THE THRESHOLD OF A NEW ERA?

> It is the sane ones, the well-adapted ones, who can, without
> qualms and without nausea, aim the missiles and press the buttons
> that will initiate the great festival of destruction that they, the sane
> ones, have prepared. No one suspects the sane, and the sane ones will
> have perfectly good reasons, logical, well-adjusted reasons for firing
> the first shot. And because of their sanity, they will have no qualms at
> all.[398]

Take a voyage around the Internet, and you can find various exhortations, promises, assurances and even workshops asserting that humanity is
spiritually ascendant. According to these hopeful voices, whether due to the
Age of Aquarius, Capitalism or the revivifying wonders of war itself,[399] there
is a teleological movement leading to greater personal freedom and stronger
spirituality.

For instance, the John Templeton Foundation holds a conference in
human spiritual progress:

> More than 400 invited professionals from across the country will attend
> the John Templeton Foundation sponsored "Spiritual Progress and Human
> Flourishing" conference . . . There experts will discuss expanding research
> on core themes from the Foundation's groundbreaking research in the ar-
> eas of Love, Joy, Gratitude, Forgiveness, Perseverance, and Health.[400]

The Foundation added: "We are witnessing a quiet revolution in research
on human flourishing." An article in the *Examiner* entitled: "Humanity is
Maturing" assured: "This growth in human awareness has happened because
millions of us bi-peds have, over time, learned from difficulties (whether
wanted or not) and matured."[401]

The Bahi'a International Community claimed:

To an extent unimaginable a decade ago, the ideal of world peace is taking on form and substance. Obstacles that long seemed immovable have collapsed in humanity's path; apparently irreconcilable conflicts have begun to surrender to processes of consultation and resolution; a willingness to counter military aggression through unified international action is emerging. The effect has been to awaken in both the masses of humanity and many world leaders a degree of hopefulness about the future of our planet that had been nearly extinguished.[402]

An article in *Utne Reader* titled "The New Renaissance" identified a fresh breed of visionaries:

[who] view recorded history and the growth of societies as phases of a much longer and more profound process of evolution . . . Most of all, the new Renaissance would spark the widespread proliferation of new modes of thinking and feeling into the far reaches of global society: true partnership between the sexes; the conviction that racial and ethnic identities are complex and valuable human options, not fixed fates; and the ever-growing sense that our daily struggles serve something greater than ourselves: a universal Higher Power toward which all religions point."[403]

And Brother Wayne Teasdale (d. 2004; a Catholic monk best known as a proponent of interfaith dialogue and social justice) called this spiritual renaissance "The Inter-spiritual Age," attributing its emergence to the maturing of the world's religions. Writing in the *Journal of Ecumenical Studies*, he proposed that "global spirituality or inter-spiritual wisdom has become possible because of a tangible sense of community among the religions and the real necessity for the religions to collaborate on the serious challenges to the world, notably the ecological crisis."[404]

This idea that humanity is "spiritually ascendant" is hardly a new one. Toward the end of the 19th century, Rudolf Steiner (d. 1925) developed Anthroposophy, which proposed that spiritual training was necessary to support the overall purpose of human evolution, the development of the mutually interdependent qualities of love and freedom. According to Steiner, there was a growth in these humors, one that could be quickened through educational and spiritual nurturing.

Wassily Kandinsky (d. 1944), an artist, was as well caught up in the spiritual hope that pre-dated World War I. In his book presenting the artist as prophet, *Concerning the Spiritual in Art* (1911), he stated that an authentic artist created art from "an internal necessity." Such a creator inhabited the tip of an upward-moving pyramid. This progressing pyramid was penetrating and proceeding into the future. The modern artist–prophet stood alone at the apex of the pyramid, making new spiritual discoveries and ushering in tomorrow's reality.[405]

And here is a note from an article in the *Christian Science Journal*, c. 1904, which captured the *zeitgeist* of that Utopian era: "Perhaps no period in ancient or modern history has contained a larger proportion of spiritually minded thinkers and workers than this in which we live."[406] These quotes concerning the growing spiritual enlightenment in the early 20th century were immediately followed by the bloodiest, most war-torn century in human history.

The belief in spiritual progress represents a noble sentiment. Sometimes these airy assurances even acknowledge the Machiavellian reality of the world, represented in one of the above quotes as "obstacles" and "apparently irreconcilable conflicts." However, in my opinion, any claim that there is spiritual movement in human history, or on a species-wide scale, is overwhelmed by the facts. The world always has been and continues to be managed by Thomas Merton's "sane" (see above), and not by those who have experienced a "growth in human awareness."

SANITY V. SPIRITUALITY

> The whole concept of sanity in a society where spiritual values
> have lost their meaning is itself meaningless.[407]

Today's spiritually realized beings gathering in conferences held by the Templeton Fund or meeting in interfaith prayer retreats simply represent examples of Machiavelli's "unarmed prophets." This well-meaning and self-certain community is surrounded by "armed prophets" who herd the hopeful and spiritually confident collective into church basements, rural mediation retreats and onto back channels of the Internet. The confidence of these spiritual adepts is in no way affected by the realities around them.

The "sane ones" — Karl Christian Rove, George W. Bush, the Super PAC funders, the morally neutered journalists, etc. — accept the world on its terms and attempt to master it. These are the social and political leaders (not the spiritual teachers); these are the ones who decide how resources are allocated, what laws are passed, what priorities are important to the short-term interests of the rich and then implement them, over whatever resistance more spiritually mature citizens may muster. Which, admittedly, is very little.

Much like the pre-World War I years, and regardless of protestations to the contrary, we do *not* rest on the threshold of a New Era. The wishful thinking of Wassily Kandinsky or the John Templeton Fund aside, humanity is as stubbornly intractable and self-destructive as ever. As Machiavelli observed, the same dynamics play out over and over again, only with greater armaments and higher potential for environmental degradation, both due to our technological progress.

Unfounded beliefs pass for "sanity," and those with a genuinely far-reaching perspective are shunted to the sidelines of the most important social, cultural and political conversations. This only further entrenches the Machiavellian princes who have been running the world since the human animal first began to walk on two legs, millions of years ago.

> Where irrational opinions hold the place of ideas, force is all-powerful. It is quite unfair to say, for example, that fascism annihilates free thought. In reality, it is the lack of free thought that makes it possible to impose by force official doctrines entirely devoid of meaning.[408]

The idea of the spiritual growth of the human animal — one that I personally have heard often from the hopeful and powerless people that inhabit the fringe of progressive, caring politics — is, in my opinion, one of the greatest hurdles to seeing our shared human history with clarity, and beginning to heal. One example of this myopic view was captured in an email that I received from a peace worker friend after the publication of my book on war and religion (*A Fatal Addiction: War in the Name of God*), who accused me of "projecting such dark qualities out of yourself and onto the sacred soul of others."[409]

His response to my thesis was that the dark qualities I perceive in the world are simply representative of my own psychosis! Would that it were so . . . for if it were just me who was the problem, the world would indeed hue far closer to his fairytale vision of peace and goodwill and look less like the Machiavellian, war-torn free-for-all that it in fact does.

Regardless of my friend's contention (in the same email) that "being in touch with diverse people around Earth, we sense a new breed of connected, young adults building something better,"[410] I believe that individuals such as this friend of mine remain a small minority of the human collective. And in terms of their influence on where we are going as a species, they are even more insignificant than their numbers would indicate — while it is certain that if one judges human spiritual and emotional movement at a certain time and place, or among like-minded friends, or with just the proper prejudice (i.e., through rose-colored glasses), it might appear that things are getting better.

But I do not believe that this is the case. Any human spiritual growth is chimerical, representing the wishes of the well intentioned rather than a careful reading of history or even the most recent newspaper reportage.

A few spare facts will bear this out. The *National Underground Railroad Freedom Center* noted that there are as many as 27 million slaves in the world today,[411] roughly equivalent to the total number of white American citizens *and* slaves living in the United States (North and South combined) at the beginning of the Civil War (1861).

In the 20th century, around 180 million people were killed in a series of wars, genocides, mass murders, exterminations, police missions, terrorist attacks and other violent interactions, equal to the total population of the United States in 1960. And, as this book shows, the Machiavellian energy underpinning human social and political interaction has hardly waned, only becoming a bit more clever and slightly less physically dangerous for participants in our times.

THINGS MAY BE GETTING WORSE

An honest assessment of the world as it is, and not as we might wish it to be, indicates that things might actually be getting worse. Far from the spiritual and emotional catharsis that the dreamers around the edges of society assure us is taking place ("don't you feel it?!" one friend of mine insistently asked), the grim reality is that we may be in the process of committing mass suicide.

We can see how little things have changed by remembering the words of the *Vishnu Purana* (c. 320; a Hindu text):

> Wealth and piety will decrease until the world will be wholly depraved. Property alone will confer rank; wealth will be the only source of devotion; passion will be the sole bond of union between the sexes; falsehood will be the only means of success in litigation; and women will be objects merely of sensual gratification. . . a man if rich will be reputed pure; dishonesty (*anyaya*) will be the universal means of subsistence, weakness the cause of dependence, menace and presumption will be substituted for learning; liberality will be devotion; mutual assent, marriage; fine clothes, dignity. He who is the strongest will reign; the people, unable to bear the heavy burden, *Kara bhara* (the load of taxes), will take refuge among the valleys . . . Thus, in the Kali age will decay constantly proceed, until the human race approaches its annihilation (*pralaya*).[412]

We are a species teetering ever closer to a certain type of cliff, flirting with crisis. We show all the control of "absolutely ignorant travellers who find themselves in a motor-car launched at full speed and driverless across broken country."[413] And our princes are merely the best "ignorant travelers," men and women who master the art of deception to the point where they, themselves, might even believe their sense of confidence and certainty. Sadly, though, any confidence that we have as individuals or as a society grows out of ignorance, not wisdom. Our most successful leaders have merely convinced the other travelers that they are in control of the runaway conveyance.

A note by the psychiatrist Georg Frankl (d. 2004; an Austrian psychoanalyst and author) echoed the earlier Hindu *Purana*:

> When universal seduction (to the power of money) prevails; when those who allow themselves to be seduced consider the word "corruption" to be merely an expression of moralistic posturing motivated by envy, it becomes a cultural climate. Then people are resigned to its inevitability, as if it were a universal law; indeed, we see that [in today's social and political climate] the so-called higher values of Truth, Beauty and intellectual honesty are considered practically useless, merely a self-indulgence.[414]

Machiavelli would have certainly concurred with these quotes, though perhaps with a bit more approbation of this dynamic, as he noted: "It is not necessary for a leader to have [moral] qualities, but it is very necessary to seem to have them."[415] True, the world is caught in a downward spiral, but for Machiavelli and his acolytes, this presents an opportunity, not a desperate challenge.

Hidden in Plain Sight

> One thing is impossible, even were you to dispose of the best public platforms, and that is to diffuse clear ideas, correct reasoning and sensible views on any wide scale.[416]

While political assassinations may be on the wane in the United States, weapons of other sorts have become the greatest signifier of humanity's collective illness. Propaganda, lies, slander, advertising, and — most importantly — the fuel for all of these, money, have replaced the duel, the midnight knife thrust and the overtly mercenary wars of past eras.

A quick overview of how money has sluiced in ever-larger amounts into the American political system demonstrates that things have definitely worsened over the past decade or so. For instance, in the 2000 election cycle, nearly three billion dollars were spent on political campaigns, while by 2012 that number had doubled, to six billion dollars. To give this some perspective, during this same time, the Dow Jones Industrial Average stood at 11,723 in mid January 2000, and 12,422 at the same time in 2012, a gain of about 6% *total* during that same time period. The American oligarchs had become a lot freer with their political donations, drawing on about the same amount of money!

And, due to the 2010 United States Supreme Court decision *Citizens United v. FEC*, prohibiting the government from placing limits on independent political spending by corporations and unions, more of this money is coming from fewer and fewer people, skewing the messages and issues of concern being discussed in the public square.

The vast majority of these massive election expenditures are employed in the Machiavellian strategies of character assassination. A *Bloomberg News* article noted that as much as 90% of campaign ads in the 2012 presidential election were negative![417]

Like much else about our ailing political system, this dynamic is hardly hidden from public view, which makes it that much more disturbing. As Rabbi Abraham Joshua Heschel averred in the shadow of the Holocaust, the opposite of good is not evil, but indifference. And we have a surplus of indifference in our culture.

In America, information on any crisis — be it ecological disaster, the ongoing oligarchation of the American political system or the horrendous emotional and economic costs of war — is always readily available. But so, too, are any number of contrary opinions, half truths and frank lies, all presented without a media that will call an untruth untrue, leaving confused members of our society to wade through a series of reports that offer both sides of any argument — regardless of how specious one of them might be — as respectable alternatives to any pressing issue.

The result is an enforced, amoral indifference, smothering the exhausted public who don't have enough time to piece the facts together into a coherent whole and are bereft of a media that will do it for them. Truth and morality are downgraded to opinion, and those who are able to best diffuse their version of events — whether independent of reality or not — control the public square.

> The reduction of principles to interests seems to be both a prerequisite and a consequence of the plurality of principles in one society . . . whatever the sincerity of men of principle — and no one should underestimate their faculty of self deception — the actual function of principles is the promotion of selfishness.[418]

Things are Getting Worse: Advertising

Although Machiavelli lived long before the advent of advertising gurus, mass media propaganda artists and political operatives with access to hundreds of millions of people for the price of a national advertisement, he would undoubtedly have heartily endorsed the schemes by which money and words have been employed to twist reality.

Character assassination, as has been variously noted, has become a staple of American political campaigns, and the vast sums of money being invested in individual candidates grows ever more pernicious each election cycle. A *Los Angeles Times* article entitled: "Negative ads increase dramatically during 2012 presidential election" noted:

> A study by Wesleyan University shows a staggering leap in negative advertising during the 2012 presidential campaign, coinciding with a huge growth in spending by outside groups eager to influence voters.

> In a campaign that already has been noted as particularly hostile, the vitriol of the rhetoric so far has reached a seemingly unprecedented level. At this point in 2008 [May], 9% of ads were classified as negative. So far in the current race, 70% of the ads have been negative ads.[419]

Linguist and social commentator Noam Chomsky (b. 1928) pointed out how ubiquitous is this dynamic in America, and who pulls the levers behind the powerful to achieve the Machiavellian images necessary to obliterate the challengers:

> As usual, the electoral campaigns [are] run by the PR industry, which in its regular vocation sells toothpaste, life-style drugs, automobiles and other commodities. Its guiding principle is deceit. They seek to delude consumers to choose their product over some virtually identical one. [Presidential campaigns] do not spend hundreds of millions of dollars to provide information. Deceit is employed to undermine democracy.[420]

This was *literally* shown to be the case above, as I noted that Mitt Romney's advertising team included men and women who had previously hawked "Colgate toothpaste, Big Macs, BMWs and Nationwide Insurance."[421]

A Spiritually Desiccated Age

Of course, one could argue that all ages are spiritually bereft times, eras during which "the so-called higher values of Truth, Beauty and intellectual honesty are considered practically useless" within the political and social realms. Even though many people of any time lament the passing of the "good old days," in point of fact, the "old days" were rarely better than the new ones, and often worse. What is memory but myth, after all? And the myth of history — propaganda written by and for the victors — is little more than a Machiavellian fraud, a narrative infused into the populace through education to secure those in power within the structure of an imagined shared past.

Our times, like all times, see the higher moral and spiritual aspects of humanity overwhelmed by lower, animal fears and desires. The amygdala trumps the neo cortex. This is represented in society. Thomas Merton, who lived his life at the highest spiritual level of Christianity, opined:

> Whether we like it or not, we have to admit that we are already living in a post-Christian era, a world in which Christian ideals and attitudes are relegated more and more to the minority. It is frightening to realize that the façade of Christianity which still generally survives has perhaps little or nothing behind it, and that what was once called "Christian society" is more purely and simply a materialistic neo-paganism with a Christian veneer.[422]

Although I might disagree with his assertion that there was a "good old days" when Merton's brand of pacifist and spiritual Christianity ever ruled in human affairs, his reading of contemporary culture certainly rings true. As peace worker Len Traubman (b. 1939) noted in a written communication to me: "unconscious egocentric humans, given choice, feel separate and threatened, and are hijacked by the reptilian brain."[423]

We live in a world in which the amygdala plays a far more important role than does the soothing rationality of the neo-cortex, or the spiritual centers of the cerebellum. Elections are still won in the realm of the "reptilian brain," regardless of how many religious appeals we hear bleated from televangelists or meditation retreats we read about on progressive spiritual blogs.

In 21st-century America, the perspective of neo-cortex based rationality becomes subsumed in empty advertising images, and morality simply represents another opinion or, even worse, a ruse used to attain votes. Max Lerner stated in his introduction to Machiavelli's collected political works:

> Ideals and ethics are important in politics as norms, but they are scarcely effective as techniques. The successful statesman is an artist, concerned with nuances of public mood, approximations of operative motives . . . religious reformers have often succeeded bringing public morale closer to some ethical norm; they have never succeeded as statesmen.[424]

Social interaction is defined by the narrow, selfish vision of Machiavellian "realpolitik" which denies any higher meaning to life, plunging our society into a quagmire, where humans truly do rule supreme.

WHERE CAN WE TURN?

> It is the good, not the evil, who are incorrigible. The evil can be
> brought to see that their glory requires action for the common benefit,
> but the good are self-sufficient and in-educable.[425]

If humankind really does make it to the next level of evolution, there will come a time when the amygdala-based worldview of our species' history is considered absurd, primitive and counterproductive. Dick Cheney, George W. Bush's Vice President and a clear and passionate advocate for realpolitik, will be considered a Neanderthal embarrassment to human social interaction.

If our progeny ever takes the next moral developmental step, there may exist a time when the heart of every nation does not bear a war memorial: an *arc de triomphe*, or an obelisk, an overgrown, erect phallus, tribute to brute masculine strength. In this imagined future, war memorials will be consigned to museums of a gloomy past in human history. Or they will have gone to seed, become overgrown meadows, testaments to a new, peaceful manner of interacting between peoples. Economies will work for all people and not just the morally shriveled oligarchy. The challenge of creating renewable and green energy will be looked at as a great, creative feast, and not an impediment to quarterly growth.

This vision of human possibility is not completely without merit. Not everyone falls meekly into line with the Machiavellian oligarchy of 21st-century America. There are Americans that are fighting back, big and small. There is a constant ferment bubbling beneath the narrative woven by the powerful and dutifully parroted by the media, where the individual *can* make a difference and working for the common good has genuine worth. An article highlighting a local group of activists in Washington D.C. that were "targeting corporate [political] donations" noted:

> Corporate contributions to D.C. political funds would be banned for the
> first time if a ballot initiative proposed by a group of city activists succeeds
> ... [Sylvia] Brown [an advisory neighborhood commissioner] said the initiative was born out of frustration that an ethics bill recently passed by the
> D.C. Council did not do enough to restrain corporate influence on elected
> officials.[426]

This hearty band of local activists is hardly the only one fighting back against the one hundred or so wealthy Americans who (often successfully) pull the strings of our electoral process.

Power Corrupts Completely

However, the hill they have to climb is high. Power corrupts completely — and the corruption seeps into the deepest recesses of a leader's world-view. As was noted in the *Guardian* (U.K.) in the summer of 2011:

> A US human rights group has called on foreign governments to pros-ecute George W. Bush and some of his senior officials for war crimes if the Obama administration fails to investigate a growing body of evidence against the former president over the use of torture. The New York-based Human Rights Watch said in a report released on Tuesday that the US authorities were legally obliged to investigate the top echelons of the Bush administration over crimes such as torture, abduction and other mistreat-ment of prisoners. It says that the former administration's legal team was part of the conspiracy in preparing opinions authorizing abuses that they knew to have no standing in US or international law.[427]

What stands out here is that President Barack Obama, the purported "antidote" to the excesses of the Bush years, turned out to be little more than a placebo. Once Obama became a member of the club, he was unwilling to take an active role in prosecuting his forerunner, understanding perhaps that some of his own actions — including a series of extra-judicial assassinations in Pakistan, Yemen and Somalia via pilotless drone aircrafts — might well be held to the same legal standard.

Contrary to the work of the hearty activists cited above, the ease with which individuals are co-opted by power represents the single greatest road-block to effecting change from within the political system. Once someone even as centered, grass-roots oriented (Obama studied community orga-nizing under Saul Alinsky in Chicago) and representative of an underclass (Obama is considered Black by American racial standards) loses his way, we (the people) must be wary of thinking that any elected politician can be trusted to center their actions in morality, once welcomed into the club.

Christopher Caldwell of the *Financial Times* noted in his article "An Expensive Clash Between the Same Janus-Faced Elite":

> The historian Anne Applebaum has observed that "when we are offered the choice between Mr. Obama and Mr. Romney, we are offered a choice be-tween two sets of elites." It would actually be more appropriate to describe these as two sides of the same Janus-faced elite. Mr. Romney represents in its acquisitive stage the same elite that Mr. Obama represents in its mana-gerial stage. Ivy League universities, as Ms. Applebaum hints, are the means whereby primitive accumulation is transformed into noblesse.[428]

It is this last sentence which holds the most fascination, as here we see specific reference to the manner in which the "primitive" impulses emitted from deep inside the human brain (in this case, to "accumulate") become civilized through the process of education at Ivy League institutions. The neo-cortex is employed not to mitigate the primal drivers, but to rationalize them, giving them the patina of social grace ("noblesse") that allows Wall Street barons and political liars to flourish in society.

We will never find recourse from our leaders. Even those that start in difficult straits — such as Barack Obama and Bill Clinton, both of whose biographies represent the gritty American dream of rising from the American middle to the very top — simply morph into members of the oligarchy, once they have been admitted into the highest echelons of America society. As George Orwell put it at the end of *Animal Farm*:

> Twelve voices were shouting in anger, and they were all alike. No question, now, what had happened to the faces of the pigs. The creatures outside looked from pig to man, and from man to pig, and from pig to man again; but already it was impossible to say which was which.[429]

Once a person enters into the pantheon of power, he — like Orwell's pigs — simply becomes one of "them."

It is the people that must stand up. True change can only be effected from outside of the halls of power, forced upon the leaders by an electorate or citizenry who bind together, and view the common good as more important than their personal, albeit infinitesimal possibility of ascension into the halls of the elite.

WHY TRY

> The present world crisis is not merely a political and economic conflict. It is a crisis of Man's spirit. It is a great religious and moral upheaval of the human race. We seek the cause of evil and find it here or there, in a particular nation, class, ideology, system. And we discharge upon this scapegoat all the virulent force of our hatred, compounded with fear and anguish. Far from curing us, this is only another paroxysm that aggravates our sickness.[430]

The first and most basic question when attempting to become an agent of change is: why bother? As Dr. Martin Luther King Jr. noted: "The guardians of the status quo are always on hand with their oxygen tents to keep the old order alive."[431] The "oxygen tents," in King Jr.'s construction, are made of money. And with money consolidated in fewer and fewer hands at the top of the economic pyramid, the rest of us are left gasping for air, while the *grandi* enjoy the fresh air beneath their gilded pavilions.

How can people such as you and I, scrabbling down here among the *largi*, expect to effect change in a world such as this? After all, the more that one looks clearly at the political and social situation — and sees how money, ignorance and greed hold sway — the less one is inclined to break their bones over attempting to save us from ourselves. "*Carpe diem*" is the cry of the erstwhile activist turned cynic after watching years of social and moral decay.

But as Simone Weil noted: "Where there is a need, there is an obligation."[432] And the Roman emperor and crypto-mystic Marcus Aurelius expanded on this idea:

> You participate in society by your existence. Then participate in its life through your actions — all your actions. Any action not directed toward a social end (directly or indirectly) is a disturbance to your life, an obstacle to wholeness, a source of dissension.[433]

Yet, despite these exhortations and assurances from great voices floating to us from out of the past, it is increasingly difficult to believe that a single citizen can make a difference, when trying to change a world in which Karl Christian Rove controls billions of dollars, and Martin Luther King Jr., Gandhi, Malcolm X, John F. Kennedy and Robert F. Kennedy were assassinated.

A Story

I am reminded of a story: A man shows up at the door one day, with a strange box-like mechanism in his hands. It has a small button on top of it.

"Here," he says, insinuating the small apparatus into the world of an otherwise normal homeowner ("you" or "me"). "It's really quite easy; all you have to do is push this button," and he points out a small red dimple on the handle atop the box, "and I will return with one million dollars. *Voilà.*"

Of course, there is a catch; there always is, so our friend standing unsurely in the doorway asks, "And?"

"Well, of course," says the man, in that knowing sort of way that certain men in ties can so easily affect. "Yes, yes — of course. If you are of the mind to hit the button, *and receive one million American dollars*, well — someone, somewhere in the world will die. Like that; unexpectedly." And here he kind of smiles. "But after all . . ."

"Who will it be?" asks the homeowner, suddenly horrified by the little device.

"I don't know," says the man, shrugging. "But we're all to die, someday. No?"

"What a horrible little gadget," says the one without the tie, shuddering.

"Be that as it may, I'll just leave it here," and he quickly places the little thing inside the door, "until you're done with it."

"But," responds the other, "What if I never push the button?"

Alas, the suit has somehow disappeared and the homeowner is left alone with his quandary.

We all know how the story ends.

It is played out again and again in households and parlors around the world on a daily basis. The price to seduce each of us into pushing that button rises and falls with all the vagaries of the stock market, but there is always a price that is barely enough, and we are always able to act with a delicious dozy indifference to that person "out there" who might well be affected by our actions. And so, push we do . . .

We Try Because We Must

Moral passivity is the most terrible danger of our time.[434]

The greatest fib of all is that we can somehow inoculate ourselves from charges of malfeasance by "taking the fifth" in life. Not asking too many questions; turning a blind eye, taking a job where one delegates moral choices to a "higher power" (i.e., their boss; not God), pushing that button anonymously and then putting the consequences out of mind.

"I have a job that is morally neutral," one might say quietly and with relief, comfortable in the knowledge that although they are not making the world better, they certainly aren't making it worse! This common mental gymnastic allows many of us to pass the vast majority of our time operating in a complete moral void, while comforting ourselves that we have no responsibility other than to our family, our friends and our job.

There is no point in becoming a positive force on the greater world community. This point of view represents one endpoint.

But as playwright Samuel Becket succinctly put it: "I can't go on. I'll go on." No matter how distressing it might feel, there is no option of moral neutrality in life. Regardless of how many people live as if they can take a moral Hippocratic Oath to do no harm when deciding on what is right about their lives and what wrong, the bottom line is that if you are not struggling to make the world a better place, you have slipped onto the side of the greedy, the narrow and the selfish.

One must go on. "Selfish indulgence is a disease."[435] So in the end, we try because we must.

Is There Hope?

There is a hole in the American system where the leadership used to be . . . The most effective answer to this leadership vacuum would be a new era of political activism by ordinary citizens. The biggest, most far-reaching changes of the past century — the labor movement, the civil rights movement, the women's movement — were not primarily the result of elective politics, but rather the hard work of committed citizen-activists fed up with the status quo.[436]

The beauty of academic and journalistic studies is that one can present all kinds of potential palliatives which are elegant, coherent and have all of the staying power of a moth wing gently touched to flame. Go to any peace-and-justice or human rights conference around the world, and you may listen to numerous presentations, even specific proposals, about how to combat the greedy and power-mad leaders that all too often rule in society.

However, when faced with the grim reality of a global economy often based on war, a massive international arms trade, political systems ruled by greed and not common sense, a propaganda machine that infiltrates not only history and the news, but reality itself — the vast majority of these fine proposals simply dissipate, and are then reborn, buried definitively in the back of academic journals and archived on library shelves.

So the question remains: is there hope?

I can answer that definitively: There *is* hope. As Albert Einstein admonished:

> All of us who are concerned with peace and the triumph of peace and justice must today be keenly aware how small an influence reason and honest good will exert upon events in the political field. However that may be, and whatever fate may have in store for us, rest assured that without the tireless efforts of those who are concerned with the welfare of humanity as a whole, the lot of humankind would be far worse than it even now is.[437]

Necessary, but not yet hopeful. After all, "things could be a lot worse" is not a stirring message of optimism. Hope comes because grass roots energy grows as it never has before. In spite of oligarchies that have metastasized from city states to nations and now to a worldwide cabal, defined by a collective of super rich internationalists who consolidate power through judicial rulings, advertising and media control, there is just as strong an organization against these few persons.

The idea of individual agency — such as that marshaled by Mahatma Gandhi and Martin Luther King Jr. — is swelling, inspiring greater numbers of people with more social media and protesting outlets, to the call for prophetic action. Now, more than ever before in human history, individual members of society believe they can gather together, form associations and advocate for the common good. Over the past few decades we have seen successful African independence movements, the fall of the Berlin Wall, Arab Spring and other socially-rejuvenating pressure groups generated from the people, yet affecting the halls of power.

Why We Can Hope

Man can find meaning in life, short and perilous as it is, only
through devoting himself to society.[438]

Citizen prophets hold the positive potential of humanity in their small but determined palms. There is enough precedent in prophetic action, and a recent history of activists who have brought together politics and the spiritual core of humanity to state that the kind of objective, truth-based social interaction that we yearn for is within our reach.

Although the amygdala is most definitely still in charge in the world, in contemporary technological civilization, following its "fight or flight" impulses no longer represents the clearest path to our species' survival. Evolution has outpaced itself, taking us far beyond the small bands of hunters and gatherers where this primitive brain structure helped keep humans safe, into a brave new era where we have become our own worst enemies.

Today, the prehensile amygdala has access to nuclear bombs, chemical toxins, horrendous vials of viruses, enough fossil fuel to turn the earth into a sweat lodge, cyber war and various other self-destructive mechanisms. However, our spiritual selves have not kept pace: our neo-cortex has remained in service to primal drivers, leading to deforestation, drone attacks, torture memos, economic anarchy and a host of other social ills which threaten to overwhelm us. In the end, there is a not-insubstantial chance that we may be in the early stages of the human endgame, as our over-engorged brains turn out to be as valuable to us as the huge girth of the dinosaurs.

As Rumi noted more than seven hundred years ago:

> Internal enemies are the real enemy. After all, external enemies are nothing. What could they be? Don't you see how thousands of unbelievers are prisoners of an unbeliever, who is their king? That one unbeliever is a prisoner of a thought. We realize thus that thoughts are to be reckoned with, since by means of one feeble, mean thought so many thousands of people are held captive.[439]

Given this reality, those who may have reached a higher spiritual station — one where the collective health of humanity is as important to them as their individual situation — must develop strategies for playing a more important role in shaping our communal life.

The small band of spiritually realized leaders that are existent even today, such as Aung San Suu Kyi of Burma, the Dalai Lama of Tibet, Nelson Mandela of South Africa, Thich Nhat Hanh of Vietnam, Michael Lerner of the United States, Jim Wallis of the United States and others, might offer the clearest path to collective survival. By developing tactics for inserting their vision of human possibility into the real-life Machiavellian free-for-all of politics and society, there might at least be a sliver of hope, the slightest possibility that humanity can overcome our vast (and often self-inflicted) challenges and make progress not just technologically, but spiritually and socially, as well.

RECLAIMING SPIRITUALITY

Only one who does not care to rule the kingdom is fit to rule it.[440]

Niccolò Machiavelli noted that fraud is equivalent if not superior to physical force as a method for ensuring princely success. And for Machiavelli, utilizing religion in general and Christianity in particular represented the extreme and therefore paradigmatic example of successful deceit in politics.

The use of religion as a cudgel to move the population toward a leader's positions is a well-practiced art in American politics. The patina of Christianity, God and Jesus is slathered over policies that rob from the poor to give to the rich, that slaughter millions in unjustified wars, that torture enemies and execute individuals for crimes and which slam the doors on the needy, the hopeless and the downtrodden, as money is funneled away from social programs and into armaments and the coffers of Wall Street.

But there is another aspect to religion that is usually absent from the center of Machiavellian politics: genuine spirituality. That place at the core of all faiths where individuals attempt to rise above their personal necessities to see themselves as a seamless part of the universal whole, where individual needs and social needs blend together.

This represents the highest aspect of the human character, and one that spiritual thinkers have been attempting (most often futilely) to insert into political and social systems since the time of Socrates (d. 399 B.C.E.). As this study moves from the Machiavellian reality of contemporary American politics to one potential antidote, these great thinkers — from Lao Tzu (c. 6th century B.C.E.), Socrates and Marcus Aurelius (d. 180) to 20th-century prophets such as Thomas Merton, Simone Weil, Mahatma Gandhi and many more — will be central to what possibilities lie latent within the political realm.

Offering a counterpoint to the American — and indeed, all Machiavellian realpolitik — systems, these men and women speaking to us from out of the past open the door to a different kind of social interaction. They offer a vision in which we don't work *against* each other for the good of a few, or where massive social decisions are ultimately decided by the amount of money behind them, but where a moral center is carved out and then inspires decision makers.

These great social philosophers have imagined a political reality where truth is not confused with the mid-point between two opposing views on an issue, where the maxims lying at the heart of all religions — such as the need for a society to help those most in need; a genuine humility in international relations; a respect for different views and religious paths; the desire to heal oneself before moving into the public square to "heal" others (often by force); a democracy shorn of oligarchic and selfish concerns — genuinely affect the manner in which a people may come together.

From out of the ideas of these great thinkers, I will build the case that what we most need in our political system is a Moral Ombudsman, a respected voice within the public square that brings together the greatest aspects of all religions, born of the place where all religions meet: at the central core of the human spirit.

I will develop the concept of an ethical governor — one that will play the role often believed to be the purview of the press — operating in the real world of mainstream and social media, which can insert truth and morality into the center of our political system. And begin to build the foundation for a true democracy, and not an oligarchy beholden to a few wealthy people and their selfish, earth-destroying interests.

CHAPTER FOUR: THE CALL FOR A MORAL OMBUDSMAN

> I know it's futile to try to shame politicians into governing and living by principle, but it's worth a try. After all, every lie an elected official tells — whether about a personal failure or a public issue — undermines the very government they're sworn to serve. It erodes the connection between citizen and servant.[441]

The illness of the American political system has been well documented. From articles buried on the inside pages of major city dailies to academic papers delivered at conferences around the world, the country's democracy has been dissected more times than a cadaver at a medical school.

However, fewer writers have come up with an antidote. Less time has been spent attempting to craft a realistic, workable legislative or activist response to a system that is essentially a democratic oligarchy — or perhaps just an oligarchy covered over with a slim veneer of democracy. Certainly, as has been outlined above (with the recent Supreme Court ruling *Citizens United v. Federal Election Commission*, 2010), the institutional structure of the United States has taken the country further from a representative democracy, not closer.

The response to Machiavelli proposed below is not simply an academic exercise. Our study now moves from examining our challenges, to providing one specific, implementable program to rectify the pooling of money and power in the highest echelons of American society. And while it might seem *Pollyannaish* to believe that something — anything — can be devised outside of the political/money driven system that we currently have which might effect change, as Fox News political commentator Bob Beckel said in the above quote, "it's worth a try."

After all, the United States is currently a country where, as Senator Bernie Sanders (I-VT) affirmed, the bottom 40% of the society controls 0.3% of its wealth,[442] while the top one percent controls 43% of the nation's riches.[443] Something must be done. And what follows is one idea that may, if successfully implemented, make a difference.

THE PROBLEM

As noted in the article "Wealth, Income and Power," few in America even appreciate the breadth of our economic illness. "Most Americans (high income or low income, female or male, young or old, Republican or Democrat) have *no* idea just how concentrated the wealth distribution actually is."[444]

The effects of this concentration of wealth among an elite can be observed not only in the manner in which the wealthiest citizens attempt to control the political process by flooding the system with money, but also in how a few rich investors and massive multi-national corporations control the media through ownership of print and broadcast outlets. As Jennifer Akin noted in her article "Mass Media":

> Currently, the majority of all media outlets in the United States and a large share of those internationally are owned by a handful of corporations . . . These companies' holdings include international news outlets, magazines, television, books, music and movies as well as large commercial subsidiaries that are not part of the media.[445]

This media domination translates directly into political power. It is not difficult to discern, for instance, how corporate control exerts pressures on the flow of news and how this skews the projected reality in our public square. As Norman Solomon (journalist and founder of the *Institute for Public Accuracy*) noted in "The Military-Industrial-Media Complex: Why war is covered from the warriors' perspective":

> Sometimes a media-owning corporation is itself a significant weapons merchant. [For instance], NBC's owner General Electric designed, manufactured or supplied parts or maintenance for nearly every major weapon system used by the U.S. during the Gulf War—including the Patriot and Tomahawk Cruise missiles, the Stealth bomber, the B-52 bomber, the AWACS plane, and the NAVSTAR spy satellite system. "In other words," we wrote in *Unreliable Sources*, "when correspondents and paid consultants on NBC television praised the performance of U.S. weapons, they were extolling equipment made by GE, the corporation that pays their salaries."[446]

All the while, those down the economic pyramid remain convinced, despite facts to the contrary, that there is some fundamental fairness, a governor or moral center, to the propagandistic information that they ingest as news or political fact. As John P. McCormick noted in *Machiavellian Democracy*:

> Absent political institutions that allow the *largi* [common people] to confidently take steps that protect the genuine freedom of all citizens, safely and without disrupting public order, "republican liberty" signifies nothing but the freedom of wolves among lambs.[447]

The current work responds with a specific program, an idea that might be implemented within our political system and, in the best of cases, offer a potential antidote to the ingathering of power and money in the top one percent of American citizens. As Machiavelli noted: "So enormous is the ambition of the great that it soon brings that city to ruin if it is not beaten down by various ways and various modes."[448]

The following pages offer one approach to beating them down.

THE AMYGDALA: REDUX

> Everything you do changes your brain. Everything. Every little thought or experience plays a role in the constant wiring and rewiring of your neural networks.[449]

At the beginning of this study, I situated the Machiavellian political dynamic within the human cortical structure, specifically in the amygdala. This small, nut shaped collection of neurons controls primal fear and emotional responses. It is also part of the primitive forebrain involved with the basic tasks of breathing, hunger and temperature control. Additionally, as noted, the amygdala is central to human expressions of aggression.

Much of the Machiavellian social and political program is based on accessing and stimulating this aspect of the human brain, thereby bringing more primal responses to the fore, instead of the higher aspects of the neocortex, seat of rational thinking and spiritual response. As this Machiavellian dynamic appears to be hardwired into the human brain, and the limbic system seems stronger than the higher functioning aspects of the cortical structure, it might look as if there can be no quantifiable change in the Machiavellian reality of human political interaction.

However, studies have shown that the brain can be reverse-engineered — that new neural connections can be made and old ones overcome. Recent research has shown that substantial changes occur in the lowest neocortical processing areas, and that these changes can profoundly alter the pattern of neuronal activation in response to experience. Neuro-scientific research indicates that experience can actually change both the brain's physical structure and functional organization.[450]

The work of this particular response to Machiavelli, then, is not only social and political, but even more importantly, cortical. New ways of seeing and experiencing political reality might potentially change brain structure and the underpinnings of thought, one person at a time. It would literally help heal the human animal, person by person.

This idea brings together political activism and neuroscience, the hopes of activists with a quantifiable social program. Wholesale, structural change to human society cannot be imposed by force. That would simply represent another Machiavellian power play. The only method by which we can truly change human civilization is to infiltrate each individual, on the structural level of people's brains.

PRACTICAL MYSTICISM — WHAT CAN WE DO?

> If God does not show more initiative in leading humans to salvation, then humans will have to take matters into their own two hands.[451]

Social action based in the common good (not personal greed and desire) can underpin a new conception of political culture. Instead of simply hoping against hope that the next corporate politician might somehow be radically different than the last, this model advocates taking matters immediately into our own hands. In this conception, partisan bickering, winner take all posturing and the lock-down grasping of the wealthy can be dissolved, and the potential for a more humanistic communal world created.

Given the contemporary era's faith in individual agency — a time unlike any prior, which respects the power and abilities of each person, regardless of gender, faith or ethnicity — our age has the *potential* to witness a novel social awakening. In 21st-century America, it is not just the white man or landowner who can exercise power. Individuals can bring help insert morality into the shared social life, in their own personal style.

> According to Gandhi, political action is not a means to acquire security and strength for one's self and one's party, but a means of witnessing to the truth and the reality of the cosmic structure by making one's own proper contribution to the order willed by God.[452]

This response to the Machiavellian political structure does not represent the plea for a spiritual elite set up against the powerful and moneyed few in the political and social realm. This would exemplify little more than a spiritual oligarchy in battle with the temporal one. Our era demands an egalitarian and democratic communal revolution, one that involves a wide range within society. And one that allows members of the public to feel that they can actually make a difference, against the deeply entrenched powers of the American oligarchy.

Today's political activist can be any one of us, and indeed the more that accept this responsibility; the better chance the political world may be changed. He or she must overcome the constant, onrushing stream of noise — the crush of information, the squawking of self-assured pundits and the failed capitalistic catharsis that defines the basest aspects of our epoch — and translate their personal yearning and anguish into action that will resonate with the sensually exhausted public. Our era cries out for people who understand the contemporary cultural milieu and speak the language of our times, while keeping the highest possibility of human social interaction forever in their sight. People who are willing, as Bob Beckel noted (above) "to try to shame politicians into governing and living by principle."

> We are living in times that have no precedent, and in our present situation, universality, which could formerly be implicit, must be fully explicit. It has to permeate our language and the whole or our way of life.[453]

Given the environmental, economic and social challenges that certainly appear to be closing in on us, we can no longer just hope against hope, eyes closed and fingers jammed into our ears, that time itself or some undefined "they" will somehow pull us through.

We, collectively and together, must push back against the Machiavellian greed that has ruled the political sphere and attempt to replace it with a social contract based on the good of humanity, not just the moneyed few.

Machiavellian Democracy

> Machiavelli's assertion that the elite's appetite to dominate is insatiable . . . necessitates the extra-electoral safeguards against them . . . as well as participation that is not only active, but also antagonistic.[454]

There are some who have thought specifically about moving beyond the glowing words of hope for a better world into the realm of action. Who have devised programs to bring fairness into the center of the political world. A few powerful leaders, such as Gandhi, Martin Luther King Jr. and Nelson Mandela, have even succeeded in effecting real and quantifiable social change within the Machiavellian brawl that we call civilization.

Professor John P. McCormick (professor of Political Science, University of Chicago) is one such thinker, reconsidering Niccolò Machiavelli's teachings in his book *Machiavellian Democracy* (Cambridge University Press, 2011). Unlike virtually every other Machiavellian scholar over the past half millennia, McCormick found in the Florentine's thought a basis for a more egalitarian democracy, and a handbook for imbuing the common man and woman with political agency.

As David Armitage (Chair of the Department of History at Harvard University) noted: "*Machiavellian Democracy* offers a radical reinterpretation of Machiavelli in the service of an equally radical critique of modern aristocratic democracy." Ian Shapiro (Sterling Professor of Political Science at Yale University) added: "John McCormick has provided a bold new reading of the great master that places his arguments at the center of contemporary debates about democracy."[455]

While McCormick does not, in the end, offer a specific, implementable program to combat our "aristocratic democracy" (he refers to his conclusions as "a heuristic proposal intended for critical but not necessarily directly practical purposes"[456]), his book offers a powerful jumping off point for developing a curriculum that is more than an academic exercise. Which is exactly what I will do in the sections following this one.

McCormick begins his exploration by noting the central issue hampering American democracy:

> A crisis of political accountability besets contemporary democracy. Mounting evidence suggests that elections, even "free and fair" ones, do not elevate to office individuals who are especially responsive to the political aspirations and expectations of their constituents. Moreover, democratic governments seem decreasingly adept at preventing society's wealthiest members from wielding excessive influence over law and policymaking.[457]

McCormick continues on to note that princely and senatorial elites are constitutionally incapable — because of their inherent appetite for oppression, disrespect for laws and inclination toward self-aggrandizement — of effectively policing the political and public square. As anyone who reads the newspaper knows, these elected officials are often the greatest perpetrators threatening the public good.[458]

> Republics are doomed, Machiavelli insists, unless the people, in addition to participating substantively and directly in lawmaking, also vigorously check the insolence of the *grandi* through accountability institutions.[459]

While his reasoning is not necessarily out of line with many past thinkers — including, according to McCormick, with Machiavelli himself — McCormick does go the extra step of developing specific ideas of how to attack this pernicious and growing problem in American democracy. He applies his reading of Machiavelli to the solution, whereas past thinkers (such as Michael Ledeen and his neo-conservative cohorts) have applied Machiavellian thinking to the aggrandizement of wealth and power among the elites.

As can be seen in the statistics of growing wealth inequality, as well as the recent passage of *Citizens United v. Federal Election Commission*, both of which concentrate more money and power in the hands of the elites, the application of Machiavellian methods can certainly work for the expansion of greed and individual success. However, McCormick states, and I emphatically agree, that Machiavellian thinking can just as easily be applied as one of the vital pressures to *prevent* the elites from consolidating power. Until now, however, it hasn't been.

Succinctly put, McCormick does not believe that the elite class in any democracy is trustworthy. Wealthy citizens, McCormick informed, "despite offering florid promises to the contrary, pursue their own interests and not those of the general populace." He then noted that this dynamic is "obviously exacerbated in electoral systems where the wealthy monopolize offices."[460]

In today's United States, the percentage of millionaires in Congress is more than 50 times higher than the percentage of millionaires in the general population.[461] To combat this undue influence of the few, McCormick found inspiration in Machiavelli's writings, as well as contemporary political theorists.

Machiavelli provides all citizens with access to formal and informal assemblies within which they deliberately transform their perhaps initially unconsidered opinion into good judgment over laws and candidates for office.[462]

Although McCormick's specific ideas are "heuristic and not necessarily practical," they provide an important jumping-off point for my concept, which is based on a lifetime spent in Washington DC, examining how outside interest groups *may* have influence over the unbridled greed of the *grandi* who populate the halls of congress, lobbying shops and the White House.

McCormick proposed that some sort of antagonistic body of representative citizens must be constituted, which might have an official role in the electoral as well as legal processes. He believed that the average voter *could* understand the issues and come to informed opinions, but not when presented only with the sound-bite advertisements, half-truths (or outright lies) and the emotional bleating that characterize contemporary American political campaigns and media reportage.

The constitution of a Machiavellian Democracy must ensure that the people's elongated learning curve is permitted to yield beneficial knowledge over time, and furthermore it must provide the means for eventually enacting legal or institutional changes on the basis of that knowledge.

McCormick proposed that the media plays an important role, and given the proper attitude, might even offer a positive one. He noted that one reason the American Founders did *not* build a safeguard into the Constitution such as a people's tribune (seen in ancient Rome) to oversee leaders and laws, was that they believed in the governing power of a widely proliferating free press, operating within an increasingly literate public sphere.[463] By most standards, the American public has a higher than 90% literacy rate and, with the explosion of news sources due to the Internet, the "widely proliferating free press" has become expansive and accessible.

However, as was earlier noted, the *grandi* have no less trouble utilizing their money to control the flow of information than they do to access the seats of power. Information in an oligarchy such as the United States has become ever more constricted, regardless of how many "outlets" for this information exist. As such, a genuinely objective, truth based clearing house for clean information is needed.

McCormick noted that in recent years, within the cloistered environs of the academic community, a number of scholars have developed and even overseen institutions that attempted to devolve power back to the people in a meaningful way. These have included citizen juries, mini-publics, people's assemblies and deliberative polls — all institutions that attempt to gather demographically diverse groups together to influence salient public policy debates. Sometimes, these small experimental bodies have even been empowered to make decisions that are legally binding within local jurisdictions.[464]

Building on these experiments, McCormick proposed to "revive the Tribune of the Plebs," which was a Roman policy for inserting the popular voice into governance. His specific proposal would gather together 51 citizens, chosen almost at random, to have some veto power over legislation, call a national referendum on a pressing issues and perhaps initiate impeachment proceedings against particularly reprobate elected leaders.[465]

He freely admitted potential problems with this system:

> The Constitutionalization of a popular ombudsman would [not] completely insulate magistrates from efforts by elites to discredit, corrupt and intimidate them. Nor does it guarantee that *grandi* will not successfully manipulate the people on occasion by appealing to religious norms and by initiating unnecessary wars.[466]

And then he noted the most daunting hurdle of any tribunal, ombudsman or clearing house that might genuinely hope to affect the political system in one such as ours: "A 'free' flow of information, especially but not only when media ownership is consolidated in increasingly fewer hands is, by itself, an insufficient popular watchdog."[467]

There is much to like about McCormick's program, as well as his fresh reading of Machiavelli's ideas. But he still freely admits that his is most probably an academic exercise, one that is not operable in the real world of Machiavellian thinkers such as Karl Christian Rove and the American oligarchs.

What follows next is one specific approach for devolving power back to the people, in a meaningful way that *may* influence the political realm. Mine is not a "heuristic" and academic thought exercise meant to spur more academic thinking on the subject, but a specific, quantifiable and, most importantly, implementable proposal that can begin the process of turning the ship of state away from the shoals of individual greed, to calmer waters representative of the needs of the majority of citizens.

A Response to Machiavelli

> When a republic empowers the people to distinguish rumor from
> fact, not only does this empowerment serve to enlighten the people,
> but also the republic benefits from the expeditious settling of partisan
> disputes and the definitive punishment of political criminals.[468]

In April 2006, I published an article entitled: "The Call for a Moral Ombudsman," in a small publication called *Reflections Magazine* out of Hibbard, Minnesota. This sparse idea became the genesis for half a decade of deep thought on how we might rescue our republic, as well as the inspiration for this study.

I agree with John McCormick that the dearth of clear and honest information in the public square represents one of the greatest obstacles to a more empowered electorate, as well as better electoral choices. Of course, this is exactly how the "guardians of the status quo" desire to have it, because an uninformed electorate is much easier to manipulate.

However, there is another way to run a democracy — one that moves far beyond the intent of the Founders. They proposed, after all, that only land-owning men could actually vote (about 10 to 15 percent of the nation's population in the late 18ᵗʰ century) and that Americans of African descent must not only be refused entrance to the electoral urns, but also that these same humans had an intrinsic "worth" that was 60% of a White person's. Nelson Mandela, an African whose worth might be more than that of the average White person, envisioned another manner of implementing democratic rule:

> Democracy means that all men are to be heard, and a decision would be taken together as a people. A minority is not to be crushed by a majority.[469]

Regardless of whether we might agree a bit more with one or the other political party, the fact remains that honest discourse and unimpeded knowledge is virtually impossible to come by in the American political panorama.

For this reason, I propose that clearly stated, honestly proposed knowledge *itself* represents the greatest potential tool supporting a genuine democracy. This is the missing link in American society. In a country where voter suppression, lying, cheating, stealing and various other methods of electoral fraud are accepted as "politics as usual," the ability to come by clear and concise information on any issue is almost impossible.

The Call for a Moral Ombudsman

> Machiavelli sought to distinguish the realm of what ought to be and the realm of what is. He rejected the first for the second. But there is a third realm: the realm of what can be . . . The measure of man is his ability to extend this sphere of the socially possible . . . We may yet find that an effective pursuit of democratic values is possible within the scope of a strong social welfare state and an unsentimental realism about human motives.[470]

A Moral Ombudsman presents one method for combating the Machiavelli American social malaise. And while many will say that it may be difficult, perhaps nearly impossible, to implement, I don't see that we have much choice but to try something, anything that might stem the smothering tide of political turpitude and economic greed that besets our culture and the world.

The Moral Ombudsman would operate within the parameters of 21ˢᵗ-century Washington D.C., acknowledging the way in which power is won and imposed. It follows the call of another great academic thinker on these issues, Philip Pettit (Laurence S. Rockefeller University Professor of Politics and Human Values, Princeton University):

> Pettit endorses "contestatory" means for challenging the policy outcomes of ordinary electoral politics. Petit frequently invokes alternative institutions through which individuals, specific subsets of the citizenry and

(more ambiguously) even the citizenry itself might variously contest, re-view or amend decisions made by the elected elites. He calls this the "edito-rial" dimension of democratic politics that must supplement the "autho-rial" dimension reflected in electoral procedures.[471]

The Moral Ombudsman would fill this role, and do so not in the halls of academe, but in the corridors of power itself — in Washington D.C., in the media and in the living rooms of voters across the country. Specifically, this is the call for the creation of a non-profit organization of the same name: "The Moral Ombudsman," to develop and insert a moral lodestar into the American political realm.

FINDING THE MORAL CENTER

> Socratic philosophy claims that the human mind can grasp the most important truths about nature and can derive guidance about human conduct. But Machiavelli argues that these are just opinions — neither better nor worse than any others.[472]

The Moral Ombudsman would center its work in the Socratic vision, not that of the Florentine philosopher. The bedrock assumption of the project would be that "the human mind can grasp the most important truths about nature and can derive guidance about human conduct." Ergo, the first and most important aspect of the program would be to derive a code of morality, which could then be applied to politicians and social actions.

The Moral Ombudsman would bring together a board of recognized religious leaders to form a non-governmental organization to provide *moral* oversight of our lawmakers, as well as the laws that they make. The rea-son that these would be mostly religious — and not political or secular social leaders — is twofold. Firstly is the religiosity of the American public. According to a 2012 Gallup poll,[473] for 81% of Americans, religion is very or fairly important. Additionally, according to a June 2013 survey, a full three quarters of Americans "say it would be positive for society if more Americans were religious."[474] Given the respect for religion in our polity, it makes per-fect sense to insert a religious, moral vision into American politics. However, as will be seen further along, this is not the tribal religion of divisive politics, but the idea of the moral vision shared by all religions.

Coupled with American's religiosity is the fact that religions offer the kind of central truths that politics never can. That is the business of reli-gion: to move beyond opinion to a sense of the absolute. Obviously, this is problematic when one religion or group claims to have the absolute truth in exclusivity, shutting all other groups out of this central fact. However, the Moral Ombudsman would represent virtually all American religions, thereby basing its ideals in a sense of morality shared between most of Amer-ica's citizenry. I will discuss below exactly how this will be done, however it should be noted that a shared sense of a moral center would be built that corresponds with the majority of Americans' religious sensibility.

To build this concept, the Moral Ombudsman would bring together representatives of all America's religious groups to constitute the governing board. It would draw leaders from the following faiths, representing the breadth of religious and even secular (though often spiritual) communities in the United States: Christianity (two each from Baptist, Pentecostal, Lutheran, Presbyterians, Methodist, Anglican, Catholic and Eastern Orthodox); Judaism (one each from Reformed, Conservative and Orthodox); Muslim (one each from Sunni, Shi'a and Sufi); two Buddhist leaders, and one each from Sikhism, Hindu, Mormon, Unitarian, Secular Humanist and Atheist.

Other potential board members might include an academic leader, an agreed upon politician, a social theorist or perhaps lay leader who would add perspective to the conversation. The final constitution of the board would represent the vast majority of American citizens. It would also acknowledge the Christian heritage of our nation by weighting the board in that direction.

The board would first be charged with developing a specific social and political moral code that would be agreed upon by *all* members of the collective. Although at first blush, this step clearly seems to present a potentially insurmountable obstacle, it is not as difficult as it might appear. At the core, virtually all religions are in accord. There are moral values shared by all creeds, which inform the hearts of every religious path.

When the beliefs of the various religions are compared to each other, an overlap is evident in certain central beliefs. A school of thought (called *Perennial or Traditional Philosophy*) has grown up around this idea, based upon the idea that all the world's great religions share the same origin (a human yearning to understand our place within the universe) and are, at root, centered on the same metaphysical principles.

Aldous Huxley (d. 1963; widely recognized to be one of the pre-eminent intellectuals of his era) described this overlap in his book *The Perennial Philosophy* (1945). And it is here, where the beliefs of the religions of the world converge, that a basis for a moral outlook that includes *all* of society can begin to be forged. And which, with the impetus of an organizational Moral Ombudsman, may be inserted into the rough-and-tumble world of Machiavellian American politics.

Huxley stated concerning the overlap of all religions:

> *Philosophia Perennis* . . . may be found among the traditional lore of primitive peoples in every region of the world, and in its fully developed forms it has a place in every one of the higher religions.[475]

And it is exactly this Perennial Philosophy that should be the basis for developing a moral center for the advocacy group. These common ideals would form the bedrock of the Moral Ombudsman's point of view.

AN AGREED-UPON MORAL CODE

> Moral and political problems are inextricable from one other, and
> it is only by some political action that we can fully satisfy the moral
> requirements that face us today.[476]

When we move beyond the pressures of politics, power and the state
(and the manner in which, as Machiavelli strongly advocates, religion is used
in service to all three), all creeds fundamentally teach that public actions
should benefit the common good. According to the teachings of all faiths,
society should not exist to enrich the few most powerful members of a society or religious leadership. This does not define the common good, though
sometimes religious institutions such as the Catholic Church or Sunni Islam
(as represented by al-Azhar University in Cairo) or Orthodox Judaism, etc.,
become hostage to powerful religious leaders such as the Pope, an Imam or
Chief Rabbi. Additionally, as has been explored in the earlier sections of this
book, religious sentiments may also be subject to influence from a powerful
secular leader such as George W. Bush, or even a charismatic self-appointed
and successful "prophet" such as Osama Bin Laden.

Regardless of the spiritual aberrations of individual political and institutional religious leaders — which the Moral Ombudsman would be created
to fight against — the common good as seen from within the heart of all
religions may, if given the opportunity and support, permeate political society with a healing, anti-Machiavellian power. As Simone Weil noted: "The
proper function of religion is to suffuse with its light all secular life, public or
private, without ever in any way dominating it."[477]

In American culture, this energy can at times be seen at work, often in
the form of specific social programs, interfaith projects and other methods of
positive communal energy that is all-too-often confined to the back pages of
newspapers or short notes at the end of broadcast news. Quietly imbuing the
public square with the anti-oligarchic energy of humble caring.

Although all religious and political leaders would scoff at the idea that
they, themselves didn't represent a moral center already, many ideals developed by the Moral Ombudsman might directly contradict aspects of American political, social and perhaps religious life. Even in cases where the social
actions or policies in today's United States are considered normal, legal and
perhaps salutary, they may run afoul of the strict ethical code of the Moral
Ombudsman.

Inserting a moral center into the social world of ethical relativity that
defines American politics will be complicated and undoubtedly occasion
much ridicule. Angelo Codevilla noted the difficulty of assaulting publicly
accepted reality with a conception of absolute truth in his introduction to
Machiavelli's *The Prince*:

> The idea that something can be true and right even when it contradicts
> a nation's laws and mocks its customs and rulers was and always will be

inherently subversive. Athens put Socrates to death and Rome resisted Socratic philosophy and Christianity [the original, non-militarized version] because of their affirmation of truths that transcend power challenged their authority.

The Moral Ombudsman would follow in the footsteps of Socrates, and the great early church fathers such as Origen (d. 254), who stated: "Christians cannot enter armies of the emperor because loyalty to Jesus forbids them to participate in war."[478] Obviously a profoundly subversive concept in a country such as the United States, where nearly 35% of the total federal budget is related to military operations, and its military expenditures represent more than the next *twenty* largest state military spenders combined.[479]

The Moral Ombudsman will not develop a Utilitarian reading of the common good (the greatest happiness for the greatest number is the measure of right), as this can just become similar to our own democracy, which sometimes appears as a tyranny of the majority of voters (which often represents only about 30% of adult Americans, due to the fact that nearly half of the country's eligible voters don't exercise their right).

In this response to Machiavelli, the ideal of a common good will have a deeper moral hue, and take into account such things as the *obligation* of those who have the means to aid those who do not; the right to adequate health care access for every citizen (hardly revolutionary, as thirty-two of the thirty-three developed nations have universal health care, with the United States being the lone exception[480]); adequate shelter; a necessary amount of nutritious food; free education; freedom of religion and association and freedom from racist or ethnically deleterious laws and behavior.

As noted in the quote by Angelo Codevilla, in many cases, the moral truth of a matter might run contrary to civil law or conventionally held opinions. For instance, handguns are not O.K. just because they have a powerful lobbying group (NRA), a majority of Americans like them, they help gun dealers reap large profits and stockholders in small arms companies are doing great. We're looking for the moral view, not the politically expedient or even legal one. Virtually all guns on the street are there to kill people — and this is ethically incorrect. Period.

The Perennial Philosophy also holds that it is an *obligation* for those who have the resources to help those who do not. This is the moral view. If congress wants to cut benefits to the poor while increasing tax advantages for those making over $100,000, as well as oil and gas companies — this is immoral. End of conversation. It may be politically savvy, it may win elections — but as far as a Moral Ombudsman would be concerned, it would be corrupt.

Here is one example of the exact kind of news notice that the Moral Ombudsman would take after, and do so with the backing of deep-thinking members of the country's faith community:

Congressional negotiators beat back efforts to expand and preserve tax refunds for poor families, even as they added $13 billion in corporate tax breaks to a package of middle class tax cuts that could come to a vote in the senate today.[481]

How Would It Work?

Everyone is aware of the difficult and menacing situation in which human society — shrunk into one community with a common fate — finds itself, but only a few act accordingly. Most people go on living their everyday life: Half frightened, half indifferent, they behold the ghostly tragicomedy that is being performed on the international stage before the eyes and the ears of the world. But on that stage, on which actors under the floodlights play their ordained roles, our fate of tomorrow, life or death of the nations, is being decided.[482]

The first and most important step for the Moral Ombudsman would be to bring the thirty or so leaders together to find a moral common ground. This represents one of the many difficult tasks of the newly constituted organization. However, despite the sense that an agreed upon moral center to our public square might be impossible to develop, I believe that such a place can be defined outside of politics, and then insinuated into the public square. Once religious and social leaders envision themselves as part of the human community, instead of a political party or specific creed, they will have an easier time finding accord.

Social issues including, but not limited to the following would be discussed and agreed upon, becoming the bedrock structure for the Moral Ombudsman's point of view and rulings. These positions would help define how politicians, their public actions and the legislation they passed, would be viewed:

- Obligation of the rich to help the poor
- Human right to health care
- Human right to adequate, nutritious food
- Human right to satisfactory housing
- Forgiveness, restitution and rehabilitation as bases for the prison system
- Minority rights
- Women's rights
- Freedom of association
- Freedom of worship
- Freedom from racism
- Freedom from hate speech
- Foreign policy based in respect and commonality
- Truth as the basis for news reporting
- Truth as the basis for political language and ideas
- Truth as the basis for political campaigns

These define just a few of the specific positions that the Moral Ombudsman *might* develop. Undoubtedly, this would be the most delicate aspect of the organization's work: coming up with agreed upon metrics on all of these issues. The scriptures of each religion provide many different teachings, from the suppression and slaughter of the "other", the veiling of women, polygamous and tribal laws, to readings that emphasize peace, respect and open-mindedness. Put bluntly, George W. Bush could find plenty in the scriptures to justify his views, as could Martin Luther King Jr.

But this is not a time to simply throw up our hands and turn sadly away from the task of inserting — nay, *forcing* — a moral center into the heart of American politics. The 30 leaders would not be culled from the most fanatic branches of their particular religions — whether *jihadi* Muslims, Zionist Jews or messianic, Evangelical Christians. The small-minded and hateful religious voices would simply not become part of the Moral Ombudsman's work. The Moral Ombudsman would be created to fight against the worldview of those voices, not to include them or in any way compromise with them.

Leaders from the various religious creeds would be sought who believed that theirs was *a* valid path and not the single road to spiritual grace. They would be leaders whose views shared much with the contemporary *zeitgeist* in respecting women's rights, the plurality of ethnic and cultural diversity and the worth of individuals (instead of holding that the religious system was more important than the rights of its constituent members).

The Moral Ombudsman would reach beyond social, economic and political barriers, speaking in the best interest of *all* Americans, all the time. At long last, there would be a consistent, publicly recognized group that could not be bought by campaign contributions or kickbacks, or frightened into silence or acquiescence. The Moral Ombudsman would be immune to fluctuations in the stock market, poll numbers and television ratings.

Issuing its decisions in policy papers, op-ed articles, newsletters, scorecards on the votes of members of congress, governors and the president, and utilizing other stratagems, this non-profit watchdog group would finally offer a true moral center from which to judge the legislation and actions of our elected princes. It would offer an examination of the American political actors, language and proposed legislation based only in truth, and the agreed upon moral center provided by the Board.

The Moral Ombudsman's positions would be unabashedly weighted toward respect, love, open-mindedness, and contrary to apocalyptic, narrow, violent and even nihilistic readings of faith that have all too often passed for "religious" in our public square. In this respect, the Moral Ombudsman could be said to have an "agenda," a specific point of view. And this would absolutely be the case: to insert a genuine ethical dimension into the American political system.

INSERTING THE MORAL CENTER

Once the moral structure was set into place, the work of the organization would be to judge specific legislators, legislation and even the media by its precepts. Each new statute coming up for a vote in Congress would be compared to the moral principles agreed upon by the Board. A grade would be issued, with a zero representing a completely immoral law (such as raising taxes on the poor so that the rich might have a lower tax burden), to a 100% (universal health care, for instance). There would be a written release issued, as well as a rating.

Each legislator would have his votes analyzed, and would receive a sumtotal number score for his moral centeredness. This method is modeled on the scores issued by NGO groups from the American Conservative Union and the NRA to the Nature Conservancy.

Additionally, the Executive Branch, military, State Department and actions of members from other governmental arms would be so judged. Pilotless drone attacks on other people's soil? Nope. No matter how much verbiage is exhaled concerning terrorism, eliciting the fear response in the amygdalae of the population, this cannot be morally justified. Secret Ops work in Latin America? Presidential pandering, military posturing, and State Department dithering? No, no and no. The Moral Ombudsman's job would not be to garner votes or make friends with the higher ups. It's job would be to begin the vital but nearly impossible work of centering American politics in some moral schema, instead of allowing it to continue to founder in the media created world of "objective reality."

Is this solution easy? Absolutely not. Is it fraught with potential problems? Yes. Oh, yes.

But we have no choice but to try.

A RESPONSE TO MACHIAVELLI — USING MACHIAVELLIAN METHODS

> According to Machiavelli, the plebian tribunate is the institution that serves as a "head" for the people at home: it directly checks noble machinations to oppress the people or to enlist the latter in uncivil schemes.[483]

Once the information was gathered and the grades issued, another vital aspect of the Moral Ombudsman's work would begin: using this information to affect the conversation in the public square, the media and national legislation. This project demands far more than just the desire to make things better. It must inspire specific and quantifiable political transformation. The Moral Ombudsman is only the foundation for the project. Social networks would be built, infiltrative methods devised and the general public and the press must be engaged and influenced.

Building the project into a socially transformative body demands political and social skills not always associated with activists. Tough and savvy, this response to Machiavelli might sometimes use Machiavellian means to achieve success. The office of the Moral Ombudsman must not only understand and address the morality of social and political interactions, but would also influence them, utilizing the basic stratagems of power to address power. As Harvey Mansfield stated in *Machiavelli's Virtue*: "Open and ingenuous force is the weapon of the existing order; it keeps the existing order in existence; it constitutes the existing order."[484]

And I am positing that the most powerful challenge to this existing order must use the same method: open and ingenuous force, in this case by wielding the words and symbols of power against itself.

Sometimes uncomfortable and off-putting, this Machiavellian style of relating to the public square will not always endear the Moral Ombudsman to either the general public or, more certainly, to the *grandi*, the members of the elite. But it can help make a difference. Understanding and managing the art of political engagement is a prerequisite for this endeavor to be successful.

HEURISTIC PROPOSALS AND SUCCESSFUL ACTIVISM

> Morality interferes with efficiency, therefore it is absurd to concern oneself with moral questions that, in any case, are practically meaningless, since the vicissitudes of the power struggle may demand at any moment that they be thrown aside as useless baggage.[485]

Perhaps the greatest single roadblock between activists and more successful endeavors is advocates' misguided sense of right and wrong. Too many morally-centered citizens believe that it is worthier to have their actions hew to some ill-defined high road and thereby attain an indefinable moral victory, instead of engaging with the society on its own terms to inspire social change. A smug sense of morality too often stops activists from using the Machiavellian methods perfected by those in power to affect those in power. They fear that by utilizing normal social and political strategies of engagement, they will be acquiescing to a corrupt society.

At an academic conference at which I spoke, I approached a professor who had just given a talk on an elegant peacekeeping method. The idea seemed to be almost completely unrealizable in the real world. I challenged him to consider that it might make more sense to devise a scheme that, though perhaps a bit less elegant, might actually effect change rather than create a schema that simply represented an academic exercise leading nowhere except to the conference podium.

He looked shocked. "We can't be just like them!" he said. "It is the obligation of the academic to stake out a moral high ground, to light a candle to which the politicians and oligarchs in the real world may aspire." "Fine," I replied — "however, they are busy ignoring you and wreaking havoc using the usual and more successful Machiavellian methods." He stomped off in a huff.

This exact dynamic of the irrelevance of many well-meaning activists has been clearly noted in the real world. The story of a Syrian agitator comes to mind. Duraid Lahham (b. 1934; a leading Syrian comedian and director), who tried to use his art to affect the political life in Syria, one of the most repressive regimes in the world at the time, once believed that he could, through his work, truly make a difference. But he was disabused of that conviction.

> For a good portion of his career, Mr. Lahham appeared on Arab-language television, challenging the region's leaders. He mocked their ideologies and railed against corruption and incompetence.
>
> But one day, he said, he realized it was all a big mistake, that his critiques did nothing but play into the hands of men in power. Dictators like to point to "freedom of criticism," he said, as a way to defend against charges that they suppress freedom of expression.
>
> "One time," Mr. Lahham recalled, "in a conversation with an Arab official we were criticizing a lot, he said to me: 'Talk all you want; we will do all we want.' "
>
> Those words seared Mr. Lahham's heart, and from that moment forward, it seemed that part of him dried up. "We had thought that artwork could shock and make change. But no, artwork, at the end of the day, even if it is critical, is entertainment."[486]

Is Mr. Lahham's experience typical of morally centered activists, be they cultural or political? Do dissenters themselves represent little more than another Machiavellian implement in the toolbox of power, in this case "proving" that a repressive regime offers "freedom of speech?"

Whether offered from the podium of an academic conference, or couched as art on TV or in the theater, are counter-oligarchic expressions little more than elegant, "heuristic" offerings that will never effect change?

REALITY: AS SEEN ON TV

> Men are so simple and so obey present necessities that he who deceives will always find someone who will let himself be deceived.[487]

This, of course, is Machiavelli's quote. But he was certainly not alone in this sentiment. Nearly thirteen centuries before the Florentine was active, Clement of Alexandria noted:

> We humans seem to be attracted to ideas based on human opinions, rather than those based on the Truth. This is so even when human opinions are contradictory. The reason that humans reject the Truth is that it is morally strict and solemn.[488]

As has been variously noted, for many people in the general public, their sense of what is true grows from what they see on television, hear from politicians, read in the newspapers, listen to on radio talk shows or ingest from other widely disseminated popular culture media. Or, even more frightening, sometimes just what they "feel" in their gut to be correct.

This dynamic is certainly no secret. A newspaper article explaining how half of America still believed that Weapons of Mass Destruction (WMD) were found in Iraq more than two years after they were *not* found there, explained:

> Experts see a raft of reasons why [people erroneously believe the WMD myth]: a drumbeat of voices from talk radio to die-hard bloggers to the Oval Office, a surprise headline here or there, a rallying around a partisan flag, and a growing need for people, in their own minds, to justify the war in Iraq.[489]

Or, as opinion analyst Steve Krull noted, people tend to become "independent of reality" in these circumstances.[490]

Very few people in our culture consider how they create and order their reality. Nor do they examine the bias or motivation of the sources for their beliefs. Most people simply ingest the never-ending series of messages from public sources, and then build their sense of objective reality from these. And when they find themselves in agreement with a majority of Americans (as seen in the latest poll numbers), any feelings of anxiety are assuaged.

This pervasive sense of a shared reality represents an insidious construction. The 20th-century prophet Thomas Merton said, in discussing this idea of a collective reality:

> The process which Kierkegaard called "leveling" is that by which the individual loses himself in the vast emptiness of a public mind. Because he identifies this abstraction with objective reality, or simply with the "truth," he abdicates his own experience and intuition.[491]

The "public mind" of which Merton speaks grows predominantly out of education, patriotic propaganda, media images and advertising messages.

Realizing this and countering this overwhelming, myopic view of reality, represent two very different things. In terms of how information is received in American culture, context is everything. Regardless of how "true" the truth of a message is, it will have little resonance with the general public unless it is presented in a format to which people are accustomed. If the Moral Ombudsman does not present its message in formats that the public is accustomed to viewing as "important," these ideas will simply be marginalized by those in the mainstream culture (like Duraid Lahham's were), shunted to the Style section of newspapers and ridiculed on TV.

FREEDOM OF INFORMATION

Authorities respect only that of which they are afraid.[492]

There are many strategies in the Machiavellian playbook that can just as well be applied to doing good, as ill. All of them must be considered for the work of the Moral Ombudsman, as the truth is irrelevant unless it can pierce the stolid reality-based (as seen on TV) consciousness of the general public. John P. McCormick noted in *Machiavellian Democracy*:

> If we are to find some semblance of objectivity and love for the common good among anyone in real world politics, it will not be in a collection of the enlightened few advanced by the philosophers ... It will be found, rather, in the body of citizens, empowered to deliberate and decide for themselves.[493]

Knowledge is the empowering tool — and information is that which is guarded so jealously by the elite. In American politics, where the highest form of fraud is obfuscation and lies, and most assassinations take place by word (as opposed to the sword), amplified by the concubine media, it is the dissemination of truth that becomes central to the task of the Moral Ombudsman.

Here, the "body of citizens" becomes empowered to make informed decisions. For as McCormick pointed out, Machiavelli "insists emphatically that it [the people's judgment] is generally superior to that of both princes and oligarchs."[494] What "the people" are lacking, in the American political system, is clear information — exactly the tool that the Moral Ombudsman offers citizens to help make their informed decisions.

And the Moral Ombudsman must overcome the desperate realization of a Duraid Lahham and utilize the Florentine master's ideas to provide the information that will allow America's citizens to draw their educated conclusions.

MACHIAVELLI FOR THE MACHIAVELLIANS

> Under the guise of *The Prince*, it is in fact the people he is addressing. This manifesto which seems to have for its sole interlocutor a future individual, is in fact addressed to the mass of common people ... A manifesto is not written for an individual, especially a non-existent individual. It is always addressed to the masses, in order to organize them into a revolutionary force.[495]

Those who have used Machiavellian methods to attain power will only respond to methods that they recognize: the very same Machiavellian modes that they have mastered. For the activist, however, many of these effective methods for leveraging social energy are considered "tainted" by their association with political operatives, business interests or other groups that moral dissidents find unsavory.

The fact that politicians and businesspersons successfully use money, advertising, war-like and patriotic language, dissemination of ideas through popular culture and the general media, and the frank application of power often compromises those avenues of infiltration for many who work for the common good. The problem with this attitude is that it leaves activists with few options to genuinely affect public discourse, relegating them to flit around the edges of the public square at poetry slams and folkloric protests.

The Moral Ombudsman, on the other hand, will most definitely apply Machiavellian methods to the public square.

Many methods of disseminating ideas and shaping public opinion considered sullied by power are, in fact, the color of water. Slick advertising, using money to produce world-class events, packaging activist ideas in a way that will attract media coverage, massaging language to fit in with the accepted social narrative, co-opting the methods of Madison Avenue, leveraging power — all of these techniques for outreach can be used for the common good just as easily as they are currently being used to destroy the world.

A discussion of Machiavellian political devices shows how they can be turned on their head, and used for the common good. These will become the basis for the outreach work of the Moral Ombudsman. Just as important as developing a moral code by which to judge new legislation, as well as the legislators, the Moral Ombudsman will influence the public square by employing pressuring techniques based on Machiavellian ideas.

What follows is an examination of specific Machiavellian methods that might be utilized by the Moral Ombudsman to influence the public square.

CO-OPTION: ADVERTISING

Far from denouncing and then turning away from existing cultural media, the Moral Ombudsman's outreach arm would infiltrate and co-opt them. There is tremendous possibility built into normative outreach mechanisms. Refusing to utilize these methods merely assures the lack of general impact of the project. The Machiavellian way is to forcibly insert these ideas into mainstream media vectors, thereby achieving far wider dissemination within the general public.

Advertising is a potent method of propagating any message, especially one with activist intent. In our society, there is no system of information distribution more ubiquitous, nor any cultural signifier that more clearly defines our shared reality. It is the one form of media that follows us virtually everywhere — from television to drug store check-out counter to elevator — and which helps delineate the shared reality of the public square.

There is absolutely no reason why this medium cannot be co-opted to influence the public square with a reality that we really *do* need. The more capable the Moral Ombudsman is at infiltrating advertising spaces, the better chance of reaching a general audience, who will be taken by surprise to find something in the medium that offers them a different and deeper perspective, instead of demanding, cajoling, bleating and shilling.

Appropriating the advertising platform with legislative scorecards, press releases, short truthful statements concerning political reality and other messages is not as hard as it might first seem. Funding would always be an issue — and while I will not address that in depth here, I am confident that funding could be provided either institutionally (i.e., if the Moral Ombudsman operated as part of an academic institution) or as a non-profit organization, through foundations such as the Ford Foundation, MacArthur Foundation or others. In any case, the ability to work in public advertising spaces is ultimately bounded only by the creativity of the activists working in the outreach capacity at the organization.

This represents another manner in which the Moral Ombudsman would stand apart from other attempts to insert a moral center into the American political spectrum. Creative thinking about how to disseminate the message would be a primary objective of the NGO. It will not be enough to simply collate the information. Expanding audience for this information will represent half of its purpose.

There are many possibilities for co-opting advertising space to disseminate this material. For example, have you seen those political mailers that crop up around election time? The Moral Ombudsman could produce one of its own — and just different enough so it would catch the eyes of the local voter. How about a series of campaign-like bumper stickers, highlighting the morality or immorality of individual lawmakers? Or taped phone calls, of the sort that the politicians themselves make, with some of these same messages?

Any mass-marketing platform that can reach people with the Moral Ombudsman's message would be utilized. Placards on busses and trains with scores on legislation or legislators; mailers through the door slot; posters exhibited in public spaces normally controlled by the business community; in bathroom stalls, elevators and stairwells; over the airwaves if the price wasn't too steep — any or all of these ideas for reaching into the public square would be appropriate.

CO-OPTION: LANGUAGE

> A prince who wishes to achieve great things must learn to deceive.[496]

Another vital tool for a Machiavellian incursion into the public square is the *lingua franca* of power. People are habituated to ingesting information in the dialect of advertising, politics and the general media. All-too-often, activists steer clear of certain words and even ideas that they feel have been abused by the powerful and greedy, as if the language itself has been degraded by its misuse. The degrading use of language does not affect the words; it only exemplifies the corrupt nature of those utilizing the vocabulary.

This is a fine line to draw. As the Chinese philosopher Chuang Tzu noted: "Words are like waves acted on by the wind; the real point of the matters discussed by them is lost."[497] Even more so when politicians and wordsmiths such as Republican operative Frank Luntz purposefully obfuscate and lie, confident that the media will hew to its own bizarre moral stricture of never calling a lie a lie.

Within the public square, language becomes completely debased. As journalist Mark Colvin noted:

> The way we use language can affect the way we think and act, and that if the misuse of language is pervasive enough, it will infect society itself. George Orwell was one of the first to say this. In his essay "Politics And The English Language", he writes: "Now, it is clear that the decline of a language must ultimately have political and economic causes: it is not due simply to the bad influence of this or that individual writer. But an effect can become a cause, reinforcing the original cause and producing the same effect in an intensified form, and so on indefinitely."[498]

Contemporary linguistic flashpoints such as "security," "God," "faith" and the bellicose vocabulary of war are used to describe everything from sports and business to politics and even fashion. This lexicon of power becomes viewed as tainted, due to its obscenely political usage, and often shunted out of the activist's dictionary because it has been utilized in service to amoral interests.

But this is not the *language's* fault. If one wants to move moral ideas and a genuine bedrock sense of truth into the mainstream, there is no more efficacious method than co-opting the language of power, thereby siphoning off some of the energy, while keeping the intent of the ideas pure.

Politicians use the language of spirituality and love to describe many social experiences, even the most horrific. As has been variously noted throughout this study, they sometimes couch bald-faced thrusts for international power as "patriotism," and wrap God and ultimate purpose together when describing even the basest of human relations, such as war. Although Leo Tolstoy noted: "to combine patriotism and peace is just as impossible as to go for a drive and to stay at home at one and the same time,"[499] politicians have no qualms with doing exactly this. As President George W. Bush said in his 2006 Veteran's Day address:

> On this Veterans Day, we honor a new generation of men and women who are defending our freedom. Since September the 11th, 2001, our Armed Forces have engaged the enemy, the terrorists on many fronts. At this moment, more than 1.4 million Americans are on active duty, serving in the cause of freedom and peace around the world.[500]

This dynamic is widespread and pervasive. For example, as was earlier noted, here is what one of the revered American leaders of the early 21st century, U. S. Senator John McCain (R-AZ) had to say about war: "The loss of every fallen soldier should hurt us lest we ever forget . . . the sublime love of those who sacrifice everything on our behalf."[501]

"Sublime love" is a mystical term. Its use in conjunction with war is sacrilegious. However, far from being called out as a godless blasphemer, Senator McCain is considered an American hero. His use of this terminology only helps to give American war and geopolitical self-interest a patina of spiritual meaning.

If a politician can have the audacity to co-opt the spiritual path, using that language to describe a man or woman whose life was sacrificed to the altar of the State, then surely the Moral Ombudsman might reinvigorate political language by attaching it to humanity's highest ideals. After all, how many morally dubious and even racist politicians have we heard — for their narrow, selfish and partisan purposes — quoting Martin Luther King, Jr., Nelson Mandela and even Gandhi? The Moral Ombudsman will be steeped in the lessons of those who hold power. The office must understand how to reach ever-larger audiences with a positive message of renewal, using the language common to the public square.

There is no reason that the Moral Ombudsman cannot adopt the same vocabulary as those against whom the organization struggles. Words such as "peace," "security," "democracy" and "freedom" — though certainly tainted by their misuse under George W. Bush and many other political leaders — stand for humanity's highest human ideals, regardless of how the language and concepts have been despoiled.

There is no reason that the Moral Ombudsman cannot express faith in God. Spiritual belief is neither more nor less respectable than atheism or secular humanism, and the majority of leaders on the board of the organization will certainly be faith-based thinkers. God is not an evil force. The way in which "God" has been co-opted for partisan and nationalistic purposes is.

To make the rulings more palatable to the press and the public, the propagandistic vocabulary of power can be turned on its head. Universal health care may be couched as a bio-defense mechanism, using examples of how it will stem vicious pathogens from running amok through middle class society; anti-torture initiatives can be wrapped with words like "muscular" and "unforgiving," and engaging with our enemies in a non-combative manner as the basis of a moral international relations may be presented as a "security measure."

One example of how language can be co-opted for the common good, instead of emptied of all moral content, comes from my own history as an activist. As the founding producer of the *Amnesty International Human Rights Art Festival*, I opened a weekend long series of art/activist events with the following speech:

> I would like to thank the political speakers this afternoon, who are here representing our honorary committee of local and national political leaders. This coming together of political leaders with advocacy artists highlights what Amnesty International represents, and what these artists are fighting for in Amnesty's name, something squarely at the heart of the American dream: human rights and justice for all. These universal values are enshrined in the Constitution of the United States of America.[502]

Co-opting the language of our conservative wing, I went on to state that these artists were "strict Constitutionalists," fighting for the most fundamental values elucidated in that document. Additionally, by highlighting the political leaders' involvement, I brought the purpose of the Art Festival — its ideals as well the activist-art presentation— directly into the mainstream of our social world.

This opening ceremony was carried live on local television, due in great part to the politicians' participation, offering an example of not only using the current language of power to fight for justice, but also how to redirect political energy in the struggle for the common good.

This may represent but a small example of how infiltrative language and popularly respected liaisons might better help diffuse an activist message, but it allows us to imagine how the Moral Ombudsman might work with the powers that be, and utilize their language, to subtly shift perceptions of them and change the power dynamics in our country.

Co-Option: Leveraging Power

> Since men love at their own pleasure and fear at the prince's pleasure, a wise prince must base himself upon that which is his, not upon that which is other men's.[503]

It is not just the language of power that will help disseminate the Moral Ombudsman's message, but the organization's relationship with politicians and other social leaders. These liaisons helped raise an activist art festival out of the realm of culture, and into the center of the social realm. The opening ceremonies were covered live due to the participation of these socially respected figures, not because of the art.

The Moral Ombudsman must utilize the same approach, going beyond simply speaking the language of power, to learning the application of force. During the *Amnesty International Human Rights Art Festival*, the inclusion of politicians, what they stand for (power) and the media and popular interest they brought with them was, frankly put, an exercise in co-option. Subtle, non-aggressive and infiltrative though it may have been, it was still a representation of how the Moral Ombudsman must think of power, and how to leverage it.

This signifies an uncomfortable aspect of a successful activist project, as activists are usually working against the temporally strong. Utilizing this energy might feel unsavory. In exercising its might, the Moral Ombudsman will find itself in direct confrontation with people who arrogantly wield their authority. There absolutely will be pushback, especially if the Moral Ombudsman is able to garner media and public interest and have an effect on the political discourse.

At the same time, however, the Moral Ombudsman must make what alliances it can in the political, business and religious worlds. These social leaders will add a popular culture *gravitas* to its positions and message. It must then use these associations to influence events.

Although representing the most delicate dance of many that the organization must undertake, the Moral Ombudsman must develop liaisons with political and business interests and, through these relationships, develop social relevance and power. There are many like-minded and dedicated political voices in the American panorama, but they are almost always ridiculed and shunted to the margins of the public square. Al Gore, with his focus on the environment, Jimmy Carter with elections, Dennis Kucinich with a focus on economic fairness and a host of other voices would undoubtedly find the project highly interesting, and be willing to add their weight and leverage to its goals. Although individually, these voices can be marginalized, when brought together with the unassailable work of the Moral Ombudsman, their political and social importance would increase.

Additionally — though certainly counter-intuitively — the Moral Ombudsman might engage business interests. Of course, in working with these public actors, the business must see some effective, corporate gain from the liaison. And they will. For instance, the Moral Ombudsman could argue that the relationship would allow the businesses to increase their customer base (just note how enterprises from Wal-Mart to Apple are scrambling to be viewed as "green," or offering living wages in far-off countries from Guatemala to China).

By working with or donating funds to the Moral Ombudsman, these businesses will be burnishing their own credentials. The Moral Ombudsman cannot turn its back on "win-win" relationships with politicians and businesses often viewed by activists as the enemy. The work of the group will take place through infiltration.

Granted, this power of association must be leveraged very judiciously. The Moral Ombudsman must never be seen as itself being co-opted, in the way that so many other respectable organizations and public figures can be. If funding is received from a Wal-Mart or Target, the decisions issued must never be tainted by this relationship. The non-profit group must always be prepared to lose the funding rather than shade or change decisions on the morality of certain behavior. A difficult stance to take (money is always central to any activity in the United States), but nonetheless, a line that must never be crossed.

CO-OPTION: HISTORY

> He who controls the present, controls the past. He who controls the past, controls the future.[504]

History is written by and for the victors. The accepted narrative of the past is simply a patchwork quilt of half-truths and important omissions stretching back into a country, ethnicity or religious path's past, defining a supposed shared legacy. This story is then parroted in history books and the contemporary media, adding to the smothering effect of generally accepted opinion and objective reality, the hobgoblin against with the truth must struggle.

In the United States, for instance, little connection is made between the ongoing apartheid suffered by Native Americans and the reviled 20th-century South African apartheid. Our narrative is one of Divine Right and Manifest Destiny, a slaughter of savages (called Amalekites and Canaanites at the time of the mass murder in the 16th-18th centuries) in the name of God and country. America, as we are told over and over again, was founded on the inalienable privileges of human rights and justice for all. The fact that the majority of America's Founding Fathers owned slaves and supported the genocide of Native Americans does not seep into the public consciousness.

History is so fungible that it is even rewritten in real time. When America's brave fighting men and women tortured human beings throughout the Iraq War (2003–2008), including waterboarding the unfortunate Khalid Sheikh Mohammed 183 times in one month,[505] it was because "they" deserved it. As late as 2010, former President George W. Bush stated: "Yeah, we waterboarded Khalid Sheikh Mohammed. I'd do it again to save lives."[506] When "they" torture "us," however, it only proves what inhuman monsters they are, and how much they deserve to be tortured.

The narrative of the State is reminiscent more of propaganda than a dispassionate, academic view of the past. There are sundry abandoned truths and forgotten histories that are central to the struggle for human rights and justice. It would be the job of the Moral Ombudsman to excavate these from the past, to help contextualize the contemporary struggle for the common good within the framework of the historical fight for fairness. Additionally, it would help set the work of the Moral Ombudsman within a historical structure. To do this history must be reclaimed.

These recovered histories — domestic, international or ancient — would become one important aspect of the work of the Center. They might be issued to counteract contemporary news stories; to situate activist endeavors within their historical context; or even to show how America once held very different ideals, much more committed to the common good than those of today's oligarchy.

For instance, the Socialist Party of America was an important political force for years. In the first decades of the 20th century, it drew significant support from many different groups, including trade unionists, progressive social reformers, populist farmers and immigrant communities. Its presidential candidate, Eugene V. Debs, ran for president five times, twice winning more than 900,000 votes (in 1912 and 1920), while the party also elected two United States Representatives, dozens of state legislators, more than a hundred mayors, and countless lesser officials.[507] American heroine Helen

Keller was an active member of this Socialist Party. How large a part of our national narrative is this story?

These histories would allow the Moral Ombudsman to "be able to take a long-term view, informed by sustained monitoring, of the costs and benefits of different [political and social] overtures."[508] Part of this "long-term view" would involve the reclaiming of history from the oligarchs, and setting the work of the Moral Ombudsman into a wider context of the people's struggle against the wealthy and powerful, both domestically and throughout world history.

The work might begin by simply unearthing past histories at odds with a contemporary narrative, progressive stories such as that of the vibrant American Socialist Party, or negative ones, like the fact that over half of the signers of the Declaration of Independence owned slaves at sometime in their life.[509] These can offer manners for inserting a question mark into the view of objective reality proposed in the public square, as well as reframing contemporary issues.

There might be an office within the Moral Ombudsman charged with just this — setting labor rights struggles, civil rights, human rights, the rights of new immigrants such as Muslim, Arab and Latinos within a historical framing, comparing them to how these groups (labor activists; new immigrants) fared 50, 100 and even 200 years ago. For instance, did you know that in 1855, Connecticut adopted the nation's first literacy test for voting? Massachusetts followed suit in 1857. The tests were implemented to discriminate against Irish-Catholic immigrants. How many of the descendants of these original immigrants are fighting for the rights of their brown and black brethren?

Unearthing these histories would greatly deepen the conversation around these issues, and fight against the mindless, sound-bit demagoguery of politicians, so often parroted by the lazy and exhausted media.

This reclamation of times past would help insert a moral center into the American public square by showing how historically human rights defenders struggled against the temporally powerful and spiritually bereft of their own time. And how the fight to reclaim their histories echoes the ongoing fight for a moral center today.

Additionally, history can evince how contemporary enmities are simply political fictions, sometimes running contrary to the real history between two people, be they Christians and Muslims or Jews and African Americans. Exhumed stories of past cooperation between contemporary enemies can become the building blocks of a new consciousness, re-conceiving the past to include the new narrative. I undertook just such a study with my counter-narrative book *Shalom/Salaam: A Story of a Mystical Fraternity*, which unearthed the virtually unknown story of a Jewish–Muslim spiritual connection going back to the founding of Islam.

In addition to expanding the understanding of the present through these investigations, it is vital that history be mined for precedents of morally based politics. These past examples can become the basis for a contemporary viewpoint. To highlight past morally based social and political actors, the Moral Ombudsman could branch out into other methods for raising awareness.

For example, the Moral Ombudsman might partner with artists, writers and other creators to emphasize the work of such Americans as Cesar Chavez, Emma Goldman, Thomas Merton, Abraham Heschel and the aforementioned Eugene Debs. They might make trading cards of forgotten heroes (numbered "1-52" most vaunted Americans), agitate for national holidays, get (nay, force) politicians to sponsor resolutions, hold belated birthday parties with invited media, create cartoon super-hero action figures and use other popular culture means of distribution, only this time for people and history embodying the ideals of the Moral Ombudsman.

Here is where the Moral Ombudsman separates itself from other activist enterprises: using creative methods to highlight its message, as well as mastering the media culture. Americans order their reality through what they read in the media, and the Moral Ombudsman would utilize numerous methods for accessing this outlet with its message.

THE MEDIA

Despite the Framers belief that a free press operating within a literate society could safeguard the rights of the citizens, what they didn't envision was the way in which a small collection of moneyed citizens could monopolize the flow of information, narrowing and twisting the vision of the citizens, and bending the political spectrum to their greedy whims. As was noted earlier, in the quotes by Republican pollster and wordsmith Frank Luntz, controlling media space and the language presented therein helps control the minds of the population.

The media can oftentimes appear to be little more than a tool of the oligarchy — even more so, since many of the main outlets are owned by vastly wealthy individuals with clear partisan agendas. As the media watchdog "Free Press" noted:

> Massive corporations dominate the U.S. media landscape. Through a history of mergers and acquisitions, these companies have concentrated their control over what we see, hear and read. In many cases, these companies are vertically integrated, controlling everything from initial production to final distribution.[510]

However that may be, the media represents the most important field in which the Moral Ombudsman must play. It is here that reality is shaped, and generally accepted opinion forms. And despite the media's feckless nature, their desire to conflate objectivity (a midpoint between two political opinions) with truth and their general laziness (the Journalist's Toolbox[511] lists various "experts" that can be accessed online, to provide quotes on a variety of subjects; what is not noted, however, is that many of these experts are self-appointed and are not vetted by any controlling authority), it still provides the surest method of reaching into the public square with a message. And to its credit, the media is as easily accessed and even manipulated by those seeking to work toward the common good as by the guardians of the status quo.

Because wealthy and powerful interests have successfully manipulated the media, those working for the common good often have looked with suspicion at it, sometimes rightfully considering the media a partisan to the narrow forces of the American oligarchy. However, the media simply follows the news — and the Moral Ombudsman, with its understanding of the media culture, will do its best to make and provide impetus for them to follow.

Thomas Merton pointed out both the intransigence of the contemporary, amoral worldview, as well as the possibility inherent in accessing the media by the Moral Ombudsman, when he stated: "The current moral climate is one of more or less resigned compliance with the worldviews popularized by the mass media."[512] What the Moral Ombudsman would realize and act upon, would be that the "worldview popularized by the mass media" can be infiltrated, using the metrics to which it is accustomed.

The Center would tweet its information, issue scorecards and press releases, partner with activist artists to collapse their ongoing process of education (which the media will not cover) into an event (which they will cover), seed websites such as "Find an Expert" with their own authorities, partner with other like-minded organizations, boil down their information into the easily digested sound-bites to which journalists are accustomed and utilize all other means of making their information relevant and easy for those gatekeepers to objective reality.

It's a War

> A leader must not have any objective, nor any thought, nor take up any other art other than the art of war . . . because it is the only art that pertains to him who leads.[513]

Make no mistake about it: the Moral Ombudsman would be embarking on a war for the soul of America. This is not to say that the organization will take up arms, or that their methods will be violent. But the language, determination and even some of the methods must be that of the steeliest fighter. Machiavelli noted:

> All armed prophets won and the unarmed came to ruin. Because beyond the things said, the nature of people is variable: it is easy to persuade them of something, but it is difficult to fix them in that persuasion.[514]

There have been only a small handful of revolutions based in the spirit in which the prophetic leader fought the battle with a warrior's will and a non-violent army. Gandhi in India, Martin Luther King Jr. in the United States and Nelson Mandela[515] in South Africa were all prophets leading non-violent armies, and all affected lasting change. More recently, the Facebook generation in Cairo and Tunisia, and the steely will of Aung San Suu Kyi toppled dictatorial governments using social media and non-violent means.

The war gear for the Moral Ombudsman has been outlined above, taken directly from Machiavelli's playbook of power. These are not cruel methods, or even immoral. What they are is time-tested methods for winning battles, be they battles of the field or of the spirit. Becoming a soldier in a political revolution is not for the weak at heart. It can be uncomfortable, demanding, humiliating and at times even personally injurious.

A prophetic leader must be focused only on two things: truth and the goal of the project. Members of the Center must not feel the compulsion to ask permission, or worry about offending either their own friends or those indifferent to the goal of the endeavor: to insert a moral center into the American politics. The Moral Ombudsman must be prepared to engage the powerful as both allies — in terms of partners of a project — or enemies, as the Moral Ombudsman marshals support to fight to change public actors driven by selfish or indifferent motivations.

It may be, in the end, that this task is simply not possible; that the sad reality of our public square makes an undertaking such as the Moral Ombudsman little more than folly.

But we won't know unless we attempt it. And given how things are going, we can't afford *not* to try.

ENDNOTES

1   Codevilla, Angelo. "Introduction." (Machiavelli, Niccolò. *The Prince.* Angelo M. Codevilla, translator). (New Haven and on: Yale University Press, 1997), p. xvi.

2   *Merriam-Webster Dictionary*, www.merriam-webster.com.

3   Machiavelli, Niccolò. *Discourses on the First Ten Books of Titus Livius* (Christian E. Detmold, translator). (New York: Random House, 1950), p. 216.

4   Jaffe, Greg. "The World is Safer, but No One will Say So." *Washington Post* (November 4, 2012), p. B1, B5.

5   Mansfield, Harvey. *Machiavelli's Virtue* (Chicago and London: University of Chicago Press, 1998), p. 55.

6   Machiavelli, Niccolò. *Discourses on the First Ten Books of Titus*, p. 117.

7   Grendler, Paul F. *The European Renaissance in American Life.* (Westport, CT: Praeger, 2006), p. 149.

8   Found at various places in the public domain.

9   Strauss, Leo. *Thoughts on Machiavelli.* (Chicago and London: The University of Chicago Press, 1978), p. 26.

10 Grendler, Paul F. *The European Renaissance in American Life*, p. 188.

11 Ibid. pp. 160-161.

12 Weil, Simone. *Simone Weil Reader* . (Wakefield, RI & London: Moyer Bell, 1977), p. 270.

13 Gregg, Richard. *The Power of Nonviolence.* (Canton, ME: Greenleaf Books, 1935), p. 112.

14 Information about the amygdala from *Science Daily*. "Science Reference: Amygdala," http://www.sciencedaily.com.

15 Machiavelli, Niccolò. *The Prince* (Angelo Codevilla, translator). (New Haven and London: Yale University Press, 1997), p. 64.

16 Quoted in Ibid. p. 102.

17 Rumi, Jallaludin. *Signs of the Unseen* (W. M. Thackston, Jr., translator). (Boston and London: Shambhala, 1999), pp. 79-80.

18 Machiavelli, Niccolò. *The Prince*, p. 65.

19 Mencius quoted in Catlin, George. *The Story of the Political Philosophers.* (New York: Tudor Publishing, 1939), p. 22.

20 Grendler, Paul F. *The European Renaissance in American Life*, pp. 194, 195, 196.

21 Ibid. p. 197.

22 Schwartz, Casey. "Science: The Age of Immorality." *Newsweek Magazine* (January 16, 2012), www.thedailybeast.com/newsweek.

23 Rumi, Jalaluddin. *Signs of the* Unseen, p. 220.

24 Lao Tzu. *The Tao Te Ching* (Stephen Mitchell, translator). (New York: HarperCollins, 1988), p. 72.

25 Sennholz, Hans F. "Machiavellian Politics." *The Freeman of the Foundation for Economic Education* (February 1996, Volume 46, Issue 2), www.thefreemanonline.org.

26 Kanai, Ryota; Felldon, Tom; Firth, Colin and Rees, Geraint. "Political Orientations Are Correlated with Brain Structure in Young Adults." *Current Biology* (Volume 21, Issue 8, April 7, 2011), pp. 677-680.

27 A social philosophy that promotes the maintenance of traditional institutions and supports, at the most, minimal and gradual change in society

28 Schaffhausen, Joanna. "The Biological Basis of Aggression." *Brain Connection.* www.brainconnection.positscience.com.

29 Kattalia, Kathryn. "The liberal brain? Scans show liberals and conservatives have different brain structures." *New York Daily News* (April 8, 2011), www.articles.nydailynews.com.

30 Jost, John T. and Amodio, David M. "Political ideology as motivated social cognition: Behavioral and neuroscientific evidence." *Motivation and Emotion* (Volume 36, Number 1, 2012), p. 55.

31 Jaffe, Greg. "The World is Safer, but No One will Say So," *Washington Post* (November 4, 2012), p. B1.

32 Gabriel, Trip. "Ryan Says Obama Policies Threaten 'Judeo-Christian' Values." *New York Times: The Caucus* (November 5, 2012), www.nytimes.com.

33 Fischer, Markus. "Machiavelli's Rapacious Republicanism." (*Machiavelli's Liberal Republican Legacy*, Paul A. Rahe, Editor. Cambridge, England: Cambridge University Press, 2006), p. li.

34 Bush, George W. "President Bush Delivers Remarks on the Protect America Act." *Washington Post* (February 13, 2008), /www.washingtonpost.com.

35 Rumi, Jalalludin. *Signs of the Unseen*, p. 60.

36 Mansfield, Harvey. *Machiavelli's Virtue*, p. 278.

37 Rettig, Jessica. "Fewer Americans See Climate Change a Threat, Caused by Humans." *US News and World Report* (August 26, 2011), www.usnews.com.

38 The Staff. "Hank Williams Jr: President Obama is a 'Muslim president who hates the US'." *The Capitol Column* (August 21, 2012), www.capitolcolumn. com.

39 Froomkin, Dan. "Yes, Iraq Definitely Had WMD, Vast Majority Of Polled Republicans Insist." *Huffington Post* (June 21, 2012), www.huffingtonpost. com.

40 Quoted in Shah, Idris. *The Way of the Sufis* (London: Penguin Books, 1991), p. 63.

41 Quoted in Achenbach, Joel. "Certificate Unlikely to Appease 'Birthers.'" *Washington Post* (April 28, 2011), p. A6.

42 Weil, Simone. *Simone Weil Reader*, p. 470.

43 Grendler, Paul F. *The European Renaissance in American Life*, p. 149.

44 Rumi, Jallaludin. *Signs of the Unseen*, p. 80.

45 Grohol, John M. "Brains of Liberals, Conservatives May Work Differently," www.psychcentral.com.

46 Confucius. *The Analects* (Arthur Waley, translator). (New York: HarperCollins, 1992), p. 169.

47 Shems-i Tabrizi. *Me and Rumi* (William C. Chittick, translator). (Louisville, KY: Fons Vitae, 2004), p. 216.

48 Rumi, Jallaludin. *Signs of the Unseen*, p. 184.

49 Aurelius, Marcus. *Meditations* (New York: Random House, 2003), p. 117.

50 Beckel, Bob and Thomas, Cal. "Would they lie to you? Umm, yes." *USA Today* (June 2, 2010), www.usatoday.com.

51 Merton, Thomas. *Mystics and Zen Masters* (New York: Farrar, Straus, Giroux, 1967), pp. 263-264.

52 Glanzberg, Michael. "Truth." *The Stanford Encyclopedia of Philosophy* (Edward N. Zalta, editor). (Spring 2009 Edition), www.plato.stanford.edu.

53 Kinsley, Michael. "Commentary: The Gaffer Speaks." *The Times* (U.K.) (April 23, 1988), www.thetimes.co.uk.

54 Weil, Simone. *Simone Weil Reader*, p. 278.

55 Ibid. p. 394.

56 Buber, Martin. *Tales of the Hasidim I* (New York: Schocken Books, 1991), p. 71.

57 Machiavelli, Niccolò. *The Prince*, p. 67.

58 Machiavelli, Niccolò. *Discourses on the First Ten Books of Titus Livius*, p. 182.

59 Weil, Simone. *Oppression and Liberty* (New York: Routledge, 2001), p. 114.

60 Nederman, Cary, "Niccolò Machiavelli." *The Stanford Encyclopedia of Philosophy* (Edward N. Zalta editor). (Fall 2009 Edition): www.plato. stanford.edu.

61 *The New Yorker* (November 26, 2012), p. 43.

62 Lord, Carnes. "Machiavelli's Realism" (Machiavelli, Niccolò. *The Prince*, Angelo M. Codevilla, translator. New Haven and London: Yale University Press, 1997), p. 115.

63 Lerner, Max. "Introduction." (Machiavelli, Niccolo. *The Prince and the Discourses on the First Ten Books of Titus Livius*, Luigi Ricci, translator. New York: Modern Library, 1950), p. xxviii.

64 Lerner, Max. "Introduction," p. xxviii.

65 Kaplan, Joshua. "Political Theory: The Classic Texts and their Continuing Relevance." *The Modern Scholar* (14 lectures in the series; lecture #7, 2005), disc 4.

66 Lerner, Max. "Introduction," pp. xliii-xliv.

67 Allen, William B. "Machiavelli and Modernity." (Machiavelli, Niccolo. *The Prince*. Angelo M. Codevilla, translator. New Haven and London: Yale University Press, 1997), p. 101.

68 Codevilla, Angelo. "Introduction," p. vii.

69 Machiavelli, Niccolò. *The Prince*, p. 57.

70 Sloan, John. "Machiavelli on War." *Xenophon Group International*, www.xenophon-mil.org.

71 Lord, Carnes. "Machiavelli's Realism," p. 117.

72 Quoted in Merton, Thomas. *On Peace*. (New York: The McCall Publishing Company, 1971), p. 49.

73 Mansfield, Harvey C. *Machiavelli's Virtue*, p. 191.

74 Codevilla, Angelo. "Introduction," p. viii.

75 Lerner, Max. "Introduction," p. xxxviii.

76 Information in the paragraph from the "Banned Books Project." *National University of Ireland, Irish Centre for Human Rights* (Galway), www.nuigalway.ie.

77 Grendler, Paul F. *The European Renaissance in American Life.*, pp. 151-152.

78 Lynch, Christopher. "Introduction." *The Art of War* (Christopher Lynch, translator. Chicago: University of Chicago Press, 2003), p. xiv.

79 Allen, William B. "Machiavelli and Modernity," p. 112.

80 Forde, Steven. "Benjamin Franklin's 'Machiavellian' Civic Virtue." *Machiavelli's Liberal Republican Legacy* (Paul A. Rahe, Editor). (Cambridge, England: Cambridge University Press, 2006), p. 148.

81 Machiavelli, Niccolò. *Discourses on the First Ten Books of Titus Livius*, p. 117.

82 Carrese, Paul. "The Machiavellian Spirit of Montesquieu's Liberal Republic." *Machiavelli's Liberal Republican Legacy* (Paul A. Rahe, Editor). (Cambridge, England: Cambridge University Press, 2006), p. 125.

83 Machiavelli, Niccolò. *The Prince*, p. 65.

84 Machiavelli, Niccolò. *Discourses on the First Ten Books of Titus Livius*, p. 139.

85 Ibid. pp. 139-139.

86 Quote and information in previous paragraph from Ledeen Michael. *Machiavelli on Modern Leadership: Why Machiavelli's Iron Rules are as Timely*

    and Important Today as Five Centuries Ago (New York: Truman Talley Books, 1999), pp. 92-93.

87 Mansfield, Harvey. *Machiavelli's Virtue*, p. 17.

88 Fischer, Markus. "Machiavelli's Rapacious Republicanism," p. xliv.

89 Strauss, Leo. *Thoughts on Machiavelli*, p. 269.

90 Pocock, J. G. A. *The Machiavellian Moment*. (Princeton, NJ and Oxford: Princeton University Press, 2003), p. 157.

91 Mansfield, Harvey. *Machiavelli's Virtue*, p. 50.

92 Rahe, Paul. "Machiavelli's Liberal Republican Legacy." (Paul A. Rahe, Editor. *Machiavelli's Liberal Republican Legacy*.) (Cambridge, England: Cambridge University Press, 2006), p. xxii.

93 Machiavelli, Niccolò. *The Prince*, p. 54.

94 Mansfield, Harvey. *Machiavelli's Virtue*, pp. 188-189.

95 Machiavelli, Niccolò. *The Prince*, p. 67.

96 Ibid. p. 66.

97 Ibid. p. 66.

98 Machiavelli, Niccolò. *Discourses on the First Ten Books of Titus Livius*, p. 147.

99 Merton, Thomas. *On Peace*, p. 246.

100 Allen, William B. "Machiavelli and Modernity," pp. 103-104.

101 Mansfield, Harvey. *Machiavelli's Virtue*, p. 45.

102 Bireley, Robert. *The Counter Reformation Prince*. (Raleigh, N.C.: University of North Carolina Press, 1990), p. 15.

103 Mulier, Eco Haitsma. "A Controversial Republican: Dutch Views of Machiavelli in the 17th and 18th Centuries." (*Machiavelli and Republicanism*. G. Bock, Q. Skinner and M. Viroli, editors. Cambridge, England: Cambridge University Press, 1993), p. 248.

104 Bireley, Robert. *The Counter Reformation Prince*, p. 17.

105 Worden, Blair. "Milton's republicanism and the Tyranny of Heaven." (*Machiavelli and Republicanism*. G. Bock, Q. Skinner and M. Viroli, editors. Cambridge, England: Cambridge University Press, 1993), p. 225.

106 Althusser, Louis. *Machiavelli and Us*. (London & New York: Verso, 1999), p. 9.

107 Ibid. p. 13.

108 Information in the paragraph from the "Banned Books Project," www. nuigalway.ie.

109 Barnett, Vincent. "Niccolò Machiavelli — the Cunning Critic of Political Reason." *History Today* (November 28 2006), www.historytoday.com.

110 Londono, Ernesto. "Brotherhood Candidate Wages Underdog Campaign in Egypt." *Washington Post* (May 17, 2012), p. A8.

111 Danford, John W. "Getting our Bearings: Machiavelli and Hume." *Machiavelli's Liberal Republican Legacy* (Paul A. Rahe, Editor). (Cambridge, England: Cambridge University Press, 2006), p. 116.

112 Thompson, C. Bradley. "John Adams Machiavellian Moment." (Paul A. Rahe, Editor. *Machiavelli's Liberal Republican Legacy*.) (Cambridge, England:

Cambridge University Press, 2006), p. 200.

113 Carrese, Paul. "The Machiavellian Spirit of Montesquieu's Liberal Republic," p. 140.

114 Ibid. p. 140.

115 Ledeen Michael. *Machiavelli on Modern Leadership: Why Machiavelli's Iron Rules are as Timely and Important Today as Five Centuries Ago*, p. 109.

116 Forde, Steven. "Benjamin Franklin's 'Machiavellian' Civic Virtue," p. 147.

117 Information concerning George Washington's Machiavellian moments taken from Spalding, Matthew. ""The American Prince?" *Machiavelli's Liberal Republican Legacy* (Paul A. Rahe, Editor). (Cambridge, England: Cambridge University Press, 2006), p. 171.

118 Mansfield, Harvey. *Machiavelli's Virtue*, p. 17.

119 Ledeen Michael. *Machiavelli on Modern Leadership: Why Machiavelli's Iron Rules are as Timely and Important Today as Five Centuries Ago*, p. 126.

120 Machiavelli, Niccolò. *The Prince*, pp. 18-19.

121 Quoted in Chomsky, Noam. "Modern-Day American Imperialism: Middle East and Beyond." *Boston University Lecture* (April 24, 2008), www.chomsky.info.

122 Rahe, Paul. "Thomas Jefferson's Machiavellian Political Science." *Machiavelli's Liberal Republican Legacy* (Paul A. Rahe, Editor). (Cambridge, England: Cambridge University Press, 2006), p. 209.

123 Ibid. p. 217.

124 Ibid. p. 214

125 Pocock, J. G. A. *The Machiavellian Moment.*, p. 211.

126 Rahe, Paul. "Thomas Jefferson's Machiavellian Political Science," pp. 214, 221.

127 Quote and information in previous paragraph from Thompson, C. Bradley. "John Adam's Machiavellian Moment," pp. 194, 201.

128 Rahe, Paul. "Machiavelli's Liberal Republican Legacy," p. xxviii.

129 Thompson, C. Bradley. "John Adam's Machiavellian Moment," p.190.

130 Information, quote and some language in this paragraph from Rosen, Gary. "James Madison's Princes and Peoples." *Machiavelli's Liberal Republican Legacy* (Paul A. Rahe, Editor). (Cambridge, England: Cambridge University Press, 2006), pp. 229-230.

131 Ibid. p. 237.

132 Walling, Karl-Friedrich. "Was Alexander Hamilton a Machiavellian Statesman?" *Machiavelli's Liberal Republican Legacy* (Paul A. Rahe, Editor). (Cambridge, England: Cambridge University Press, 2006), p. 255.

133 Lamberton, John. *American Machiavelli: Alexander Hamilton and the Origins of U.S. Foreign Policy*. (Cambridge, England: Cambridge University Press, 2004), pp. 271-272.

134 Mansfield, Harvey. *Machiavelli's Virtue*, p. 298.

135 The Economist. "Niccolò Machiavelli: Founding Father." *The Economist*

(May 3, 2007), www.economist.com.

136 Jewell, Jim. "Machiavelli Reigns: Dirty campaigns beg the question: 'Is everything fair game in American politics?'" *Rooftop* (November 8, 2010), www.therooftopblog.wordpress.com.

137 Ledeen Michael. *Machiavelli on Modern Leadership: Why Machiavelli's Iron Rules are as Timely and Important Today as Five Centuries Ago*, p. 158.

138 Ibid. pp. 185-186.

139 Machiavelli, Niccolò. *Discourses on the First Ten Books of Titus Livius*, p. 139.

140 Grendler, Paul F. *The European Renaissance in American Life*, p. 168.

141 Strauss, Leo. *Thoughts on Machiavelli*, p. 13.

142 Redstone, Julia. "The Language of War." *World Watch* (September 24, 2001), www.lightomega.org.

143 Lane, Charles. "No More 'War.'" *Washington Post* (March 13, 2012), p. A15.

144 Editors. "The War President." *Mother Jones* (May/June 2012), p. 8.

145 Ibid. p. 8.

146 Lane, Charles. "No More 'War,'" A15.

147 Weil, Simone. *The Simone Weil Reader*, p. 308.

148 Information and quote in this paragraph from McCrummen, Stephanie. "Gingrich Delivers 'Wild and Woolly.'" *Washington Post* (January 30, 2012), p. A1, 7.

149 Marinucci, Carla. "Jerry Brown's applies 'Art of War' to new tenure." *San Francisco Chronicle* (March 11, 2001), www.sfgate.com.

150 Eskow, Richard. "2011: The Year of Resistance to Conservatism's 'War of the Words.'" *Huffington Post* (December 31, 2011), www.huffingtonpost.com.

151 Schaub, Diana. "Machiavelli's Realism." *The National Interest* (Fall 1998), www.findarticles.com.

152 Quoted in Ibid.

153 Clement of Alexandria. *The One Who Knows God* (William Wilson, Translator). (Tyler Texas: Scroll Publishing, 1990), p. 119.

154 Machiavelli, Niccolò. *The Prince*, p. 22.

155 Lane, Charles. "No More 'War,'" p. A15.

156 www.luntzglobal.com.

157 Luntz, Frank. "Interview: Frank Luntz." *Frontline* (November 9, 2004), www.pbs.org.

158 Information on Luntz and Orwell, as well as quote from Gross, Terry. "Frank Luntz Explains 'Words That Work.'" *Terry Gross Show* (January 9, 2007), www.npr.org.

159 Rucker, Philip. "Romney Team Tries to Make Pitch-Perfect Ads." *Washington Post* (August 24, 2012), p. A1.

160 Urban, Hugh B. "Machiavelli meets the religious right: Michael Ledeen, the neoconservatives, and the political uses of fundamentalism." *Journal of Ecumenical Studies* 2007 42(1), p. 78.

161 Mansfield, Harvey. *Machiavelli's Virtue*, p. 27.

162 Ledeen Michael. *Machiavelli on Modern Leadership: Why Machiavelli's Iron Rules are as Timely and Important Today as Five Centuries Ago*, p. 117.

163 Priest, Dana. "From an ex-CIA Official, a blunt defense of Harsh Interrogation." *Washington Post* (April 25, 2012), pp. C1, 9.

164 CNN Political Unit. "CNN Poll: George W. Bush only living ex-president under 50%." (June 7, 2012), www.cnn.com.

165 McCain, John. "Eulogy for Pat Tillman." (May 3, 2004): www.mccain. senate.gov.

166 Tolstoy, Leo. *On Civil Disobedience and Non-Violence*. (New York: Bergman Publishers, 1967), p. 75.

167 Machiavelli, Niccolò. *Discourses on the First Ten Books of Titus Livius*, p. 182.

168 Strauss, Leo. *Thoughts on Machiavelli*, p. 189.

169 Kamen, Al. "George W. Bush and the G-Word." *Washington Post* (October 14, 2005), www.washingtonpost.com.

170 Lewis, Neal. "Red Cross Finds Detainee Abuse in Guantanamo." *New York Times*, (November 20, 2004), p. A1, A14.

171 Spencer, Nick. "Machiavelli's The Prince, part 8: a lingering love of justice." *Guardian, U.K.* (May 14, 2012), www.guardian.co.uk.

172 Quoted in Waters, David. "On Faith: Examining McCain's God and Country." *Washington Post* (October 7, 2008), www.washingtonpost.com.

173 Smith, Eric Drummond. "Machiavellian and Hobbesian Concepts of Power and Its Relationship to Politics." *Smith's Blue Book*, www.smithsbluebook. com.

174 Varela, Felix. *Letters to Elpidio* (New York: Paulist Press, 1989), p. 43.

175 Mansfield, Harvey. *Machiavelli's Virtue*, p. 164.

176 Metzler, Rebekah. "Mitt Romney Ramps Up Right-leaning Rhetoric." *US News and World Report* (July 19, 2012), www.usnews.com.

177 Balta, Victor. "Commentary: Obama doesn't hate America, conservatives hate American workers." *The Current* (July 19, 2012), www.current.com.

178 Marcus, Lloyd. "Evil Democrat Paradigms." *The American Thinker* (September 10, 2010), www.americanthinker.com.

179 Pull-out quote and this quote from Stoeltje, Melissa Fletcher. "'God and Country' service features faith, patriotism, political hopefuls." *San Antonio Express-News* (May 27, 2012), www.mysanantonio.com.

180 Miller, Lisa. "One Nation Under God." *Newsweek Magazine* (December 9, 2010), www.thedailybeast.com/newsweek.

181 Tashman, Brian. "God Tells Robertson that 'Radical' Obama will Bring Down America." *Right Wing Watch* (January 3, 2012), www.rightwingwatch.org.

182 Cannon, Carl. "Patriot Games." *Real Clear Politics* (July 13, 2012), www. realclearpolitics.com.

183 Downing, Brian. "Fundamentalism at the US's corps." *Asia Times* (May 15, 2012), www.atimes.com.

184 Carlson, Peter. "Max Cleland: Political Veteran." *Washington Post* (July 3, 2003), pp. C1, C4.

185 Orwell, George. "Politics and the English Language." (in the public domain)

186 Pocock, J. G. A. *The Machiavellian Moment.*, p. 196.

187 Strauss, Leo. *Thoughts on Machiavelli*, p. 274.

188 Schuster, M.A.; Franke, T.M.; Bastian, A.M.; Sor, S; Halfon, N. "Firearm storage patterns in US homes with children." *American Journal of Public Health* (2000: 90), p. 588– 594.

189 Hamby, Peter. "Romney courts gun owners and pivots to general election." *CNN* (April 13, 2012), www.cnn.com.

190 Rahe, Paul. "Machiavelli's Liberal Republican Legacy," p. xxii.

191 Colonel Dan. "God, Guts and Guns." *The Price of Liberty* (April 7, 2008), www.thepriceofliberty.org.

192 Chiaramonte, Perry. "Gun sales explode as election looms." *Fox News* (March 22, 2012), www.foxnews.com.

193 Machiavelli, Niccolò. *The Prince*, p. 54.

194 Machiavelli, Niccolò. *History of Florence from the Earliest Times to the Death of Lorenzo the Magnificent.* (London & New York: The Colonial Press, 1901), p. 143.

195 Henneberger, Melinda. "Truth Seldom Yields Applause Lines." *Washington Post* (March 23, 2012), p. A2.

196 Fallows, James. "Paul Ryan and the Post-Truth Convention Speech." *The Atlantic* (August 30, 2012), www.theatlantic.com.

197 Beckel, Bob and Thomas, Cal. "Would they lie to you? Umm, yes," www.usatoday.com.

198 Henneberger, Melinda. "Truth Seldom Yields Applause Lines," p. A2.

199 Cardinal Richelieu (Armand Jean du Plessis Richelieu (d. 1642). In the public domain; found at multiple sources.

200 Stalin, Josef.

201 Thomas, Will. "Rigged." *Stolen Election 2004* (October 10, 2004), www.takeoverworld.info.

202 Ibid.

203 Goodman, Susannah; Mulder, Michelle and Smith, Pamela. "Counting Votes 2012: A State by State Look at Election Preparedness." *Verified Voting Foundation* (2012), www.verifiedvoting.org.

204 Simon, Howard L. "Restricting Voter Rights Is the Threat to Democracy, not Fraud." *US News* (June 13, 2012), www.usnews.com.

205 Thompson, Krissah. "Report: Laws May Cut Latino Voting." *Washington Post* (September 23, 2012), p. A3.

206 Demby, Gene. "Pennsylvania Voter ID Law: Mike Turzai Repeats Debunked Myth About Election Fraud." *Huffington Post* (August 16, 2012), www.huffingtonpost.com.

207 Machiavelli, Niccolò. *Discourses on the First Ten Books of Titus Livius*, p. 228.

208 Hartmann, Thom. "If You Want To Win An Election, Just Control The Voting Machines." *Common Dreams* (January 31, 2003), www.commondreams.org.

209 Strauss, Leo. *Thoughts on Machiavelli*, p. 82.

210 Ruhe, Brian. *Freeing the Buddha: Diversity on a Sacred Path* (Vancouver, BC: Buddhist Spectrum Study Group, 1999), p. 264.

211 Ibid. p. 264.

212 Lerner, Max. "Introduction," p. xxxiv.

213 Drake, Russell M. "Bush-Hitler: Hypnotizing The Masses." *Information Clearing House* (July 21, 2004), www.informationclearinghouse.info.

214 Urban, Hugh B. "Machiavelli meets the religious right: Michael Ledeen, the neoconservatives, and the political uses of fundamentalism," p. 93.

215 Mansfield, Harvey. *Machiavelli's Virtue*, p. 22.

216 Strauss, Leo. *Thoughts on Machiavelli*, p. 192.

217 Fischer, Markus. "Machiavelli's Rapacious Republicanism," p. xlii.

218 "A major telephone poll put out by *Rasmussen Reports* in December of 2009 asked 1,000 Americans if waterboarding and other harsh interrogation techniques should be used on terrorists. Fifty-eight percent answered yes." Sacco, Jeffrey B. "Waterboarding: An American Dilemma." *University of Nebraska at Kearney Summer Student Research Program* (Summer 2010), p. 11.

219 Marrapodi, Eric. "Poll: Many Americans Uncomfortable with Muslims." *CNN* (September 6, 2011), www.cnn.com.

220 The Center on Budget and Policy Priorities states that the tax cuts have conferred the "largest benefits, by far on the highest income households." Friedman, Joel and Shapiro, Isaac. "Tax Returns: A Comprehensive Assessment of the Bush Administration's Record on Cutting Taxes." *Center on Budget and Policy Priorities* (April 23, 2004), www.cbpp.org.

221 In March 2008, after eight years of the Bush–Cheney administration, "the number of Americans who believe the Earth is warming has dropped." Keim, Brandon. "The Climate Change Attitude Mystery." *Wired* (March 14, 2008), www.wired.com.

222 Lawrence, Dr. Gary C. "Charity, Gratitude and the Role of Government." *Audience Alliance Pictures* (April 7, 2010), www.audiencealliance.com.

223 "The Bush administration considered most treaties to be too restrictive of US sovereignty." Bender, Bryan. "Obama may face fight on treaties." *Boston Globe* (October 25, 2009), www.boston.com.

224 Skinner, Richard M. "George W. Bush and the Partisan Presidency" Political Science Quarterly 123.4 (2009), pp. 605-622.

225 Martin, Patrick. "Bush budget targets the poor." *World Socialist Website* (February 13, 2003), www.wsws.org.

226 Lerner, Max. "Introduction," p. xlv.

227 Suskind, Ron. "Faith, Certainty and the Presidency of George W. Bush." *New York Times* (October 17, 2004), p. 64.

228 Machiavelli, Niccolò. *Discourses on the First Ten Books of Titus Livius*, p. 182.

229 Allen, William B. "Machiavelli and Modernity," p. 108.

230 Holguin, Jaime. "A Rare Glimpse Inside Bush's Cabinet." *CBS News "60 Minutes"* (February 11, 2009), www.cbsnews.com.

231 Corn, David. "The Other Lies of George W. Bush." *The Nation* (October 13, 2003), www.commondreams.org.

232 Ibid.

233 Strauss, Leo. *Thoughts on Machiavelli*, p. 216.

234 Suskind, Ron. "Faith, Certainty and the Presidency of George W. Bush," p. 51

235 Machiavelli, Niccolò. *Discourses on the First Ten Books of Titus Livius*, p. 222.

236 Suskind, Ron. "Faith, Certainty and the Presidency of George W. Bush," p. 47

237 Quoted in Ibid. pg. 46

238 Mansfield, Harvey. *Machiavelli's Virtue*, p. 76.

239 Allen, William B. "Machiavelli and Modernity," p. 109.

240 Strauss, Leo. *Thoughts on Machiavelli*, p. 186.

241 Cromwell, David. "In God he trusts - how George Bush infused the White House with a religious spirit." *The Independent (U.K.)* (February 21, 2003), www.independent.co.uk.

242 Hassan, Salah D. "Enemy Arabs." *Socialism and Democracy* (2003), www.sdonline.org.

243 Machiavelli, Niccolò. *The Prince*, p. 67.

244 Lampman, Jane. "New scrutiny of role of religion in Bush's policies." *Christian Science Monitor* (March 17, 2003), www.csmonitor.com.

245 Machiavelli, Niccolò. *The Prince*, p. 67.

246 Bush, George W. "Transcript of Debate Between Bush and Kerry, With Domestic Policy the Topic." *New York Times* (October 13, 2004), www.nytimes.com.

247 Yost, Pete. "Bush E-mails Found: 22 Million Missing E-mails From George W. Bush White House Recovered." *Huffington Post* (December 14, 2009), www.huffingtonpost.com.

248 Machiavelli, Niccolò. *The Prince*, p. 67.

249 Beiner, Ronald. *Civil Religion: A Dialogue in the History of Political Philosophy.* (Cambridge, England: Cambridge University Press, 2011), p. 20.

250 Carver, Tom. "Bush puts God on his side." *BBC News* (April 6, 2003), www.news.bbc.co.uk.

251 Allen, Mike and Gellman, Barton. "Preemptive Strikes Part Of U.S. Strategic Doctrine." *Washington Post* (December 11, 2002), p. A1.

252 Woodward, Bob. "Bush at War: A Course of 'Confident Action.'" *Washington Post* (November 19, 2002), www.washingtonpost.com.

253 Cornwell, Rupert. "Bush: God Told Me to Invade Iraq." *The Independent* (U.K.). (October 7, 2005), www.independent.co.uk.

254 Machiavelli, Niccolò. *Discourses on the First Ten Books of Titus Livius*, p. 147.

255 Machiavelli, Niccolò. *The Prince*, p. 62.

256 Holt, Doug. "The Role of the Amygdala in Fear and Panic." *Serendip* (Bryn

Mawr College, January 8, 2008), www.serendip.brynmawr.edu.

257 Morgan, David. "Bush Spy Bill Stance Called Fear-Mongering." *CBS News* (February 11, 2009), www.cbsnews.com.

258 Holt, Doug. "The Role of the Amygdala in Fear and Panic."

259 Merton, Thomas. *On Peace*, p. 127.

260 Arkes, Hadley. "Machiavelli and America." (Machiavelli, Niccolo. *The Prince.* Angelo M. Codevilla, translator. New Haven and London: Yale University Press, 1997), pp. 130-131.

261 Christopher Hudson quoted in Frankl, George. *Foundations of Morality.* (London: Open Gate Press, 2000), p. 23.

262 Merton, Thomas. *On Peace*, p. 230.

263 Chad, Norman. "Repeat After Me: It's Only a Game." *Washington Post* (November 22, 2004), p. D2.

264 CNN. "Cheney: Kerry win risks terror attack." (September 7, 2004), www.cnn.com.

265 Medved, Michael. "Rick Santorum's Momentum Shouldn't Convert GOP Into a 'God Squad.'" *Daily Beast* (March 14, 2012), www.thedailybeast.com.

266 Blumenthal, Max. "The Little-Known, Inside Story About How Newt Became the Man He Is." *Alter Net* (December 18, 2011), www.alternet.org.

267 Dionne, E. J. "Revenge of the Base." *Washington Post* (December 19, 2011), p. A19.

268 Gowans, Alison. "Gingrich Asks Iowans To Punish Negative Politicians at Waterloo Stop." *Iowa City Patch* (January 2, 2012), www.iowacity.patch.com.

269 Edward Lazarus in Ibid.

270 Holloway, Carson. "Cruelty Well Used: Machiavelli, Walker, and Romney?" *Public Discourse* (June 6, 2012), www.thepublicdiscourse.com.

271 Ibid.

272 Dimaggio, Anthony. "American Empire and the Legacy of Machiavelli." *Illinois State University* (2004), www.pol.illinoisstate.edu.

273 Greenwald, Glenn. "Attorney General Holder defends execution without Charges." *Salon* (March 6, 2012), www.salon.com.

274 Mansfield, Harvey. *Machiavelli's Virtue*, p. 299.

275 Page, Clarence. "Decision-making behind drone attacks needs review." *Chicago Tribune* (June 19, 2012), www.recordnet.com.

276 Machiavelli, Niccolò. *The Prince*, p. 61.

277 Page, Clarence. "Decision-making behind drone attacks needs review."

278 Ibid.

279 Quoted in Miller, Lisa. "Finding His Faith." *Newsweek Magazine* (July 11, 2008), www.thedailybeast.com/newsweek.

280 Machiavelli, Niccolò. *The Prince*, p. 67.

281 Grendler, Paul F. *The European Renaissance in American Life*, p. 149.

282 Ibid. p. 153.

283 Randolph, Eleanor. "The Political Legacy of Baaad Boy Atwater." *New York Times* (September, 19, 2008), www.nytimes.com.

284 Quoted by Eleanor Randolph, ibid.

285 Caraballo, Alex. "Romney's Welfare Attack Ads Are Racist, Desperate." *The Minaret* (September 6, 2012), www.theminaretonline.com.

286 Eckel, Mike. "From Willie Horton to windsurfing: Five top political attack ads." *Christian Science Monitor* (May 24, 2012), www.csmonitor.com.

287 Jaffe, Ina. "An Inside Look at the Dark Art of Politics." *National Public Radio* (November 3, 2011), www.npr.org.

288 Ibid.

289 Shrum, Robert. "In Defense of Karl Rove." *The Week* (August 18, 2011), www.theweek.com.

290 A "push-poll" is a political campaign technique in which an individual or organization attempts to influence or alter the view of respondents under the guise of conducting a poll.

291 Anderson, Paul. *Machiavelli's Shadow: The Rise and Fall of Karl Rove.* (New York: Rodale, 2008), p. 13.

292 Machiavelli, Niccolò. *Discourses on the First Ten Books of Titus Livius*, p. 182.

293 Charles Green quoted in Hendrix, Steve. "Whispered Attacks Speak Volumes about S.C. Politics." *Washington Post* (January 12, 2012), p. A8.

294 Ibid.

295 Smith, Ben. "Oppo: From dark art to daily tool." *Politico.* (August 4, 2011), www.politico.com.

296 Wallsten, Peter. "GOP Readies its Plan of Attack." *Washington Post* (January 2, 2012), p. A6.

297 Sherwell, Philip. "'Now it's time to rock 'em and sock 'em.'" *The Telegraph* (U.K.) (October 17, 2004), www.telegraph.co.uk.

298 Nagourney, Adam. "2 Character Models for a Single Cinematic Point: Winning Elections at Any Cost." *New York Times* (December 8, 2011), p. A22.

299 Ibid. p. A22.

300 Ledeen Michael. *Machiavelli on Modern Leadership: Why Machiavelli's Iron Rules are as Timely and Important Today as Five Centuries Ago*, p. 188.

301 Birchall, Jonathan. "Using the dark arts of land-use politics to defeat NIMBYs." *Los Angeles Times* (November 23, 2009), www.articles.latimes.com.

302 Mansfield, Harvey. *Machiavelli's Virtue*, pp. 270-271.

303 Rove, Karl. "Karl Rove Reads." www.rove.com.

304 Anderson, Paul. *Machiavelli's Shadow: The Rise and Fall of Karl Rove*, p. 13.

305 "Bush may Talk to God, but He Listens to Karl Rove." *Believers Against Bush* (March 21, 2004), www.believersagainstbush.org.

306 Zernike, Kate and Rutenberg, Jim. "Friendly Fire: The Birth of an Anti-Kerry Ad." *New York Times* (August 20, 2004), www.nytimes.com.

307 Alexander, Paul. *Machiavelli's Shadow: The Rise and Fall of Karl Rove* (Emmaus, PA: Rodale Books, 2008), publisher's summary.

308 Machiavelli, Niccolò. *Discourses on the First Ten Books of Titus Livius*, pp. 138-139.

309 Wulfhorst, Ellen. "Karl Rove in Running for Time's Person of the Year." *Reuters News Service* (November 16, 2004), www.democraticunderground. com.

310 Madsen, Wayne. "Exposing Karl Rove." *Counterpunch* (October 31 - November 02, 2002), www.counterpunch.org.

311 Schouten, Fredreka. "Karl Rove-affiliated groups target President Obama." *USA Today* (March 1, 2011), www.usatoday.com.

312 McDonald, Greg. "Karl Rove's Super PAC Targets Five Democrats With Ads." *Newsmax* (November 10, 2011), www.newsmax.com.

313 Gallagher, Bill. "They'd Be More Truthful If They Called Themselves 'Swift Boat Veterans for Lies'." *Niagara Falls Reporter* (August 24, 2004), www. commondreams.org.

314 Zernike, Kate. "Kerry Pressing Swift Boat Case Long After Loss." *New York Times* (May 28, 2006), www.nytimes.com.

315 Ibid.

316 N.C. & M.J. "The new Swift Boat Vets ad is wrong — but you wouldn't know it from watching FOX." *Media Matters* (September 22, 2004), www. mediamatters.org.

317 Bankston, Susan DuQuesnay. "Swift Boat Veteran's for . . . Crossroads." *Juanita Jean: A Professional Political Organization* (April 23, 2012), www. juanitajean.com.

318 Mansfield, Harvey. *Machiavelli's Virtue*, p. 27.

319 Hallmark, Clayton. "Karl Rove, Michael Ledeen Spies Procured Forged Niger Documents." *Bella Ciao* (July 29, 2005), www.bellaciao.org.

320 Ibid.

321 Ledeen, Michael. *Machiavelli on Modern Leadership: Why Machiavelli's Iron Rules are as Timely and Important Today as Five Centuries Ago*, p. 31.

322 Hallmark, Clayton. "Karl Rove, Michael Ledeen Spies Procured Forged Niger Documents," www.bellaciao.org.

323 Quote and information in previous paragraph from Ledeen, Michael. *Machiavelli on Modern Leadership: Why Machiavelli's Iron Rules are as Timely and Important Today as Five Centuries Ago*, p. 2.

324 Ibid. pp. 159-160.

325 Ibid. p. 71.

326 Hallmark, Clayton. "Karl Rove, Michael Ledeen Spies Procured Forged Niger Documents," www.bellaciao.org.

327 Grendler, Paul. *The European Renaissance in American Life*, p. 166.

328 Ledeen, Michael. *Machiavelli on Modern Leadership: Why Machiavelli's Iron Rules are as Timely and Important Today as Five Centuries Ago*, p. 112.

329 Ibid. p. 115.

330 Jonathan Schell of the Nation quoted in Urban, Hugh B. *The Secrets of the Kingdom: Religion and Concealment in the Bush Administration.* (Lanham, MD: Rowman and Littlefield Publishers, 2007), p. 133.

331 Urban, Hugh B. *The Secrets of the Kingdom: Religion and Concealment in the Bush Administration*, p. 128.

332 Ledeen, Michael. *Machiavelli on Modern Leadership: Why Machiavelli's Iron Rules are as Timely and Important Today as Five Centuries Ago*, pp. 117-118.

333 Ibid. p. 159.

334 Heer, Jeet and Wagner, Dave. "Man of the World: Michael Ledeen's adventures in history." *Boston Globe* (October 10, 2004), www.boston.com.

335 Borger, Julian. "Aide says White House mocked evangelicals." *The Guardian* (U.K.) (October 13, 2006), www.guardian.co.uk.

336 Strauss, Leo. *Thoughts on Machiavelli*, pp. 269-270.

337 Weil, Simone. *The Simone Weil Reader*, p. 364.

338 McCormick, John P. *Machiavellian Democracy.* (Cambridge, England: Cambridge University Press, 2011), p. 179.

339 Quote from the following two articles: Turque, Bill. "Small Group Makes Big Dent on Super PAC Individual Donations." *Washington Post* (August 2, 2012), p. A13 and Klein, Ezra. "Disclosing the Deeper Ills of Campaign Finance." *Washington Post* (July 28, 2012), p. A2.

340 Machiavelli, Niccolò. *The Prince*, p. 67.

341 Eggen, Dan and Farnam, T. W. "Romney Relying on Small Group of Big Donors." *Washington Post* (February 2, 2012), p. A4.

342 "The World Fact Book: Budget." *Central Intelligence Agency.* www.cia.gov.

343 McCormick, John P. *Machiavellian Democracy*, p. 137.

344 Skelton, George. "Special-interest money and politics: the American way." *Los Angeles Times* (April 26, 2012), www.articles.latimes.com.

345 Milstein, Andrew. "Plugging Leaks in the Dam: The Future [and Past] of Campaign Finance Reform and the Effects of Money in Federal Elections." *Geneva NY League of Women Voters Luncheon* (April 3, 2007), www.geneva. ny.lwvnet.org.

346 Younge, Gary. "US elections: no matter who you vote for, money always wins." *The Guardian* (U.K.) (January 29, 2012), www.guardian.co.uk.

347 Quoted in Ibid.

348 Krugman, Paul. "Oligarchy, American Style." *New York Times* (November 4, 2011), p. A31.

349 www.merriam-webster.com/dictionary.

350 Quoted in Eggen, Dan. "Super PACs Outspend Campaigns 2 to 1 in S.C." *Washington Post* (January 17, 2012), p. A6.

351 Farnam, T. W. "Super PACs let Big Donors Give Even More to their Candidates." *Washington Post* (January 9, 2012), p. A4.

352 Mundy, Alicia. "Adelson Says He Could Give $100 Million More to Help

Gingrich." *Washington Wire* (blog of *The Wall Street Journal*). (February 21, 2012), www.blogs.wsj.com.

353 McCormick, John P. *Machiavellian Democracy*, p. 155.

354 Marcus, Ruth. "It's the Super PAC Era." *Washington Post* (January 4, 2012), p. A17.

355 Farnam, T. W. "Super PACs let Big Donors Give Even More to their Candidates."

356 Eggen, Dan. "Are Iowa Caucuses a Harbinger of the 'Super PAC' Era?" *Washington Post* (January 4, 2012), p. A6.

357 Machiavelli, Niccolò. *The Prince*, p. 37.

358 A satirically pejorative phrase coined by John J. DiIulio Jr., Ph.D., a former George W. Bush administration staffer who ran the President's Faith-Based Initiative. After DiIulio resigned from his White House post in late 2001, journalist Ron Suskind quoted him in an *Esquire* magazine article describing the administration of the Bush White House as follows: "What you've got is everything—and I mean everything—being run by the political arm. It's the reign of the Mayberry Machiavellis."

359 Clift, Theresa. "Two Texas billionaires are nation's top Super PAC donors." *San Antonio Express-News* (June 27, 2012), www.blog.chron.com.

360 Polk, Laray. "Harold Simmons Is Dallas' Most Evil Genius." *D Magazine* (February 2010), www.dmagazine.com.

361 Clift, Theresa. "Two Texas billionaires are nation's top Super PAC donors."

362 Kirkpatrick, David D. "The 2004 Campaign: The Conservatives: Club of the Most Powerful Gathers in Strictest Privacy." *New York Times* (August 28, 2004), www.nytimes.com.

363 www.cfnp.org.

364 Eggen, Dan and Farnam, T. W. "Romney Relying on Small Group of Big Donors," p. A4.

365 CNN Money. "Top super PAC donors." *CNN* (June 2012), www.money.cnn.com.

366 Eggen, Dan. "Are Iowa Caucuses a Harbinger of the 'Super PAC' Era?"

367 Blumenthal, Paul. "Super PAC Mega-Donors Increase Their Influence In May." *Huffington Post* (June 27, 2012), www.huffingtonpost.com.

368 Sonmez, Felicia. "Negative ads: Is it the campaigns, or the super PACs." *Washington Post Election 2012 Blog* (March 22, 2012), www.washingtonpost.com.

369 Jackson, Brooks. "American Crossroads/Crossroads GPS." *FactCheck.org: A Project of the Annenberg Public Policy Center* (September 18, 2011), www.factcheck.org.

370 Henneberger, Melinda. "We are all Fact-checkers." *Washington Post* (August 31, 2012), p. A2.

371 Helederman, Rosalind. "Fact Checkers Face Quick Push-Back on Ryan Speech." *Washington Post* (August 31, 2012), p. A10.

372 Kessler, Glenn. "Fact check: Context missing in GOP's repeated 'we-built it' theme." *Seattle Times* (August 29, 2012), www.seattletimes.com.

373 Mandela, Nelson. *A Long Walk to Freedom* (Boston: Little Brown and Company, 1995), p. 177.

374 Ibid. p. 177.

375 Mansfield, Harvey. *Machiavelli's Virtue*, p. 236.

376 Cillizza, Chris. "The Political Fight on Health Care is Over: Republicans Won." *Washington Post* (June 21, 2012), p. A4.

377 Quoted in Zaller, John. "A Theory of Media Politics." *Miller-Converse Lecture, University of Michigan* (April 14, 1997), p. 1.

378 Quoted in Ibid. p. 1.

379 Moyers, Bill. "Buying the War." *Bill Moyers Journal*. www.pbs.org/moyers/journal.

380 Mann, Thomas E. and Ornstein, Norman J. "Let's Just Say It: The Republicans are the Problem." www.washingtonpost.com.

381 R.S. "Who? Media Turns Its Back On Experts Who Blame GOP For Political Gridlock." *Media Matters* (May 18, 2012), www.mediamatters.org.

382 Harwood, John. "If Fox Is Partisan, It Is Not Alone." *New York Times* (November 2, 2009), p. A12.

383 Machiavelli, Niccolò. *The Prince*, p. 50.

384 Ledeen, Michael. *Machiavelli on Modern Leadership: Why Machiavelli's Iron Rules are as Timely and Important Today as Five Centuries Ago*, p. 30.

385 Kurtz, Howard. "Should We Blame Sarah Palin for Gabrielle Giffords' Shooting?" *The Daily Beast* (January 8, 2011), www.thedailybeast.com.

386 Allen, William B. "Machiavelli and Modernity," p. 104.

387 Merton, Thomas. *On Peace*, p. 241.

388 Pitney Jr., John Jay. "Military Language in Politics Proves Resilient." *National Review* (March 29, 2011), www.nationalreview.com.

389 Agence France Presse. "Leading US Daily Admits Underplaying Stories Critical of White House Push for Iraq War." *Common Dreams* (August 12, 2004), www.commondreams.org.

390 Dadge, David. *The War in Iraq and Why the Media Failed Us*. (Westport, CT: Praeger Publishers, 2006), back jacket cover.

391 Heschel, Abraham Joshua quoted in Heschel, Susannah. "God and Society in Heschel and King." *The Shalom Center* (September 8, 2001), www.theshalomcenter.org.

392 Bader, Sharon. "The Media: Objectivity." *Environment in Crisis*. www.herinst.org.

393 Vanden Heuvel, Katrina. "Three Issues that Could Decide the Election." *Washington Post* (January 3, 2012), p. A13.

394 FAIR (Fairness in Accuracy and Reporting). "NYT to Readers: Can You Handle the Truth?" (January 12, 2002), www.fair.org.

395 Ibid.

396 Editorial Page. "These Charges Are False ..." *Los Angeles Times* (August 24, 2008).

397 Taibbi, Matt. "Hacks R Us, Interview." *On the Media* (November 12, 2004), www.onthemedia.org.

398 Merton, Thomas. *On Peace*, p. 161.

399 "Why War is Good, or War, Progress and Civilization." www.quotations.hubpages.com

400 *The Human Spirit: Human Flourishing Conference.* www.acelebrationofspirit.org.

401 Marshall, Jacqueline. "Humanity is Maturing." *The Examiner* (May 8, 2011), www.examiner.com.

402 "The Prosperity of Humankind." *A statement prepared by the Bahá'í International Community Office of Public Information, Haifa* (March 3, 1995), www.statements.bahai.org.

403 Spayde, Jon. "The New Renaissance." *Utne Reader* (Jan-Feb 1998), p. 43.

404 Teasdale, Wayne. "The Interspiritual Age: Practical Mysticism for the Third Millennium." *Council on Spiritual Practices* (1999), www.csp.org.

405 Kandinsky, Wassily. *Concerning the Spiritual in Art* (M. T. H. Sadler, translator). (Mineola, NY: Dover Publications, 1977).

406 Verrall, Richard. "Human Nature and Spiritual Progress." *The Christian Science Journal* (October 1904), www.journal.christianscience.com.

407 Merton, Thomas. *On Peace*, p. 161.

408 Weil, Simone. *Simone Weil Reader*, p. 38.

409 Traubman, Len. Communication via email (September 8, 2012).

410 Ibid.

411 www.freedomcenter.org.

412 Wilkins, W. J. *Hindu Mythology, Vedic and Puranic.* (Calcutta & London: Thacker, Spink. & Co, 1900), p. 622.

413 Weil, Simone. *Oppression and Liberty*, p. 114.

414 Frankl, Georg. *Foundations of Morality*, p. 15.

415 Lerner, Max. "Introduction," p. xxxii.

416 Weil, Simone. *Simone Weil Reader*, p. 38.

417 Giroux, Greg. "Obama, Romney Bash Each Other With 90% Negative Ads." *Bloomberg News* (July 16, 2012), www.bloomberg.com.

418 Mansfield, Harvey. *Machiavelli's Virtue*, p. 80.

419 Little, Morgan. "Negative ads increase dramatically during 2012 presidential election." *Los Angeles Times* (May 3, 2012), www.latimes.com.

420 Chomsky, Noam. "2004 Elections." *Chomsky Info* (November 29, 2004), www.chomsky.info.

421 Rucker, Philip. "Romney Teams Tries to Make Pitch-Perfect Ads." *Washington Post* (August 24, 2012), A1.

422 Merton, Thomas. *Peace in a Post-Christian Era.* (Maryknoll, NY: Orbis, 2004), pp. xxi-xxii.

423 Traubman, Len. Communication via email (September 8, 2012).

424 Lerner, Max. "Introduction," p. xliv.

425 Mansfield, Harvey. *Machiavelli's Virtue*, p. 29.

426 DeBonis, Mike. "D.C. Activists Target Corporate Donations." *Washington Post* (January 18, 2012, p. B1.

427 McGreal, Chris. "George W Bush should be prosecuted over torture, says human rights group." *Guardian Newspaper* (U.K.) (July 11, 2011), p. 20.

428 Caldwell, Christopher. "An Expensive Clash Between the same Janus-Faced Elite." *Financial Times* (July 14-15, 2012), p. 11.

429 Orwell, George. *Animal Farm*. www.gutenberg.net.au.

430 Merton, Thomas. *Peace in the Post-Christian Era*, p. 127.

431 King Jr., Martin Luther. *The Papers of Martin Luther King, Jr., Volume V* (Berkeley, CA: University of California Press, 2005), p. 280.

432 Weil, Simone. *Waiting for God*. (New York: Harper & Row Publishers, 1992), p. 99.

433 Aurelius, Marcus. *Meditations*, p. 123.

434 Merton, Thomas. *On Peace*, p. 117.

435 Chuang Tzu. *The Genius of the Absurd*. (Arranged from the work of James Legge by Clae Waltham). (New York: Ace Books, 1971), p. 275.

436 Herbert, Bob. "Real Citizens Would March into the Arena." (*News and Observer*, Raleigh, NC), January 26, 2007.

437 Einstein, Albert. *The Einstein Reader*. (New York: Kensington Publishing Corp., 1984), p. 132.

438 Einstein, Albert. *Einstein on Humanism*. (New York: Carol Publishing Group, 1993), p. 5.

439 Rumi, Jallaludin. *Signs of the Unseen*, p.60.

440 Chuang Tzu. *Genius of the Absurd*, p. 318.

441 Beckel, Bob and Thomas, Cal. "Would they lie to you? Umm, yes."

442 Sanders, Senator Bernie. "Speech on the floor of the U.S. Senate." (June 29, 2012), www.upworthy.com.

443 Dunn, Alan. "Average America vs the One Percent." *Forbes* (March 21, 2012), www.forbes.com.

444 Domhoff, G. William. "Wealth, Income and Power." *Who Rules America*. (March 2012), www2.ucsc.edu.

445 Akin, Jennifer. "Mass Media." *Beyond Intractability* (March 2005), www.beyondintractability.org.

446 Solomon, Norman. "The Military-Industrial-Media Complex: Why war is covered from the warriors' perspective." *FAIR* (July/August 2005), www.fair.org.

447 McCormick, John P. *Machiavellian Democracy*, p. 114.

448 Machiavelli, Niccolò. *Discourses on the First Ten Books of Titus Livius*, p. 211.

449 Stafford, Tom. "Does the internet rewire your brain?" *BBC News* (April 24, 2012), www.bbc.com.

450 Chaney, Warren H. *The Dynamic Mind* (Las Vegas: Houghton-Brace Publishing Company, 2007), pp. 33-35.

451 Mandela, Nelson. *A Long Walk to Freedom*, p. 265.

452 Merton, Thomas. *On Peace*, p. 181.

453 Weil, Simone. *Simone Weil Reader*, pp. 113-114.

454 McCormick, John P. *Machiavellian Democracy*, p. 146.

455 Both quotes from back jacket cover, Ibid.

456 Ibid. p. 183.

457 Ibid. p. vii.

458 Ibid. p. 162.

459 Ibid. p. 6.

460 Ibid. p. 92.

461 "12 Facts About Money And Congress That Are So Outrageous That It Is Hard To Believe That They Are Actually True." *The Economic Collapse* (November 8, 2011), www.theeconomiccollapseblog.com.

462 McCormick, John P. *Machiavellian Democracy*, p. 67.

463 Ibid. p. 179.

464 Ibid. p. 160.

465 Ibid. pp. 183-185.

466 Ibid. p. 180.

467 Ibid. p. 180.

468 Ibid. p. 69.

469 Mandela, Nelson. *Long Walk to Freedom*, p. 22.

470 Lerner, Max. "Introduction." *The Prince and the Discourses*, p. xlvi.

471 McCormick, John. *Machiavellian Democracy*, p. 149.

472 Codevilla, Angelo. "Introduction," p. xiv.

473 http://www.gallup.com/poll/1690/religion.aspx

474 Newport, Frank. "Americans Say More Religion in U.S. Would Be Positive." *Gallup*, www.gallup.com

475 Huxley, Aldous. *The Perennial Philosophy*. (New York: Harper and Row, 1970), p. vii.

476 Merton, Thomas. *On Peace*, p. 87.

477 Weil, Simone. *Simone Weil Reader*, p. 202.

478 Origen quoted in Sibley, Mulford. *The Quiet Battle: Writings on the Theory and Practice of Non-Violent Resistance* (Chicago: Quadrangle Books, 1963), p. 13.

479 "Worldwide Military Expenditures 2011." *Global Security*, www.globalsecurity.org.

480 Hartmann, Thom. "Medicare 'Part E'- for Everybody." *Truthout* (December 13, 2010), www.archive.truthout.org.

481 Weisman, Jonathan. "Bid to Save Tax Refunds for the Poor Is Blocked." *Washington Post* (September 23, 2004), p. A4.

482 Einstein, Albert. *Einstein on Humanism*, p. 68.

483 McCormick, John P. *Machiavellian Democracy*, p. 30.

484 Mansfield, Harvey. *Machiavelli's Virtue*, p. 62.

485 Merton, Thomas. *On Peace*, p. 49.

486 Slackman, Michael. "An Arab Artist Says All the World Really Isn't a Stage." *New York Times*, (August 19, 2006) www.nytimes.com.

487 Machiavelli, Niccolò. *The Prince*, p. 66.

488 Clement of Alexandria. *The One Who Knows God*, p. 119.

489 Hanley, Charles J. "Half of U.S. Still Believes Iraq Had WMD." *The Associated Press* (April 7, 2006).

490 Ibid.

491 Merton, Thomas. *Mystics and Zen Masters*, pp. 263-264.

492 Mandela, Nelson. *Long Walk to Freedom*, p. 409.

493 McCormick, John P. *Machiavellian Democracy*, p. 169.

494 Ibid. p. 75.

495 Althusser, Louis. *Machiavelli and Us*, p. 25.

496 Xenophon quoted in Machiavelli, Niccolò. *Discourses on the First Ten Books of Titus Livius*, p. 319.

497 Chuang Tzu. *Genius of the Absurd*, p. 72.

498 Colvin, Mark. "Some key learnings about the debasement of language." *The Punch* (September 30, 2009), www.thepunch.com.au.

499 Tolstoy, Leo. *On Civil Disobedience and Non-Violence*, p. 104.

500 Bush, George. "Veteran's Day Address." *USA Patriotism* (November 11, 2006), www.usa-patriotism.com.

501 McCain, John. "Eulogy for Pat Tillman." (May 3, 2004), www.mccain.senate.gov.

502 From Tom Block's welcome speech to the first ever *Amnesty International Human Rights Art Festival*, April 23, 2010.

503 Machiavelli, Niccolò. *The Prince*, p. 64.

504 Orwell, George. *1984*. (London: Penguin Books, Signet Classic, 1977), p. 248.

505 Sunday Times. 2009. "September 11 Mastermind Khalid Sheikh Mohammed 'Waterboarded' 183 Times." *The Times* (UK). April 20, 2009.

506 Owen, Paul. "George Bush admits US waterboarded 9/11 mastermind." *The Guardian* (U.K.). (June 3, 2010), www.guardian.co.uk.

507 Weinstein, James. *The Decline of Socialism in America, 1912-1925* (New York: Vintage Books, 1969), pp. 116–118.

508 Quoted in McCormick, John P. *Machiavellian Democracy*, p. 156.

509 According to *The Monticello Classroom*, www.classroom.monticello.org.

510 Free Press. "Who Owns the Media?" www.freepress.net.

511 "Expert Sources," www.journaliststoolbox.org.

512 Merton, Thomas. *On Peace*, p. 24.

513 Machiavelli, Niccolò. *The Prince*, p. 54.

514 Ibid. p. 22.

515 Though Mandela did advocate aggression against state installations, he was strident in his protection of human life.

Bibliography

Abeshouse, Bob. "Koch Brothers." *alJazeera* (March 29, 2012): www.aljazeera. com.

Achenbach, Joel. "Certificate Unlikely to Appease 'Birthers.'" *Washington Post* (April 28, 2011): p. A6.

Agence France Presse. "Leading US Daily Admits Underplaying Stories Critical of White House Push for Iraq War." *Common Dreams* (August 12, 2004): www.commondreams.org.

Akin, Jennifer. "Mass Media." *Beyond Intractability* (March 2005: www.beyondintractability.org.

Alexander, Paul. *Machiavelli's Shadow: The Rise and Fall of Karl Rove*. Emmaus, PA: Rodale Books, 2008.

Allen, Mike (and Gellman, Barton). "Preemptive Strikes Part Of U.S. Strategic Doctrine." *Washington Post* (December 11, 2002): A1.

——"Rove suspected Gore aide of DUI leak." *Politico*. (March 7, 2010): www. politico.com.

Allen, William B. "Machiavelli and Modernity." (Machiavelli, Niccolo. *The Prince*. Angelo M. Codevilla, translator). New Haven and London: Yale University Press (1997): 101-113.

Almond, Ian. *Sufism and Deconstruction: A Comparative Study of Derrida and Ibn Arabi*. London: Routledge, 2004.

Althusser, Louis. *Machiavelli and Us* (Gregory Elliott, translator). London & Brooklyn, NY: Verso, 1999.

Anderson, Paul. *Machiavelli's Shadow: The Rise and Fall of Karl Rove*. New York: Rodale, 2008.

Arkes, Hadley. "Machiavelli and America." (Machiavelli, Niccolo. *The Prince.* Angelo M. Codevilla, translator). New Haven and London: Yale University Press (1997): 124-153.

Aurelius, Marcus. *Meditations.* New York: Random House, 2003.

Bader, Sharon. "The Media: Objectivity." *Environment in Crisis,* www.herinst. org.

Balta, Victor. "Commentary: Obama doesn't hate America, conservatives hate American workers." *The Current* (July 19, 2012): www.current.com.

Bankston, Susan DuQuesnay. "Swift Boat Veteran's for . . . Crossroads." *Juanita Jean: A Professional Political Organization* (April 23, 2012): www.juanita-jean.com.

Barnett, Vincent. "Niccolo Machiavelli — the Cunning Critic of Political Reason." *History Today* (November 28 2006): www.historytoday.com.

Baumann, Nick. "White House Emails Case Nearing Settlement." *Mother Jones* (December 11, 2009): www.motherjones.com.

Beckel, Bob and Thomas, Cal. "Would they lie to you? Umm, yes." *USA Today* (June 2, 2010): www.usatoday.com.

Beiner, Ronald. *Civil Religion: A Dialogue in the History of Political Philosophy.* Cambridge, England: Cambridge University Press, 2011.

Believers Against Bush. "Bush may Talk to God, but He Listens to Karl Rove." *Believers Against Bush* (March 21, 2004): www.believersagainstbush.org.

Bender, Bryan. "Obama may face fight on treaties." *Boston Globe* (October 25, 2009): www.boston.com.

Birchall, Jonathan. "Using the dark arts of land-use politics to defeat NIMBYs." *Los Angeles Times* (November 23, 2009): www.articles.latimes.com.

Bireley, Robert. *The Counter Reformation Prince.* Raleigh, N.C.: University of North Carolina Press, 1990.

Blumenthal, Max. "The Little-Known, Inside Story About How Newt Became the Man He Is." *Alter Net* (December 18, 2011): www.alternet.org.

Blumenthal, Paul. "Sheldon Adelson Gives $5 Million To Super PAC Backing House Republicans." *Huffington Post* (April 16, 2012): www.huffington-post.com.

——"Super PAC Mega-Donors Increase Their Influence In May." *Huffington Post* (June 27, 2012): www.huffingtonpost.com.

Bock, Gisela; Skinner, Quentin and Viroli, Maurizio. *Machiavelli and Republicanism.* Cambridge: Cambridge University Press, 1993.

Borger, Julian. "Aide says White House mocked evangelicals." *The Guardian* (U.K.) (October 13, 2006): www.guardian.co.uk.

Buber, Martin. *Tales of the Hasidim I & II.* New York: Schocken Books, 1991.

Bush, George W. *A Charge to Keep.* New York: William Morrow, 1999.

——"President Bush Delivers Remarks on the Protect America Act." *Washington Post* (February 13, 2008): www.washingtonpost.com.

——"Transcript of Debate Between Bush and Kerry, With Domestic Policy the Topic." *New York Times* (October 13, 2004): www.nytimes.com.

——"Veteran's Day Address." *USA Patriotism* (November 11, 2006), www.usa-patriotism.com.

Cannon, Carl. "Patriot Games." *Real Clear Politics* (July 13, 2012): www.real-clearpolitics.com.

Caldwell, Christopher. "An Expensive Clash Between the same Janus-Faced Elite." *Financial Times* (July 14-15, 2012): p. 11.

Carlson, Peter. "Max Cleland: Political Veteran." *Washington Post* (July 3, 2003): C1, C4.

Carrese, Paul. Carrese, Paul. "The Machiavellian Spirit of Montesquieu's Liberal Republic." *Machiavelli's Liberal Republican Legacy* (Paul A. Rahe, Editor). Cambridge, England: Cambridge University Press (2006): 121-142.

Caraballo, Alex. "Romney's Welfare Attack Ads Are Racist, Desperate." *The Minaret* (September 6, 2012): www.theminaretonline.com.

Carver, Tom. "Bush puts God on his side." *BBC News* (April 6, 2003): www.news.bbc.co.uk.

Catlin, George. *The Story of the Political Philosophers.* New York: Tudor Publishing, 1939.

Caulfield, Philip. "George W. Bush rakes in $15 million in speaking fees since leaving office: report." *New York Daily News* (May 22, 2011).

Chad, Norman. "Repeat After Me: It's Only a Game." *Washington Post* (November 22, 2004): D2.

Chaney, Warren H. *The Dynamic Mind.* Las Vegas: Houghton-Brace Publishing Company, 2007.

Chiaramonte, Perry. "Gun sales explode as election looms." *Fox News* (March 22, 2012): www.foxnews.com.

Chomsky, Noam. "2004 Elections." (November 29, 2004): www.chomsky.info.

——"Modern-Day American Imperialism: Middle East and Beyond." *Boston University Lecture* (April 24, 2008): www.chomsky.info.

Chuang Tzu. *The Genius of the Absurd.* (Arranged from the work of James Legge by Clae Waltham). New York: Ace Books, 1971.

CIA. "The World Fact Book: Budget." *Central Intelligence Agency.* www.cia.gov.

Cillizza, Chris. "The Political Fight on Health Care is Over: Republicans Won." *Washington Post* (June 21, 2012): A4.

——(and Blake, Aaron). "Super PACs are Saving Romney." *Washington Post* (July 25, 2012): A6.

Clausewitz, Carl von. *On War* (Anatol Rapaport, editor). London: Penguin Books, 1968.

Clement of Alexendria. *The One Who Knows God* (William Wilson, Translator). Tyler Texas: Scroll Publishing, 1990.

Clift, Theresa. "Two Texas billionaires are nation's top Super PAC donors." *San Antonio Express-News* (June 27, 2012): www.blog.chron.com.

Cline, Austin. "West Virginia: Liberals to Ban Bibles." *About.com Agnosticism/Atheism* (September 20, 2004): www.atheism.about.com.

CNN. "Cheney: Kerry win risks terror attack." (September 7, 2004): www.cnn.com.

——"CNN Poll: George W. Bush only living ex-president under 50%." (June 7, 2012): www.cnn.com.

——"Top super PAC donors." (June 2012): www.money.cnn.com.

Codevilla, Angelo. "Introduction." Machiavelli, Niccolo. *The Prince*. (Angelo M. Codevilla, translator). New Haven and London: Yale University Press (1997): xii-xviii.

——"Words and Power." Machiavelli, Niccolo. *The Prince*. (Angelo M. Codevilla, translator). New Haven and London: Yale University Press (1997): xix-xxxviii.

Colonel Dan. "God, Guts and Guns." *The Price of Liberty* (April 7, 2008): www.thepriceofliberty.org.

Colvin, Mark. "Some key learnings about the debasement of language." *The Punch* (September 30, 2009): www.thepunch.com.au.

Confucius. *The Analects* (Arthur Waley, translator). New York: HarperCollins, 1992.

Corn, David. "The Other Lies of George W. Bush." *The Nation* (October 13, 2003): www.commondreams.org.

Cornwell, Rupert. "Bush: God Told Me to Invade Iraq." *The Independent* (U.K.) (October 7, 2005): www.independent.co.uk.

Cromwell, David. "In God he trusts - how George Bush infused the White House with a religious spirit." *The Independent* (U.K.) (February 21, 2003): www.independent.co.uk.

Dadge, David. *The War in Iraq and Why the Media Failed Us*. Westport, CT: Praeger Publishers, 2006.

Danford, John W. "Getting our Bearings: Machiavelli and Hume." *Machiavelli's Liberal Republican Legacy* (Paul A. Rahe, Editor). Cambridge, England: Cambridge University Press (2006): 94-120.

DeBonis, Mike. "D.C. Activists Target Corporate Donations." *Washington Post* (January 18, 2012): B1, B4.

Demby, Gene. "Pennsylvania Voter ID Law: Mike Turzai Repeats Debunked Myth About Election Fraud." *Huffington Post* (August 16, 2012): www.huffingtonpost.com.

Dimaggio, Anthony. "American Empire and the Legacy of Machiavelli." *Illinois State University* (2004): www.pol.illinoisstate.edu.

Dionne, E. J. "Revenge of the Base." *Washington Post* (December 19, 2011): p. A19.

Domhoff, G. William. "Wealth, Income and Power." *Who Rules America* (March 2012): www2.ucsc.edu.

Downing, Brian. "Fundamentalism at the US's corps." *Asia Times* (May 15, 2012), www.atimes.com.

Drake, Russell M. "Bush-Hitler: Hypnotizing The Masses." *Information Clearing House* (July 21, 2004): www.informationclearinghouse.info.

Dunn, Alan. "Average America vs the One Percent." *Forbes* (March 21, 2012): www.forbes.com.

Eckel, Mike. "From Willie Horton to windsurfing: Five top political attack ads." *Christian Science Monitor* (May 24, 2012): www.csmonitor.com.

Eckhart, Meister. *Meister Eckhart* (Raymond. B. Blakney, translator). New York: Harper and Row Publishers, 1941.

——*Selected Writings* (Oliver Davis, translator). London: Penguin Books, 1994.

Economic Collapse Blog. "12 Facts About Money And Congress That Are So Outrageous That It Is Hard To Believe That They Are Actually True." *The Economic Collapse* (November 8, 2011): www.theeconomiccollapseblog. com.

Economist, The. "Niccolo Machiavelli: Founding Father." *The Economist* (May 3, 2007): www.economist.com.

Einstein, Albert. *The Einstein Reader*. New York: Kensington Publishing Corp., 1984.

——*Einstein on Humanism*. New York: Carol Publishing Group, 1993.

Eisenstein, Elizabeth. *The Printing Press as an Agent of Change*. Cambridge: Cambridge University Press, 1980.

Eggen, Dan, "Are Iowa Caucuses a Harbinger of the 'Super PAC' Era?" *Washington Post* (January 4, 2012): A6.

——(and Farnam, T. W.). "Romney Relying on Small Group of Big Donors." *Washington Post* (February 2, 2012): A4.

——"Super PACs Outspend Campaigns 2 to 1 in S.C." *Washington Post* (January 17, 2012): A6.

Eskow, Richard. "2011: The Year of Resistance to Conservatism's 'War of the Words.'" *Huffington Post* (December 31, 2011): www.huffingtonpost.com.

Fadiman, James & Frager, Robert (editors). *Essential Sufism*. New York: HarperCollins, 1997.

FactCheck.org. "About Us." www.factcheck.org.

——"Cheney & Edwards Mangle Facts." *FactCheck.org* (November 8, 2004): www.factcheck.org.

FAIR (Fairness in Accuracy and Reporting). "NYT to Readers: Can You Handle the Truth?" (January 12, 2002): www.fair.org.

Fallows, James. "Paul Ryan and the Post-Truth Convention Speech." *The Atlantic* (August 30, 2012): www.theatlantic.com.

Farnam, T. W. "Mystery Donor gives $10 million for Attack Ads." *Washington Post* (April 14, 2012): A6.

——"Super PACs let Big Donors Give Even More to their Candidates." *Washington Post* (January 9, 2012): A4.

Fischer, Markus. "Machiavelli's Rapacious Republicanism." *Machiavelli's Liberal Republican Legacy*, (Paul A. Rahe, Editor). Cambridge, England: Cambridge University Press,(2006): xxxi-lxii.

Forde, Steven. "Benjamin Franklin's 'Machiavellian' Civic Virtue." *Machiavelli's Liberal Republican Legacy*, (Paul A. Rahe, Editor). Cambridge, England: Cambridge University Press (2006): 143-166.

Frankl, George. *Foundations of Morality.* London: Open Gate Press, 2000.

Free Press. "Who Owns the Media?" www.freepress.net.

Friedman, Joel and Shapiro, Isaac. "Tax Returns: A Comprehensive Assessment of the Bush Administration's Record on Cutting Taxes." *Center on Budget and Policy Priorities* (April 23, 2004): www.cbpp.org.

Froomkin, Dan. "Yes, Iraq Definitely Had WMD, Vast Majority Of Polled Republicans Insist." *Huffington Post* (June 21, 2012) www.huffingtonpost.com.

Gabriel, Trip. "Ryan Says Obama Policies Threaten 'Judeo-Christian' Values." *New York Times: The Caucus* (November 5, 2012): www.nytimes.com.

Gallagher, Bill. "They'd Be More Truthful If They Called Themselves 'Swift Boat Veterans for Lies'." *Niagara Falls Reporter* (August 24, 2004), www.commondreams.org.

Gandhi, Mohandas K. *Gandhi on Nonviolence* (Thomas Merton, editor). New York: New Directions Publishing Corporation, 1964.

Gelb, Leslie H. *Power Rules: How Common Sense can Rescue American Foreign Policy.* New York: HarperCollins, 2009.

Giroux, Greg. "Obama, Romney Bash Each Other With 90% Negative Ads." *Bloomberg News* (July 16, 2012): www.bloomberg.com.

Gladstone, Brooke. "Hacks R Us, Interview." *On the Media* (November 12, 2004): www.onthemedia.org.

Glanzberg, Michael. "Truth." *The Stanford Encyclopedia of Philosophy* (Edward N. Zalta, editor). (Spring 2009 Edition): www.plato.stanford.edu.

Global Security. "Worldwide Military Expenditures 2011." *Global Security.* www.globalsecurity.org.

Goodman, Susannah; Mulder, Michelle and Smith, Pamela. "Counting Votes 2012: A State by State Look at Election Preparedness." *Verified Voting Foundation* (2012): www.verifiedvoting.org.

Gowans, Alison. "Gingrich Asks Iowans To Punish Negative Politicians at Waterloo Stop." *Iowa City Patch* (January 2, 2012): www.iowacity.patch.com.

Greenwald, Glenn. "Attorney General Holder defends execution without Charges." *Salon* (March 6, 2012): www.salon.com.

Gregg, Richard. *The Power of Nonviolence.* Canton, ME: Greenleaf Books, 1935.

Grendler, Paul F. *The European Renaissance in American Life.* Westport, CT: Praeger, 2006.

Grohol, John M. "Brains of Liberals, Conservatives May Work Differently." *Psych Central* (December 20, 2007): www.psychcentral.com.

Gross, Terry. "Frank Luntz Explains 'Words That Work.'" *Terry Gross Show* (January 9, 2007): www.npr.org.

Hallmark, Clayton. "Karl Rove, Michael Ledeen Spies Procured Forged Niger Documents." *Bella Ciao* (July 29, 2005): www.bellaciao.org.

Hamby, Peter. "Romney courts gun owners and pivots to general election." *CNN* (April 13, 2012): www.cnn.com.

Hanley, Charles J. "Half of U.S. Still Believes Iraq Had WMD." *The Associated Press* (April 7, 2006).

Hartmann, Thom. "If You Want To Win An Election, Just Control The Voting Machines." *Common Dreams* (January 31, 2003): www.commondreams.org.

——"Medicare 'Part E'- for Everybody." *Truthout* (December 13, 2010): www.archive.truthout.org.

Harwood, John. "If Fox Is Partisan, It Is Not Alone." *New York Times* (November 2, 2009): A12.

Hassan, Salah D. "Enemy Arabs." *Socialism and Democracy* (2003): www.sdonline.org.

Heer, Jeet and Wagner, Dave. "Man of the World: Michael Ledeen's adventures in history." *Boston Globe* (October 10, 2004): www.boston.com.

Helderman, Rosalind S. "Fact Checkers Face Quick Pushback on Ryan Speech." *Washington Post* (August 31, 2012): A1, 10.

Hendrix, Steve. "Whispered Attacks Speak Volumes about S.C. Politics." *Washington Post* (January 12, 2012): A8.

Henneberger, Melinda. "Truth Seldom Yields Applause Lines." *Washington Post* (March 23, 2012): A2.

——"We are all Fact-checkers." *Washington Post* (August 31, 2012): A2.

Herbert, Bob. "Real Citizens Would March into the Arena." *Raleigh NC News and Observer* (January 26, 2007): www.newsobserver.com.

Heschel, Susannah. "God and Society in Heschel and King." *The Shalom Center* (September 8, 2001): www.theshalomcenter.org.

Hillman, James. *A Terrible Love of War*. New York: Penguin Books, 2004.

Holguin, Jaime. "A Rare Glimpse Inside Bush's Cabinet." *CBS News "60 Minutes"* (February 11, 2009): www.cbsnews.com.

Holloway, Carson. "Cruelty Well Used: Machiavelli, Walker, and Romney?" *Public Discourse* (June 6, 2012): www.thepublicdiscourse.com.

Holt, Doug. "The Role of the Amygdala in Fear and Panic." *Serendip* (Bryn Mawr College, January 8, 2008): www.serendip.brynmawr.edu.

Huffington Post. "George W. Bush Reaps $15 Million Post-Presidency" (July 20, 2011): www.huffingtonpost.com.

Human Rights Watch. "Background on Women's Status in Iraq Prior to the Fall of the Saddam Hussein Government" (November 2003): www.hrw.org.

Hussein, Saddam. "A Speech delivered by President Saddam Hussein." *Third Conference of the General Federation of Iraq Women* (April 17, 1971): www. reformation.org.

Huxley, Aldous. *The Perennial Philosophy.* New York: Harper and Row, 1970.

Irish Center for Human Rights. "Banned Books Project." *National University of Ireland, Irish Centre for Human Rights* (Galway), www.nuigalway.ie.

Jackson, Brooks. "American Crossroads/Crossroads GPS." *FactCheck.org: A Project of the Annenberg Public Policy Center* (September 18, 2011): www. factcheck.org.

Jackson, Richard. "Language Power and Politics: Critical Discourse Analysis and the War on Terrorism." *49ᵗʰ Parallel: An Interdisciplinary Journal of North American Studies* (Birmingham, England: University of Birmingham, Issue 15, Spring 2005).

Jaffe, Greg. "The World is Safer, but No One will Say So." *Washington Post* (November 4, 2012): B1, B5.

Jaffe, Ina. "An Inside Look at the Dark Art of Politics." *National Public Radio* (November 3, 2011): www.npr.org.

Jewell, Jim. "Machiavelli Reigns: Dirty campaigns beg the question: 'Is everything fair game in American politics?'" *Rooftop* (November 8, 2010): www. therooftopblog.wordpress.com.

Jost, John T. and Amodio, David M. "Political ideology as motivated social cognition: Behavioral and neuroscientific evidence." *Motivation and Emotion* (Volume 36, Number 1, 2012): 55-64.

Kamen, Al. "George W. Bush and the G-Word." *Washington Post* (October 14, 2005): www.washingtonpost.com.

Kanai, Ryota; Felldon, Tom; Firth, Colin and Rees, Geraint. "Political Orientations Are Correlated with Brain Structure in Young Adults." *Current Biology* (Volume 21, Issue 8, April 7, 2011): 677-680.

Kandinsky, Wassily. *Concerning the Spiritual in Art* (M. T. H. Sadler, translator). Mineola, NY: Dover Publications, 1977.

Kaplan, Joshua. "Political Theory: The Classic Texts and their Continuing Relevance." *The Modern Scholar* (14 lectures in the series; lecture #7; 2005): disc 4.

Kattalia, Kathryn. "The liberal brain? Scans show liberals and conservatives have different brain structures." *New York Daily News* (April 8, 2011): www.articles.nydailynews.com.

Keim, Brandon. "The Climate Change Attitude Mystery." *Wired* (March 14, 2008): www.wired.com.

Kessler, Glenn and Slevin, Peter. "Cheney is Fulcrum of Foreign Policy." *Washington Post* (October 13, 2002): A1, A16.

——"Fact check: Context missing in GOP's repeated 'we-built it' theme." *Seattle Times* (August 29, 2012): www.seattletimes.com.

King Jr., Martin Luther. *I Have a Dream: Writings and Speeches that Changed the World.* San Francisco: HarperSanFrancisco, 1992.

——*The Papers of Martin Luther King, Jr., Volume V.* Berkeley, CA: University of California Press, 2005.

Kinsley, Michael. "Commentary: The Gaffer Speaks." *The Times* (U.K.) (April 23, 1988): www.thetimes.co.uk.

Kirk, Chris. "Obama's 262 Drone Strikes in Pakistan." *Slate Magazine* (Friday, June 8, 2012): www.slate.com.

Kirkpatrick, David D. "The 2004 Campaign: The Conservatives: Club of the Most Powerful Gathers in Strictest Privacy." *New York Times* (August 28, 2004): www.nytimes.com.

Klein, Ezra. "Disclosing the Deeper Ills of Campaign Finance." *Washington Post* (July 28, 2012): A2.

Krasner, Jonathan B. and Sarna, Jonathan D. *The History of the Jewish People: A Story of Tradition and Change, Volume 2.* Springfield, NJ: Behrman House Publishers, 2007.

Krugman, Paul. "Oligarchy, American Style." *New York Times* (November 4, 2011): A31.

Kurtz, Howard. "Should We Blame Sarah Palin for Gabrielle Giffords' Shooting?" *The Daily Beast* (January 8, 2011): www.thedailybeast.com.

Lamberton, John. *American Machiavelli: Alexander Hamilton and the Origins of U.S. Foreign Policy.* Cambridge, England: Cambridge University Press, 2004.

Lampman, Jane. "New scrutiny of role of religion in Bush's policies." *Christian Science Monitor* (March 17, 2003): www.csmonitor.com.

Lane, Charles. "No More 'War.'" *Washington Post* (March 13, 2012): A15.

Lao Tzu. *The Tao Te Ching* (Stephen Mitchell, translator). New York: Harper-Collins, 1988.

Lawrence, Dr. Gary C. "Charity, Gratitude and the Role of Government." *Audience Alliance Pictures* (April 7, 2010): www.audiencealliance.com.

Ledeen Michael. *Machiavelli on Modern Leadership: Why Machiavelli's Iron Rules are as Timely and Important Today as Five Centuries Ago.* New York: Truman Talley Books, 1999.

Lerner, Max. "Introduction." (Machiavelli, Niccolo. *The Prince and the Discourses*, Luigi Ricci, translator). New York: Modern Library (1950): xxv-xlvi.

Lewis, Neal. "Red Cross Finds Detainee Abuse in Guantanamo." *New York Times*, (November 20, 2004): A1, A14.

Little, Morgan. "Negative ads increase dramatically during 2012 presidential election." *Los Angeles Times* (May 3, 2012): www.latimes.com.

Londono, Ernesto. "Brotherhood Candidate Wages Underdog Campaign in Egypt." *Washington Post* (May 17, 2012): A1, A8.

Lord, Carnes. "Machiavelli's Realism." (Machiavelli, Niccolo. *The Prince*, Angelo M. Codevilla, translator). New Haven and London: Yale University Press (1997): 114-123.

Los Angeles Time Editorial Page. "These Charges Are False . . ." *Los Angeles Times* (August 24, 2008).

Luntz, Frank. "Frank Luntz Explains 'Words That Work.'" *Terry Gross Show* (January 9, 2007): www.npr.org.

——"Interview: Frank Luntz." *Frontline* (November 9, 2004): www.pbs.org.

——www.luntglobal.com

Lynch, Christopher. "Introduction." Machiavelli, Niccolo. *The Art of War* (Christopher Lynch, translator). Chicago: University of Chicago Press (2003): xiii-xxxiv.

Machiavelli, Niccolo. *Discourses on the First Ten Books of Titus Livius* (Christian E. Detmold, translator). New York: Random House, 1950.

——*History of Florence from the Earliest Times to the Death of Lorenzo the Magnificent*. London & New York: The Colonial Press, 1901.

——*The Prince* (Angelo Codevilla, translator). New Haven and London: Yale University Press, 1997.

Madsen, Wayne. "Exposing Karl Rove." *Counterpunch* (October 31 - November 02, 2002): www.counterpunch.org.

Mandela, Nelson. *Long Walk to Freedom*. New York: Back Bay Books, 1995.

Mann, Thomas E. and Ornstein, Norman J. "Let's Just Say It: The Republicans are the Problem." *Washington Post* (April, 27, 2012): www.washingtonpost.com.

Mansfield, Harvey. *Machiavelli's Virtue*. Chicago and London: University of Chicago Press, 1998.

Marcus, Lloyd. "Evil Democrat Paradigms." *The American Thinker* (September 10, 2010): www.americanthinker.com.

Marcus, Ruth. "It's the Super PAC Era." *Washington Post* (January 4, 2012): A17.

Marinucci, Carla. "Jerry Brown's applies 'Art of War' to new tenure." *San Francisco Chronicle* (March 11, 2001): www.sfgate.com.

Marrapodi, Eric. "Poll: Many Americans Uncomfortable with Muslims." *CNN* (September 6, 2011): www.cnn.com.

Marshall, Jacqueline. "Humanity is Maturing." *The Examiner* (May 8, 2011): www.examiner.com.

Martin, Patrick. "Bush budget targets the poor." *World Socialist Website* (February 13, 2003): www.wsws.org.

Marx, Steven. "Moses and Machiavellism." *Journal of the American Academy of Religion* (Volume 65, Issue 3, Fall October 1, 1997): 551-572.

McAlpine, Alistair. *The New Machiavelli*. New York: John Wiley and Sons, Inc., 1998.

McCain, John. "Eulogy for Pat Tillman." (May 3, 2004): www.mccain.senate.gov.

McCormick, John P. *Machiavellian Democracy*. New York: Cambridge University Press, 2011.

McCrummen, Stephanie. "Gingrich Delivers 'Wild and Woolly.'" *Washington Post* (January 30, 2012): p. A1, 7.

McDonald, Greg. "Karl Rove's Super PAC Targets Five Democrats With Ads." *Newsmax* (November 10, 2011): www.newsmax.com.

McGreal, Chris. "George W Bush should be prosecuted over torture, says human rights group." *Guardian Newspaper* (U.K.) (July 11, 2011), p. 20.

Medved, Michael. "Rick Santorum's Momentum Shouldn't Convert GOP Into a 'God Squad.'" *Daily Beast* (March 14, 2012): www.thedailybeast.com.

Mencius. *Mencius* (D. C. Lau, translator). Hong Kong: The Chinese University Press, 2003.

Merton, Thomas. *Mystics and Zen Masters.* New York: Farrar, Straus, Giroux, 1967.

——*On Peace.* New York: The McCall Publishing Company, 1971.

——*Peace in the Post-Christian Era.* Maryknoll, NY: Orbis, 2004.

——*Raids on the Unspeakable.* New York: New Directions Publishing Corp., 1964.

Metzler, Rebekah. "Mitt Romney Ramps Up Right-leaning Rhetoric." *US News and World Report* (July 19, 2012): www.usnews.com.

Milbank, Dana and VandeHei, Jim. "From Bush, Unprecedented Negativity." *Washington Post* (May 31, 2004): A1, A32.

Miller, Lisa. "Finding His Faith." *Newsweek Magazine* (July 11, 2008): www.the-dailybeast.com/newsweek.

——"One Nation Under God." *Newsweek Magazine* (December 9, 2010): www.thedailybeast.com/newsweek.

Milstein, Andrew. "Plugging Leaks in the Dam: The Future [and Past] of Campaign Finance Reform and the Effects of Money in Federal Elections." *Geneva NY League of Women Voters Luncheon* (April 3, 2007): www.geneva.ny.lwvnet.org.

Morgan, David. "Bush Spy Bill Stance Called Fear-Mongering." *CBS News* (February 11, 2009): www.cbsnews.com.

Moyers, Bill. "Buying the War." *Bill Moyers Journal.* www.pbs.org/moyers/journal.

Mulier, Eco Haitsma. "A Controversial Republican: Dutch Views of Machiavelli in the 17th and 18th Centuries." *Machiavelli and Republicanism* (G. Bock, Q. Skinner and M. Viroli, editors). Cambridge, England: Cambridge University Press (1993): 247-264.

Mundy, Alicia. "Adelson Says He Could Give $100 Million More to Help Gingrich." *Washington Wire* (blog of *The Wall Street Journal*). (February 21, 2012): www.blogs.wsj.com.

Nagourney, Adam. "2 Character Models for a Single Cinematic Point: Winning Elections at Any Cost." *New York Times* (December 8, 2011): A22.

N.C. & M.J. "The new Swift Boat Vets ad is wrong ——but you wouldn't know it from watching FOX." *Media Matters* (September 22, 2004): www.mediamatters.org.

Nederman, Cary. "Niccolò Machiavelli." *The Stanford Encyclopedia of Philosophy* (Edward N. Zalta editor). (Fall 2009 Edition): www.plato.stanford.edu.

Nunberg, Geoffrey. "Simpler Terms; If It's 'Orwellian,' It's Probably Not." *New York Times* (June 22, 2003): www.nytimes.com.

Orwell, George. *1984*. London: Penguin Books, Signet Classic, 1977.

——*Animal Farm*. www.gutenberg.net.au.

——"Politics and the English Language." *Fifty Essays by George Orwell* (Australia: Project Gutenberg of Australia, 2010): www.gutenberg.net.au.

Owen, Paul. "George Bush admits US waterboarded 9/11 mastermind." *The Guardian* (U.K.). (June 3, 2010): www.guardian.co.uk.

Page, Clarence. "Decision-making behind drone attacks needs review." *Chicago Tribune* (June 19, 2012). www.recordnet.com.

Patterson, David. *Greatest Jewish Stories*. New York: Jonathan David Publishers, 2001.

Pew Research Center. "The American-Western European Values Gap." *Pew Global Attitudes Project* (February 29, 2012): www.pewglobal.org.

Pitney Jr., John Jay. "Military Language in Politics Proves Resilient." *National Review* (March 29, 2011): www.nationalreview.com.

Pocock, J. G. A. *The Machiavellian Moment*. Princeton, NJ and Oxford: Princeton University Press, 2003.

Polk, Laray. "Harold Simmons Is Dallas' Most Evil Genius." *D Magazine* (February 2010): www.dmagazine.com.

Polsby, Daniel D. and Brennen, Dennis. "Taking Aim at Gun Control." *Heartland Policy Institute* (October 30, 1995): www.catb.org.

Priest, Dana. "From an ex-CIA Official, a blunt defense of Harsh Interrogation." *Washington Post* (April 25, 2012): C1, 9.

Publius. "American Oligarchy and Our Machiavellian Moment by Publius." *Eagle Historical Review* (August 19, 2011): www.eaglehistoricalreview.com.

Rahe, Paul. "Machiavelli's Liberal Republican Legacy." *Machiavelli's Liberal Republican Legacy* (Paul A. Rahe, Editor). Cambridge, England: Cambridge University Press (2006): xix-xxx.

——(editor). *Machiavelli's Liberal Republican Legacy*. Cambridge, England: Cambridge University Press, 2006.

——"Thomas Jefferson's Machiavellian Political Science." *Machiavelli's Liberal Republican Legacy* (Paul A. Rahe, Editor). Cambridge, England: Cambridge University Press (2006): 208-228.

Randolph, Eleanor. "The Political Legacy of Baaad Boy Atwater." *New York Times* (September, 19, 2008): www.nytimes.com.

Rawls, John. ""The Law of Peoples." *The Politics of Human Rights* (Obrad Savic, editor). (London and New York: Verso, 1999): 16-45.

Rauscher, Dick. "Spiritual Growth: The Primitive Ego Grows Up." *Dick Rauscher — Stonyhill*. www.stonyhill.com.

Redstone, Julia. "The Language of War." *World Watch* (September 24, 2001): www.lightomega.org.

Rettig, Jessica. "Fewer Americans See Climate Change a Threat, Caused by Humans." *US News and World Report* (August 26, 2011): www.usnews.com.

Roarke, John T. and Boyer, Mark A. *World Politics: International Politics on the World Stage*. New York: McGraw Hill College, 2001.

Rosen, Gary. "James Madison's Princes and Peoples." *Machiavelli's Liberal Republican Legacy* (Paul A. Rahe, Editor). (Cambridge, England: Cambridge University Press, 2006): 229-253.

Rosenthal, Andrew. "Secrets and Lies." *New York Times Editorial Page Editor's Blog* (March 29, 2012): www.takingnote.blogs.nytimes.com.

Rove, Karl. "Karl Rove Reads." www.rove.com.

R.S. "Who? Media Turns Its Back On Experts Who Blame GOP For Political Gridlock." *Media Matters* (May 18, 2012), www.mediamatters.org.

Rucker, Philip. "Romney Team Tries to Make Pitch-Perfect Ads." *Washington Post* (August 24, 2012): A1, 10.

Ruhe, Brian. *Freeing the Buddha: Diversity on a Sacred Path*. Vancouver, BC: Buddhist Spectrum Study Group, 1999.

Rumi, Jalaluddin. *Signs of the Unseen* (W. M. Thackston, Jr., translator). Boston and London: Shambhala, 1999.

——*The Essential Rumi* (Coleman Barks, translator). NewYork: HarperCollins, 1995.

Russell, Bertrand. *Bertrand Russell's Best*. New York: Routledge, 2009.

Sacco, Jeffrey B. "Waterboarding: An American Dilemma." *University of Nebraska at Kearney Summer Student Research Program* (Summer 2010).

Salmon, Jacqueline L. "Most Americans Believe in Higher Power, Poll Finds." *Washington Post* (June 24, 2008): A2.

Sanders, Senator Bernie. "Speech on the floor of the U.S. Senate." (June 29, 2012): www.upworthy.com.

Sargent, Greg. "The Plum Line." *Washington Post* (May 14, 2012), www.washingtonpost.com.

Savic, Obrad (editor, for the Belgrade Circle). *The Politics of Human Rights*. New York and London: Verso, 1999.

Schaffhausen, Joanna. "The Biological Basis of Aggression." *Brain Connection*. www.brainconnection.positscience.com.

Schaub, Diana. "Machiavelli's Realism." *The National Interest* (Fall 1998): www.findarticles.com.

Schlesinger Jr. Arthur. "Diane Rehm Show." *National Public Radio* (September 29, 2004): www.thedianerehmshow.org.

Schouten, Fredreka. "Karl Rove-affiliated groups target President Obama." *USA Today* (March 1, 2011): www.usatoday.com.

——"Several Bush officials work in areas related to former jobs." *USA Today* (May 20, 2009): www.usatoday.com.

Schuster, M.A.; Franke, T.M.; Bastian, A.M.; Sor, S; Halfon, N. "Firearm storage patterns in US homes with children." *American Journal of Public Health* (2000: 90): 588– 594.

Schwartz, Casey. "Science: The Age of Immorality." *Newsweek Magazine* (January 16, 2012): www.thedailybeast.com/newsweek.

Schwartz, Regina M. *The Curse of Cain: The Violent Legacy of Monotheism*. Chicago: University of Chicago Press, 1997.

Sennholz, Hans F. "Machiavellian Politics." *The Freeman of the Foundation for Economic Education* (February 1996, Volume 46, Issue 2): www.thefreemanonline.org.

Shah, Idris. *The Sufis*. London, England: Octagon Press, 2001.

——*The Way of the Sufis*. London: Penguin Books, 1991.

Shams-i Tabrizi. *Me and Rumi: The Autobiography of Shams-I Tabrizi* (William C. Chittick, translator). Louisville, KY: Fons Vitae, 2004.

Sherwell, Philip. "'Now it's time to rock 'em and sock 'em.'" *The Telegraph* (U.K.) (October 17, 2004): www.telegraph.co.uk.

Shrum, Robert. "In Defense of Karl Rove." *The Week* (August 18, 2011): www.theweek.com.

Sibley, Mulford. *The Quiet Battle: Writings on the Theory and Practice of Non-Violent Resistance*. Chicago: Quadrangle Books, 1963.

Simon, Howard L. "Restricting Voter Rights Is the Threat to Democracy, not Fraud." *US News* (June 13, 2012): www.usnews.com.

Skelton, George. "Special-interest money and politics: the American way." *Los Angeles Times* (April 26, 2012): www.articles.latimes.com.

Skinner, Richard M. "George W. Bush and the Partisan Presidency" Political Science Quarterly 123.4 (2009): 605-622.

Slackman, Michael. "An Arab Artist Says All the World Really Isn't a Stage." *New York Times* (August 19, 2006): www.nytimes.com.

Sloan, John. "Machiavelli on War." *Xenophon Group International*, www.xenophon-mil.org.

Smith, Ben. "Oppo: From dark art to daily tool." *Politico*. (August 4, 2011): www.politico.com.

Smith, Eric Drummond. "Machiavellian and Hobbesian Concepts of Power and Its Relationship to Politics." *Smith's Blue Book*, www.smithsbluebook.com.

Solomon, Norman. "The Military-Industrial-Media Complex: Why war is covered from the warriors' perspective." *FAIR* (July/August 2005): www.fair.org.

Spalding, Matthew. ""The American Prince?" *Machiavelli's Liberal Republican Legacy* (Paul A. Rahe, Editor). Cambridge, England: Cambridge University Press (2006): 170-188.

Sonmez, Felicia. "Negative ads: Is it the campaigns, or the super PACs." *Washington Post Election 2012 Blog* (March 22, 2012): www.washingtonpost.com.

Spayde, Jon. "The New Renaissance." *Utne Reader* (Jan-Feb 1998): p. 43.

Spencer, Nick. "Machiavelli's The Prince, part 8: a lingering love of justice." *Guardian, U.K.* (May 14, 2012): www.guardian.co.uk.

The Staff. "Hank Williams Jr: President Obama is a 'Muslim president who hates the US'." *The Capitol Column* (August 21, 2012): www.capitolcolumn. com.

Stafford, Tom. "Does the internet rewire your brain?" *BBC News* (April 24, 2012): www.bbc.com.

Stoeltje, Melissa Fletcher. "'God and Country' service features faith, patriotism, political hopefuls." *San Antonio Express-News* (May 27, 2012): www. mysanantonio.com.

Strauss, Leo. *Thoughts on Machiavelli.* Chicago and London: The University of Chicago Press, 1978.

Suskind, Ron. "Faith, Certainty and the Presidency of George W. Bush." *New York Times* (October 17, 2004): Sunday Magazine, cover story.

Taibbi, Matt. "Hacks R Us, Interview." *On the Media* (November 12, 2004): www.onthemedia.org.

Tashman, Brian. "God Tells Robertson that 'Radical' Obama will Bring Down America." *Right Wing Watch* (January 3, 2012): www.rightwingwatch.org.

Teasdale, Wayne. "The Interspiritual Age: Practical Mysticism for the Third Millennium." *Council on Spiritual Practices* (1999): www.csp.org.

Thomas, Will. "Rigged." *Stolen Election 2004* (October 10, 2004), www.take-overworld.info.

Thompson, C. Bradley. "John Adams Machiavellian Moment." *Machiavelli's Liberal Republican Legacy* (Paul A. Rahe, Editor). Cambridge, England: Cambridge University Press (2006): 189-207.

Thompson, Krissah. "Report: Laws May Cut Latino Voting." *Washington Post* (September 23, 2012): p. A3.

Times, Sunday. "September 11 Mastermind Khalid Sheikh Mohammed 'Waterboarded' 183 Times." *The Times* (UK). April 20, 2009.

Tolstoy, Leo. *On Civil Disobedience and Non-Violence.* New York: Bergman Publishers, 1967.

Turque, Bill. Small Group Makes Big Dent on Super PAC Individual Donations." *Washington Post* (August 2, 2012): A13.

Urban, Hugh B. "Machiavelli meets the religious right: Michael Ledeen, the neoconservatives, and the political uses of fundamentalism." *Journal of Ecumenical Studies* 2007, 42(1): 76-97.

——*The Secrets of the Kingdom: Religion and Concealment in the Bush Administration.* Lanham, MD: Rowman and Littlefield Publishers, 2007.

USA Today Editorial Writers. "The Campaign Goes Negative." *USA Today* (May 3, 2012): 6A.

Vanden Heuvel, Katrina. "Three Issues that Could Decide the Election." *Washington Post* (January 3, 2012): p. A13.

Varela, Felix. *Letters to Elpidio.* New York: Paulist Press, 1989.

Verrall, Richard. "Human Nature and Spiritual Progress." *The Christian Science Journal* (October 1904): www.journal.christianscience.com.

Walling, Karl-Friedrich. "Was Alexander Hamilton a Machiavellian Statesman?" *Machiavelli's Liberal Republican Legacy* (Paul A. Rahe, Editor). (Cambridge, England: Cambridge University Press (2006): 254-278.

Wallsten, Peter. "GOP Readies its Plan of Attack." *Washington Post* (January 2, 2012): A1, A6.

Waters, David. "On Faith: Examining McCain's God and Country." *Washington Post* (October 7, 2008): www.washingtonpost.com.

Weil, Simone. *An Anthology*. New York: Grove Press, 1986.

———*Oppression and Liberty*. New York: Routledge, 2001.

———*Simone Weil Reader*. Wakefield, RI & London: Moyer Bell, 1977.

———*Waiting for God*. New York: Harper & Row Publishers, 1992.

Weinstein, James. *The Decline of Socialism in America, 1912-1925*. New York: Vintage Books, 1969.

Weisberger, Bernard A. *America Afire: Jefferson, Adams, and the First Contested Election*. New York: William Morrow Paperbacks, 2001.

Weisman, Jonathan. "Bid to Save Tax Refunds for the Poor Is Blocked." *Washington Post* (September 23, 2004): A4.

Wilkins, W. J. *Hindu Mythology, Vedic and Puranic*. Calcutta & London: Thacker, Spink. & Co, 1900.

Woodward, Bob. "Bush at War: A Course of 'Confident Action.'" *Washington Post* (November 19, 2002): www.washingtonpost.com.

Worden, Blair. "Milton's republicanism and the Tyranny of Heaven." *Machiavelli and Republicanism* (G. Bock, Q. Skinner and M. Viroli, editors). Cambridge, England: Cambridge University Press (1993): 225-246.

Wulfhorst, Ellen. "Karl Rove in Running for Time's Person of the Year." *Reuters News Service* (November 16, 2004): www.democraticunderground.com.

Yost, Pete. "Bush E-mails Found: 22 Million Missing E-mails From George W. Bush White House Recovered." *Huffington Post* (December 14, 2009): www.huffingtonpost.com.

Younge, Gary. "US elections: no matter who you vote for, money always wins." *The Guardian* (U.K.) (January 29, 2012): www.guardian.co.uk.

Zaller, John. "A Theory of Media Politics." *Miller-Converse Lecture, University of Michigan* (April 14, 1997).

Zernike, Kate (and Rutenberg, Jim). "Friendly Fire: The Birth of an Anti-Kerry Ad." *New York Times* (August 20, 2004), www.nytimes.com.

———"Kerry Pressing Swift Boat Case Long After Loss." *New York Times* (May 28, 2006): www.nytimes.com.

INDEX